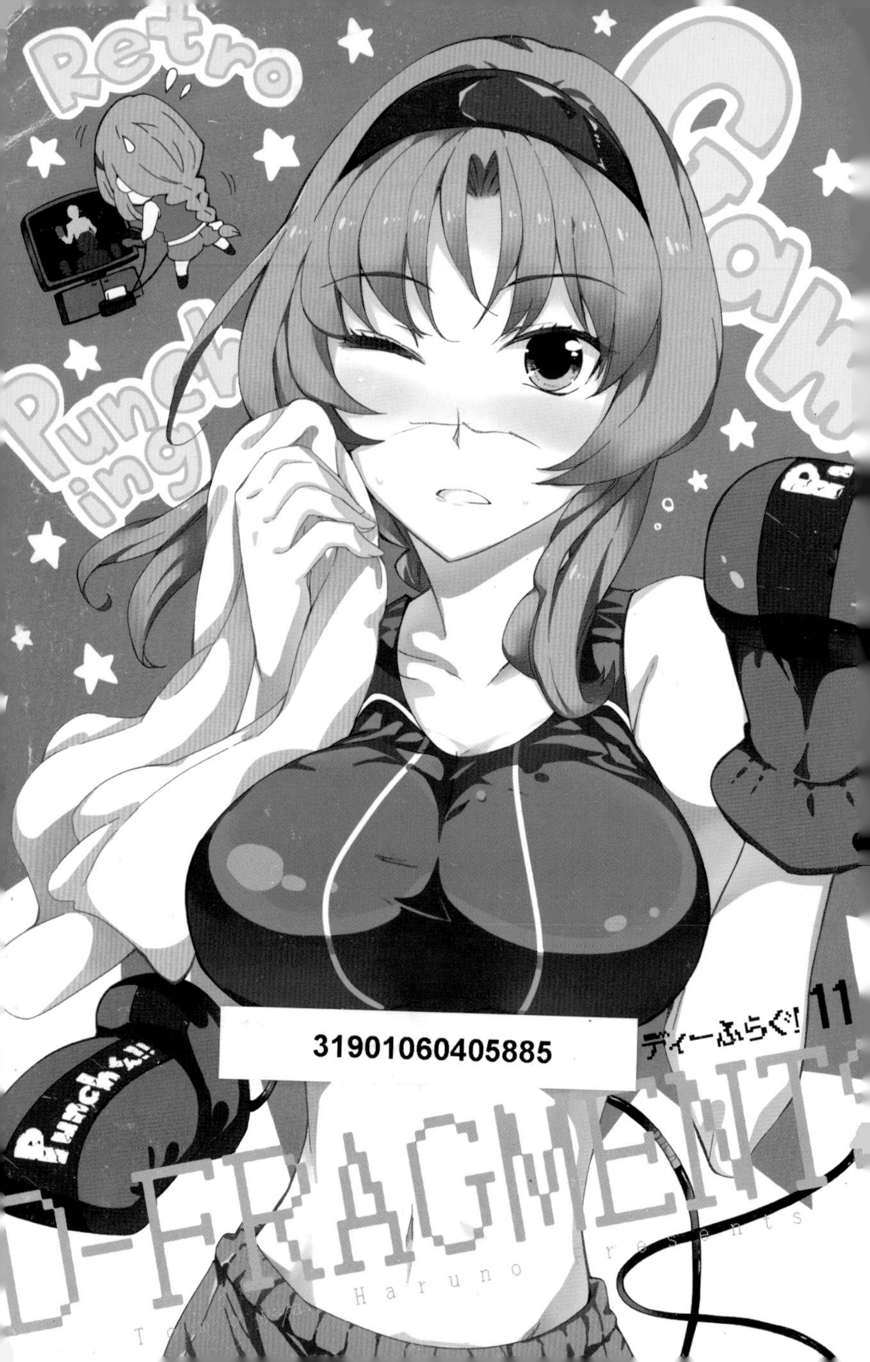
Retro
Punching
Punch
ディーふらぐ! 11
D-FRAGMENTS
Haruno

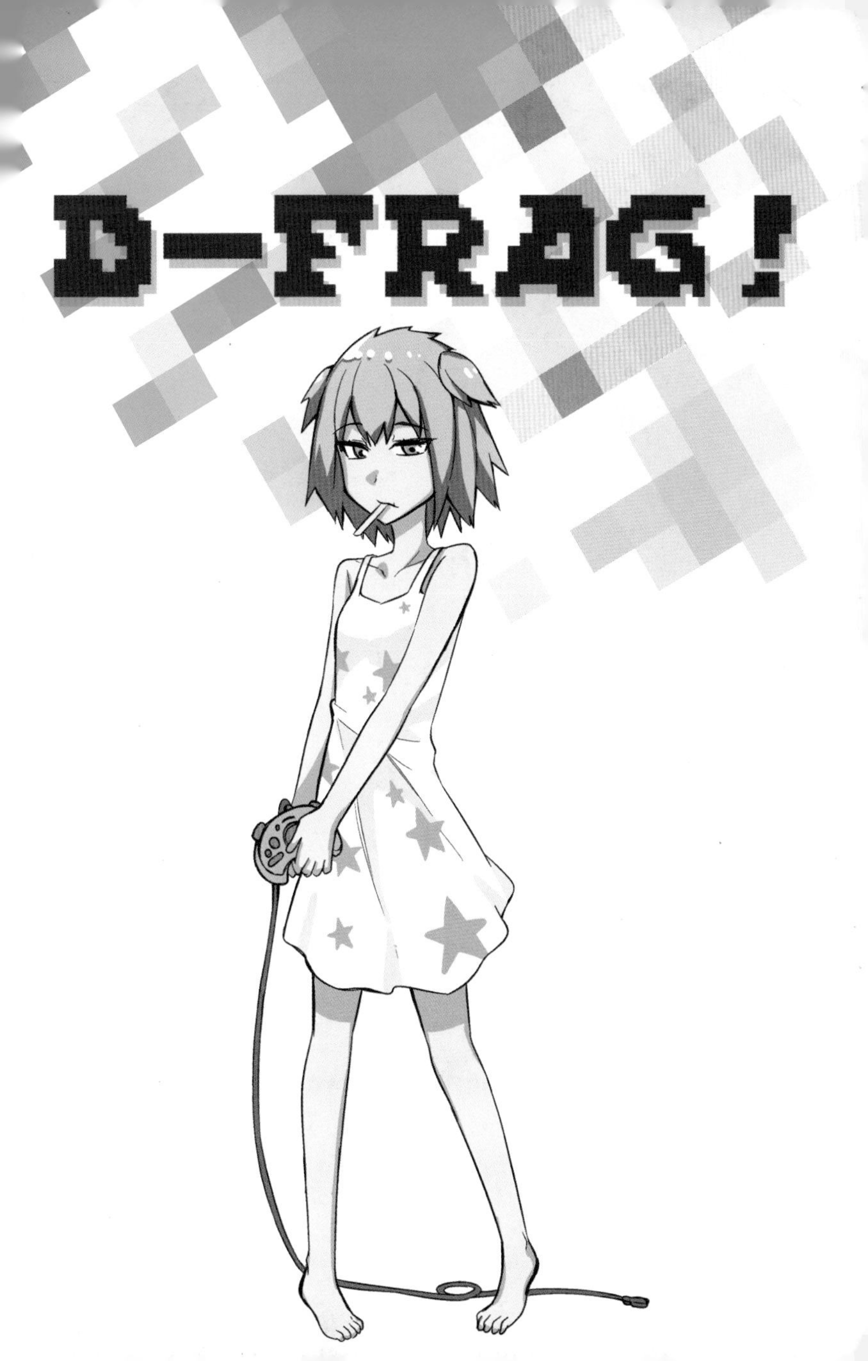
D-FRAG!

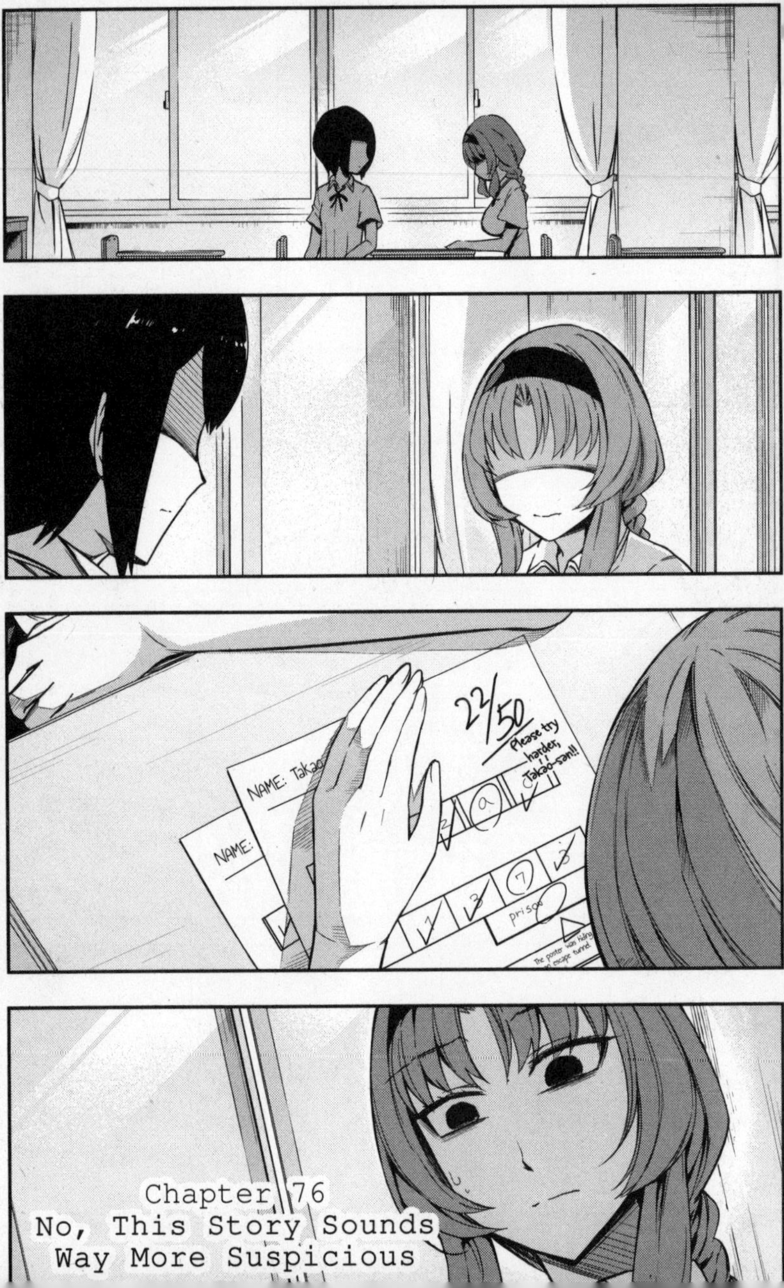
22/50
Please try harder, Takao-san!!
NAME: Takao
NAME:
prison
Chapter 76
No, This Story Sounds Way More Suspicious

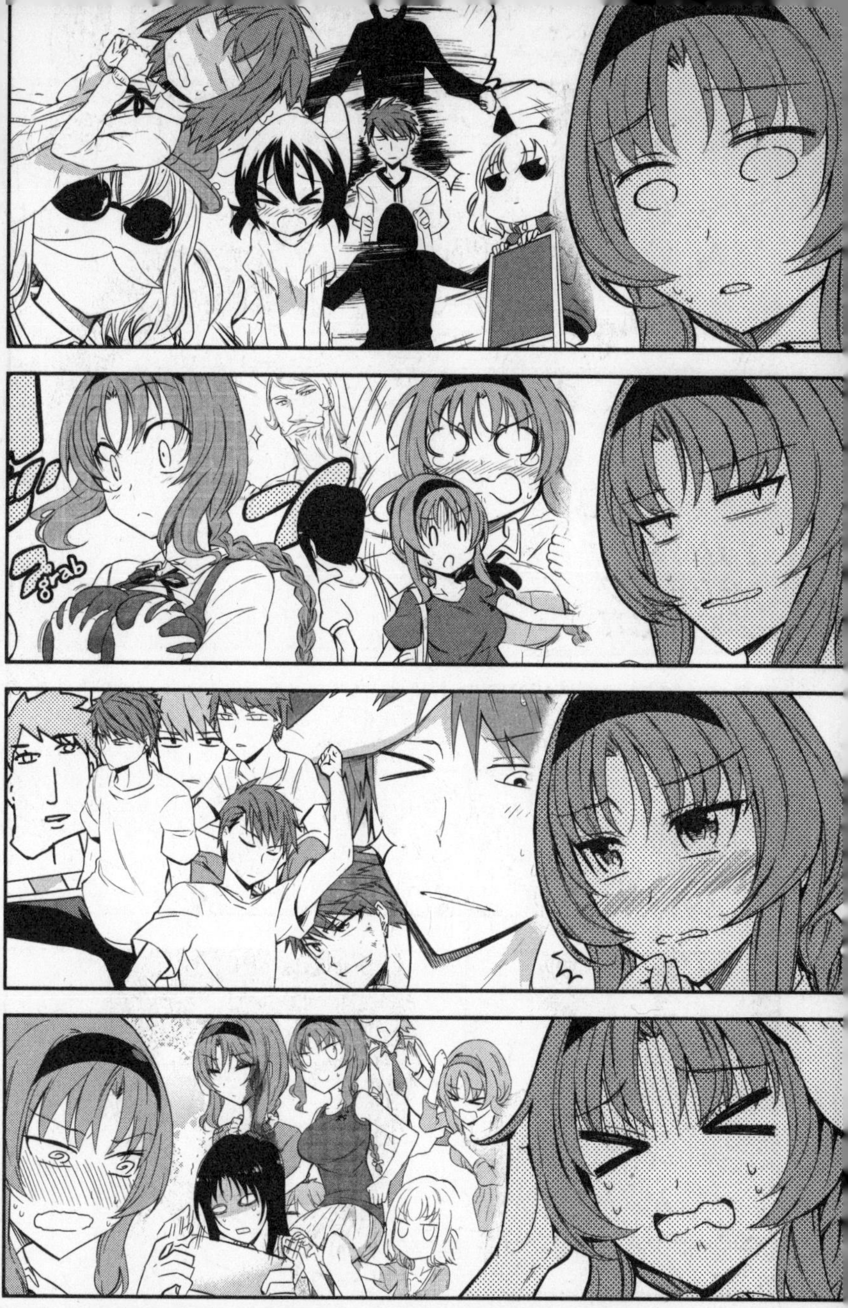
grab

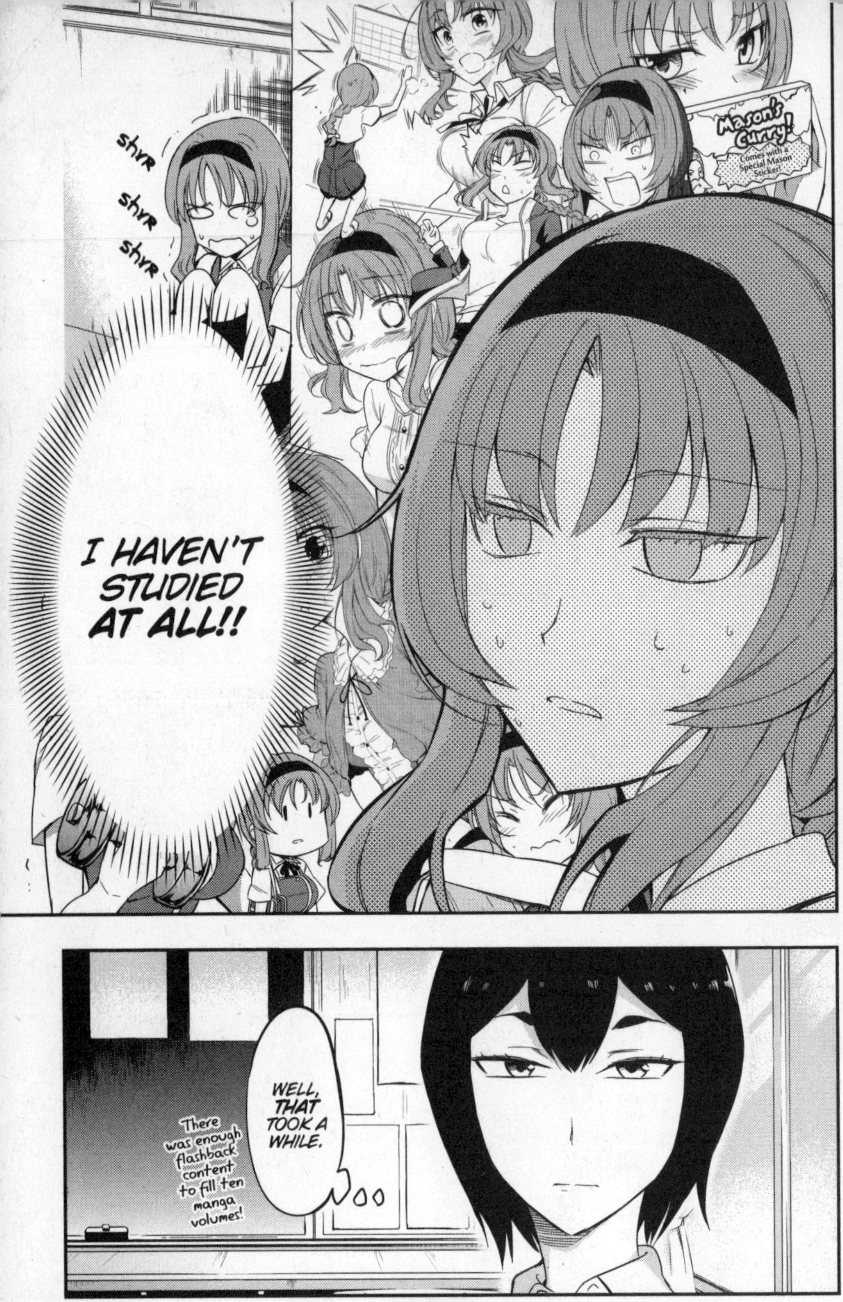

Mason's Curry!
Comes with a Special Mason Sticker!
shvr
shvr
shvr
I HAVEN'T STUDIED AT ALL!!
WELL, THAT TOOK A WHILE.
There was enough flashback content to fill ten manga volumes!

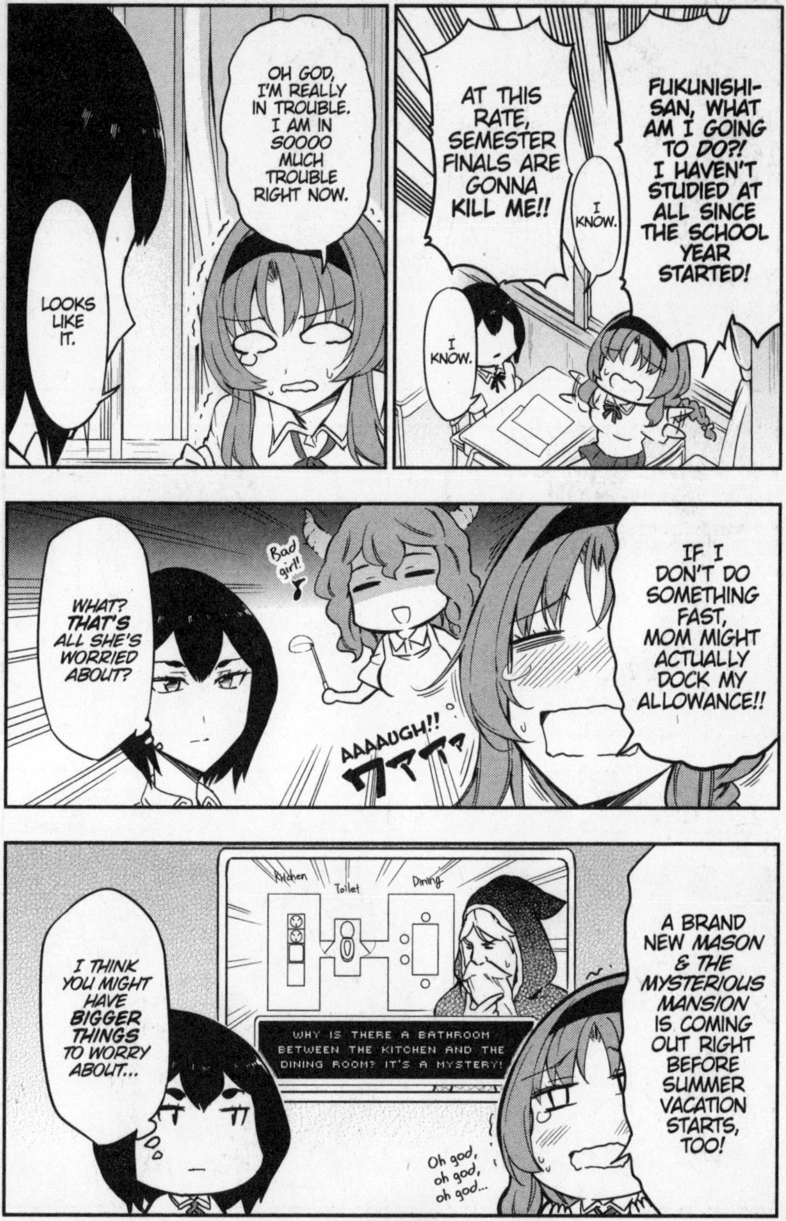
FUKUNISHI-SAN, WHAT AM I GOING TO DO?! I HAVEN'T STUDIED AT ALL SINCE THE SCHOOL YEAR STARTED!
I KNOW.
AT THIS RATE, SEMESTER FINALS ARE GONNA KILL ME!!
I KNOW.
OH GOD, I'M REALLY IN TROUBLE. I AM IN SOOOO MUCH TROUBLE RIGHT NOW.
LOOKS LIKE IT.
IF I DON'T DO SOMETHING FAST, MOM MIGHT ACTUALLY DOCK MY ALLOWANCE!!
AAAAUGH!!
ワアアァ
Bad girl!
WHAT? THAT'S ALL SHE'S WORRIED ABOUT?
A BRAND NEW MASON & THE MYSTERIOUS MANSION IS COMING OUT RIGHT BEFORE SUMMER VACATION STARTS, TOO!
Oh god, oh god, oh god...
Kitchen
Toilet
Dining
WHY IS THERE A BATHROOM BETWEEN THE KITCHEN AND THE DINING ROOM? IT'S A MYSTERY!
I THINK YOU MIGHT HAVE BIGGER THINGS TO WORRY ABOUT...

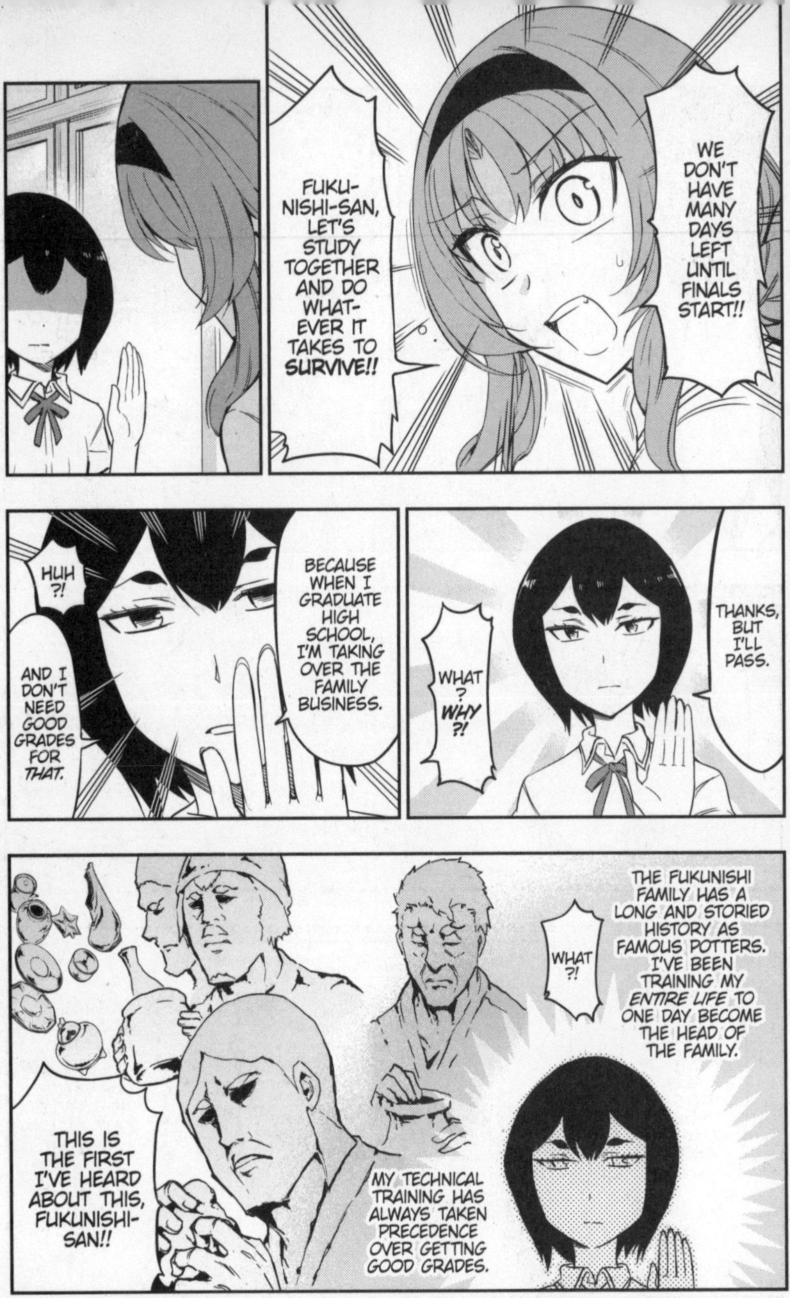
WE DON'T HAVE MANY DAYS LEFT UNTIL FINALS START!!
FUKUNISHI-SAN, LET'S STUDY TOGETHER AND DO WHATEVER IT TAKES TO SURVIVE!!
THANKS, BUT I'LL PASS.
WHAT? WHY?!
BECAUSE WHEN I GRADUATE HIGH SCHOOL, I'M TAKING OVER THE FAMILY BUSINESS.
HUH?!
AND I DON'T NEED GOOD GRADES FOR THAT.
THE FUKUNISHI FAMILY HAS A LONG AND STORIED HISTORY AS FAMOUS POTTERS. I'VE BEEN TRAINING MY ENTIRE LIFE TO ONE DAY BECOME THE HEAD OF THE FAMILY.
WHAT?!
MY TECHNICAL TRAINING HAS ALWAYS TAKEN PRECEDENCE OVER GETTING GOOD GRADES.
THIS IS THE FIRST I'VE HEARD ABOUT THIS, FUKUNISHI-SAN!!

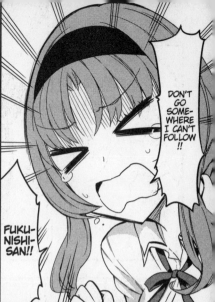

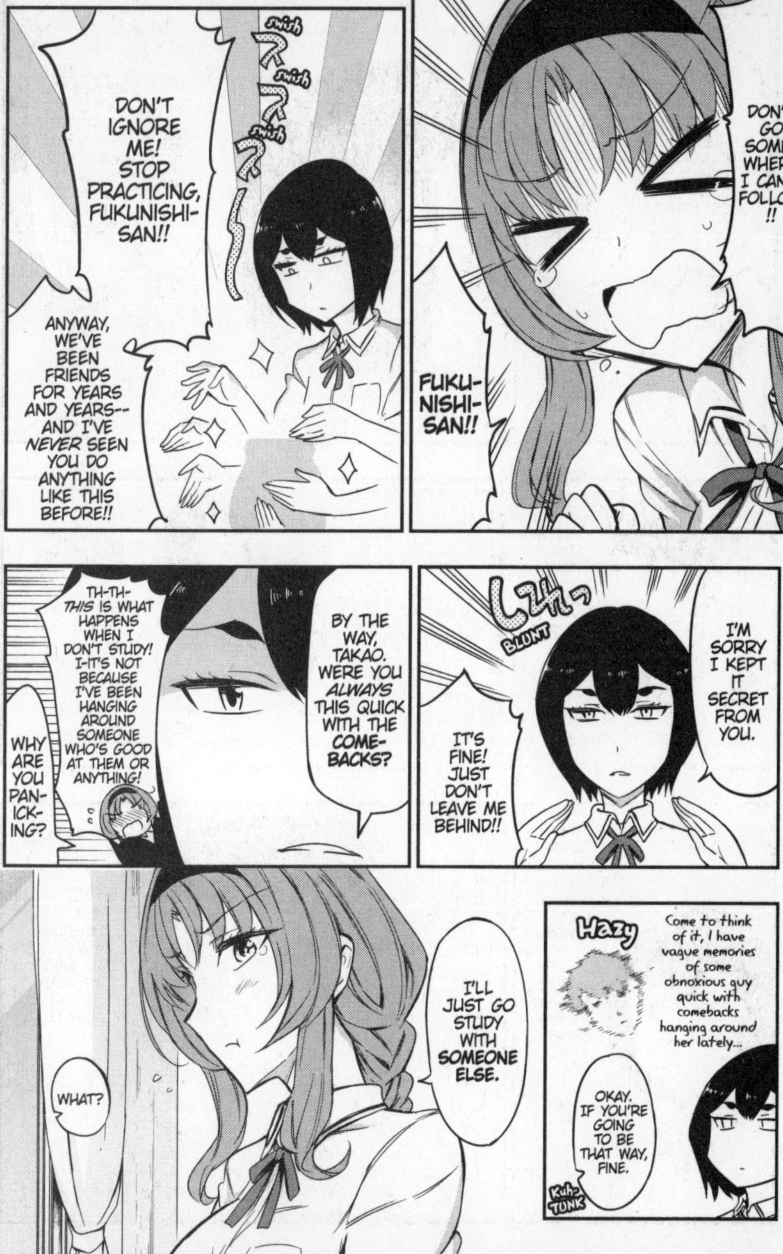
DON'T GO SOMEWHERE I CAN'T FOLLOW!!
FUKUNISHI-SAN!!
swish
swish
swish
DON'T IGNORE ME! STOP PRACTICING, FUKUNISHI-SAN!!
ANYWAY, WE'VE BEEN FRIENDS FOR YEARS AND YEARS-- AND I'VE *NEVER* SEEN YOU DO ANYTHING LIKE THIS BEFORE!!
BLUNT
I'M SORRY I KEPT IT SECRET FROM YOU.
IT'S FINE! JUST DON'T LEAVE ME BEHIND!!
BY THE WAY, TAKAO. WERE YOU *ALWAYS* THIS QUICK WITH THE COMEBACKS?
TH-TH-*THIS* IS WHAT HAPPENS WHEN I DON'T STUDY! I-IT'S NOT BECAUSE I'VE BEEN HANGING AROUND SOMEONE WHO'S GOOD AT THEM OR ANYTHING!
WHY ARE YOU PANICKING?
Hazy
Come to think of it, I have vague memories of some obnoxious guy quick with comebacks hanging around her lately...
OKAY. IF YOU'RE GOING TO BE THAT WAY, FINE.
Kuh-TUNK
I'LL JUST GO STUDY WITH SOMEONE ELSE.
WHAT?

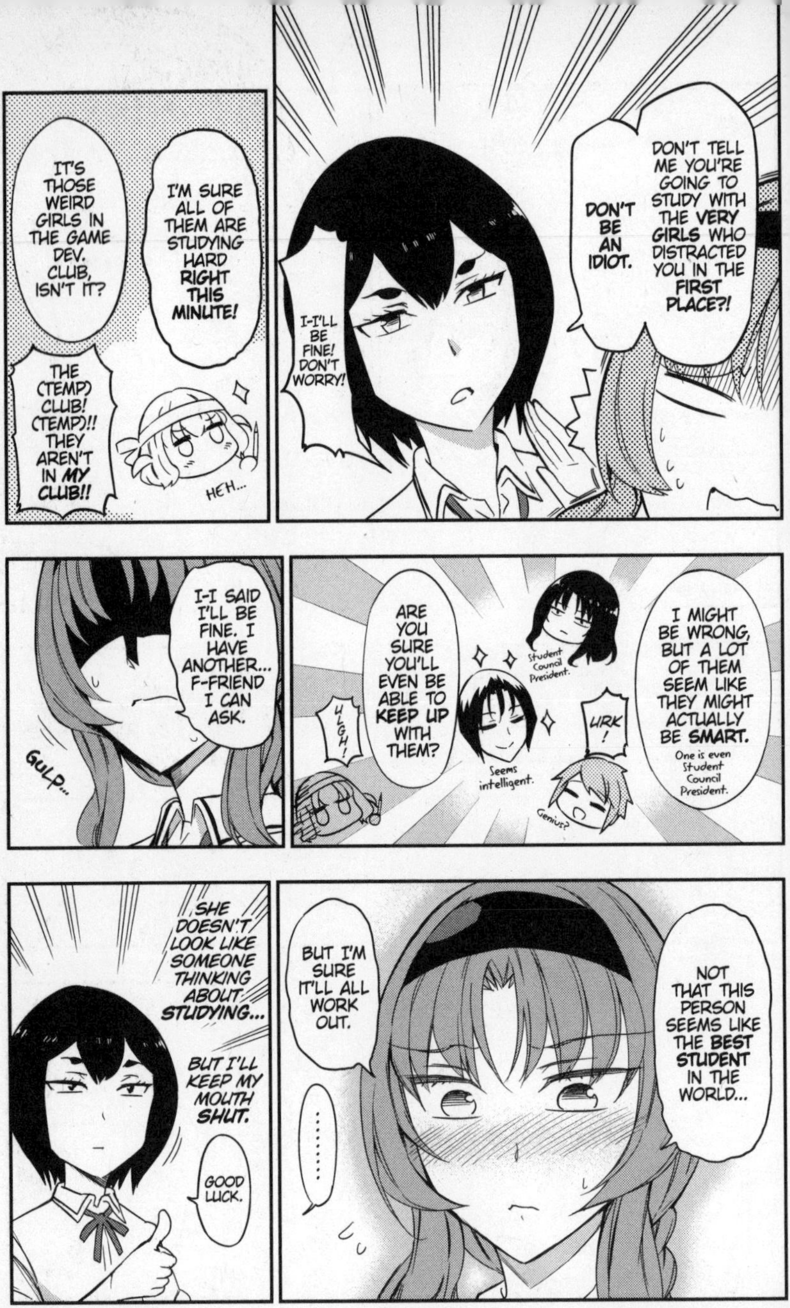
DON'T TELL ME YOU'RE GOING TO STUDY WITH THE VERY GIRLS WHO DISTRACTED YOU IN THE FIRST PLACE?!
DON'T BE AN IDIOT.
I-I'LL BE FINE! DON'T WORRY!
I'M SURE ALL OF THEM ARE STUDYING HARD RIGHT THIS MINUTE!
IT'S THOSE WEIRD GIRLS IN THE GAME DEV. CLUB, ISN'T IT?
THE (TEMP) CLUB! (TEMP)!! THEY AREN'T IN MY CLUB!!
HEH...
I MIGHT BE WRONG, BUT A LOT OF THEM SEEM LIKE THEY MIGHT ACTUALLY BE SMART.
One is even Student Council President.
URK!
Student Council President.
Seems intelligent.
Genius?
ARE YOU SURE YOU'LL EVEN BE ABLE TO KEEP UP WITH THEM?
ULGH!
I-I SAID I'LL BE FINE. I HAVE ANOTHER... F-FRIEND I CAN ASK.
GULP...
NOT THAT THIS PERSON SEEMS LIKE THE BEST STUDENT IN THE WORLD...
BUT I'M SURE IT'LL ALL WORK OUT.
....
SHE DOESN'T LOOK LIKE SOMEONE THINKING ABOUT STUDYING...
BUT I'LL KEEP MY MOUTH SHUT.
GOOD LUCK.

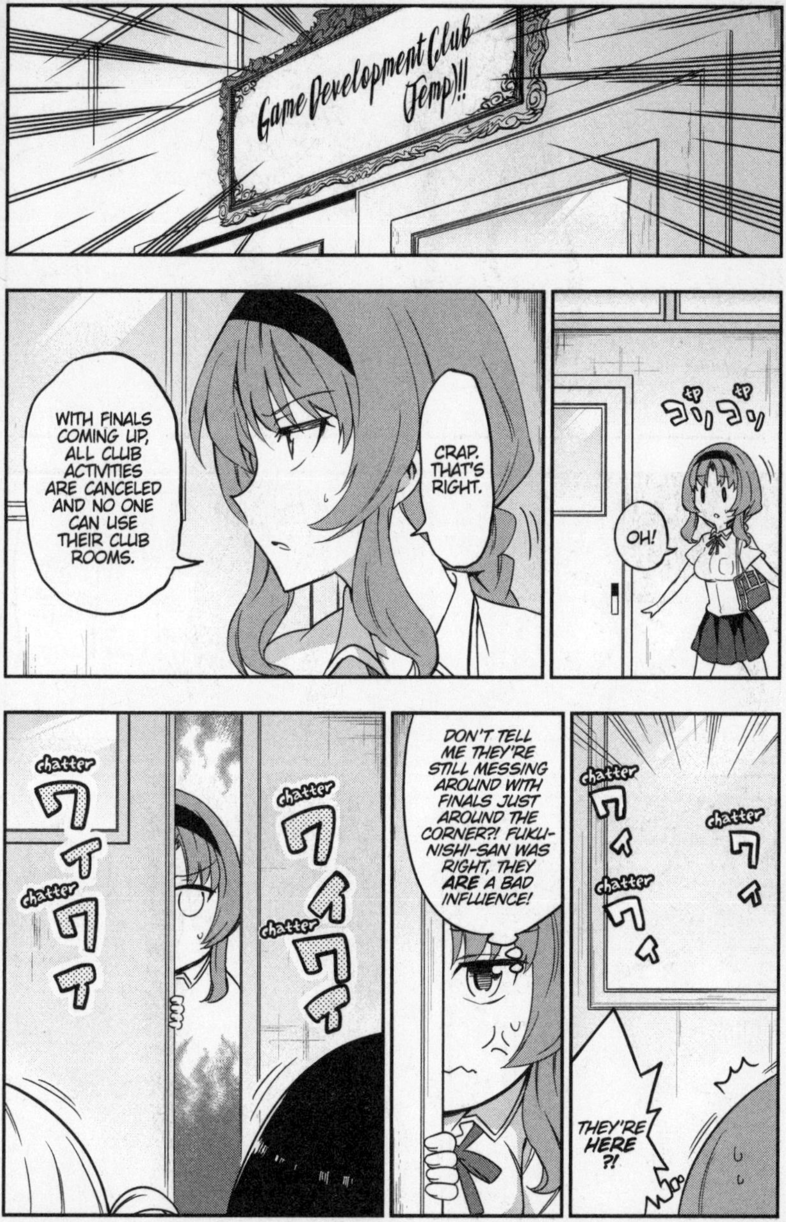
Game Development Club (Temp)!!
tp tp
OH!
CRAP. THAT'S RIGHT.
WITH FINALS COMING UP, ALL CLUB ACTIVITIES ARE CANCELED AND NO ONE CAN USE THEIR CLUB ROOMS.
chatter
chatter
chatter
THEY'RE HERE?!
DON'T TELL ME THEY'RE STILL MESSING AROUND WITH FINALS JUST AROUND THE CORNER?! FUKU-NISHI-SAN WAS RIGHT, THEY ARE A BAD INFLUENCE!
chatter
chatter
chatter
chatter

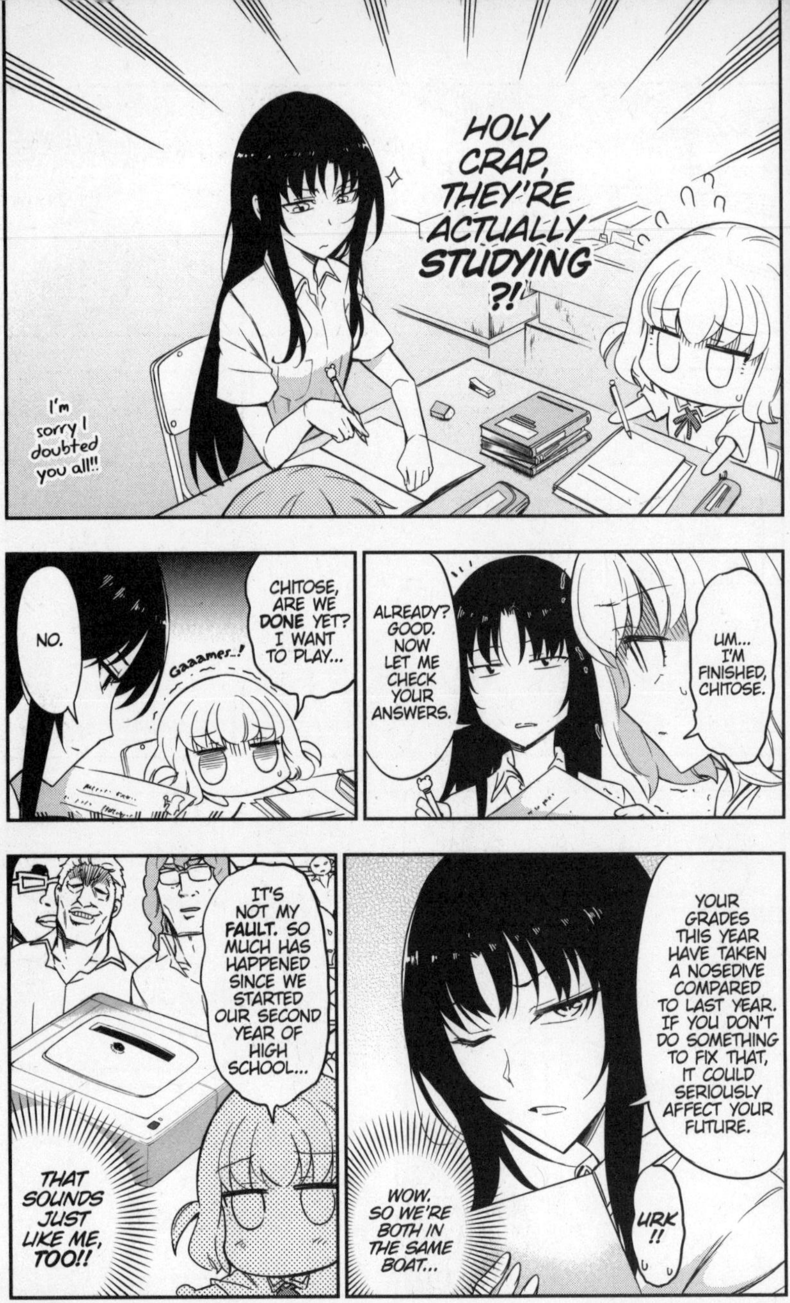
HOLY CRAP, THEY'RE ACTUALLY STUDYING?!
I'm sorry I doubted you all!!
UM... I'M FINISHED, CHITOSE.
ALREADY? GOOD. NOW LET ME CHECK YOUR ANSWERS.
CHITOSE, ARE WE DONE YET? I WANT TO PLAY...
Gaaames...!
NO.
YOUR GRADES THIS YEAR HAVE TAKEN A NOSEDIVE COMPARED TO LAST YEAR. IF YOU DON'T DO SOMETHING TO FIX THAT, IT COULD SERIOUSLY AFFECT YOUR FUTURE.
URK!!
WOW. SO WE'RE BOTH IN THE SAME BOAT...
IT'S NOT MY FAULT. SO MUCH HAS HAPPENED SINCE WE STARTED OUR SECOND YEAR OF HIGH SCHOOL...
THAT SOUNDS JUST LIKE ME, TOO!!

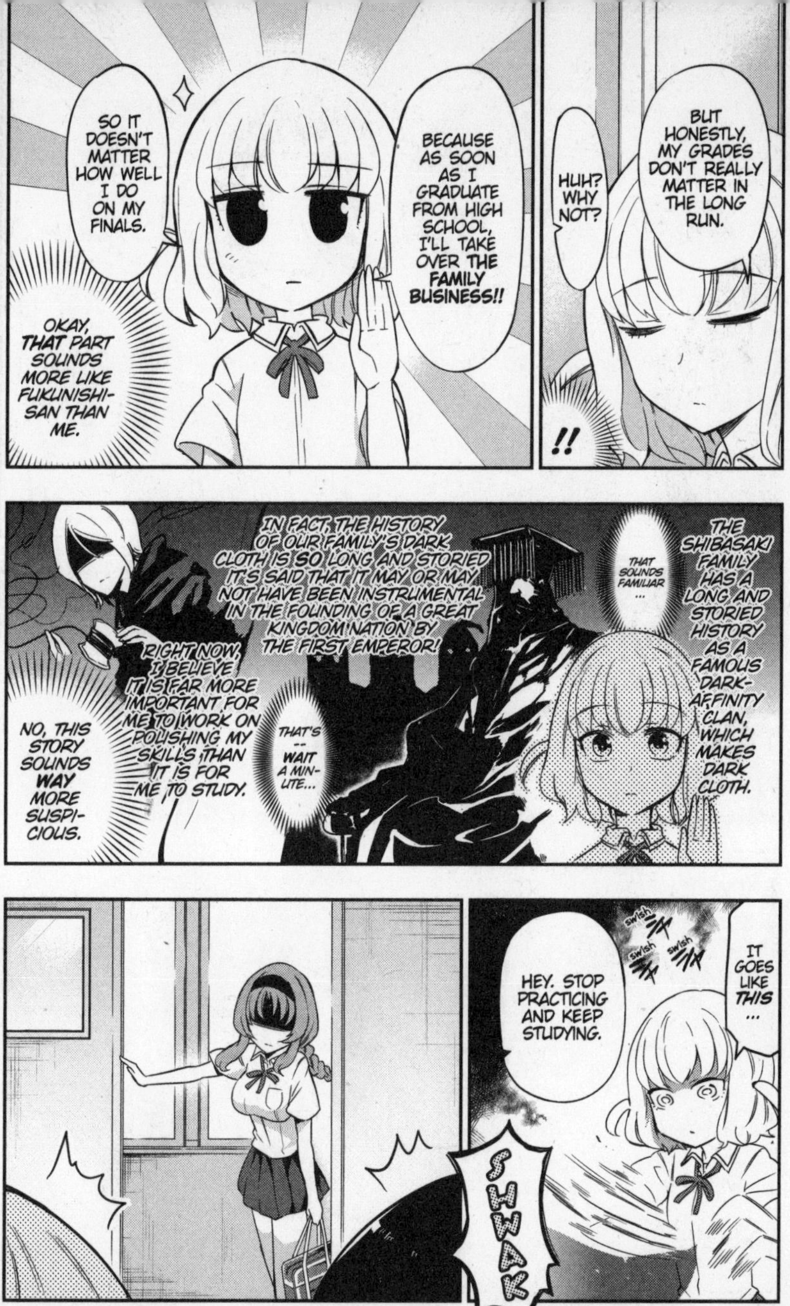
BUT HONESTLY, MY GRADES DON'T REALLY MATTER IN THE LONG RUN.
HUH? WHY NOT?
!!
BECAUSE AS SOON AS I GRADUATE FROM HIGH SCHOOL, I'LL TAKE OVER THE FAMILY BUSINESS!!
SO IT DOESN'T MATTER HOW WELL I DO ON MY FINALS.
OKAY, THAT PART SOUNDS MORE LIKE FUKUNISHI-SAN THAN ME.
THE SHIBASAKI FAMILY HAS A LONG AND STORIED HISTORY AS A FAMOUS DARK-AFFINITY CLAN, WHICH MAKES DARK CLOTH.
THAT SOUNDS FAMILIAR...
IN FACT, THE HISTORY OF OUR FAMILY'S DARK CLOTH IS SO LONG AND STORIED IT'S SAID THAT IT MAY OR MAY NOT HAVE BEEN INSTRUMENTAL IN THE FOUNDING OF A GREAT KINGDOM NATION BY THE FIRST EMPEROR!
THAT'S -- WAIT A MIN-UTE...
RIGHT NOW, I BELIEVE IT IS FAR MORE IMPORTANT FOR ME TO WORK ON POLISHING MY SKILLS THAN IT IS FOR ME TO STUDY.
NO, THIS STORY SOUNDS WAY MORE SUSPI-CIOUS.
IT GOES LIKE THIS...
swish
swish
swish
HEY. STOP PRACTICING AND KEEP STUDYING.
SWAK

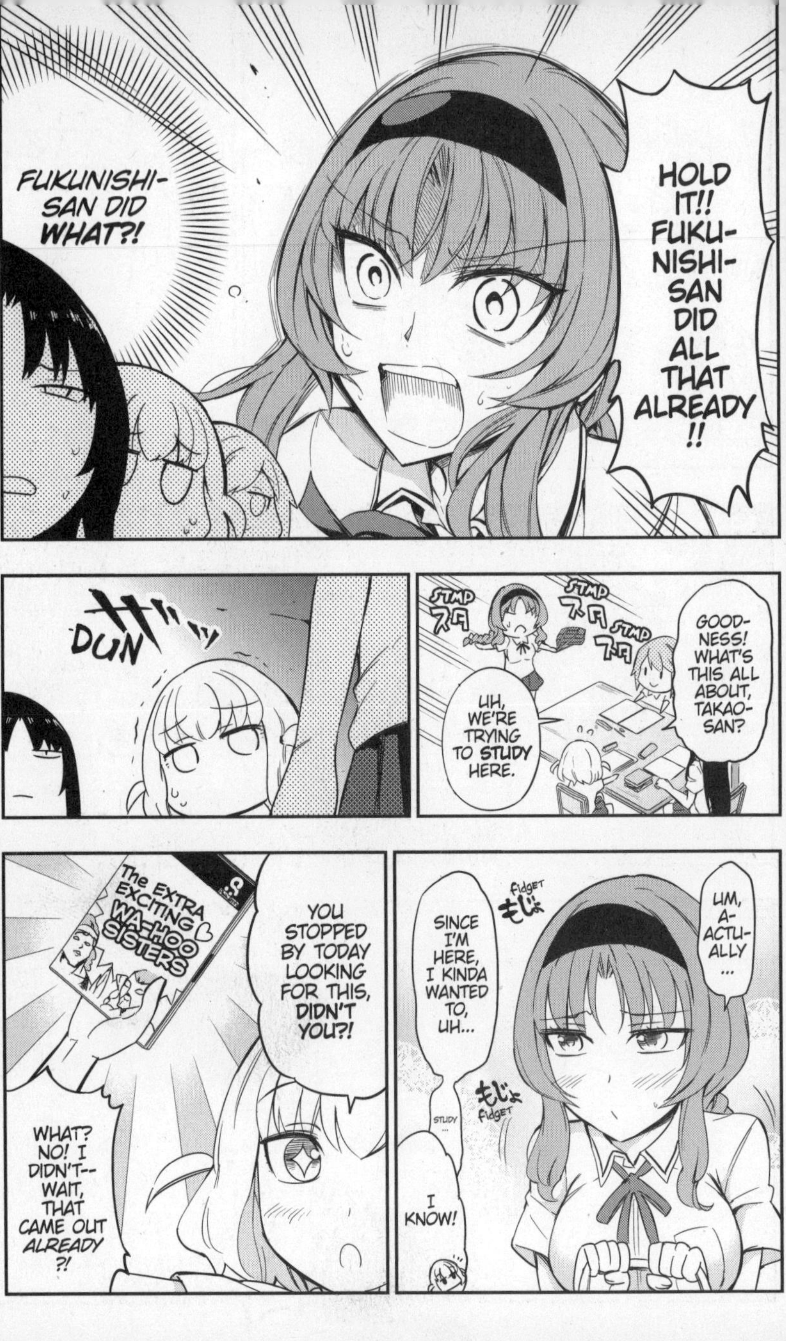
HOLD IT!! FUKUNISHI-SAN DID ALL THAT ALREADY!!
FUKUNISHI-SAN DID WHAT?!
STMP
STMP
STMP
GOODNESS! WHAT'S THIS ALL ABOUT, TAKAO-SAN?
UH, WE'RE TRYING TO STUDY HERE.
DUN
UM, A-ACTUALLY...
fidget
SINCE I'M HERE, I KINDA WANTED TO, UH...
fidget
STUDY...
I KNOW!
YOU STOPPED BY TODAY LOOKING FOR THIS, DIDN'T YOU?!
The EXTRA EXCITING WA-HOO SISTERS
WHAT? NO! I DIDN'T-- WAIT, THAT CAME OUT ALREADY?!

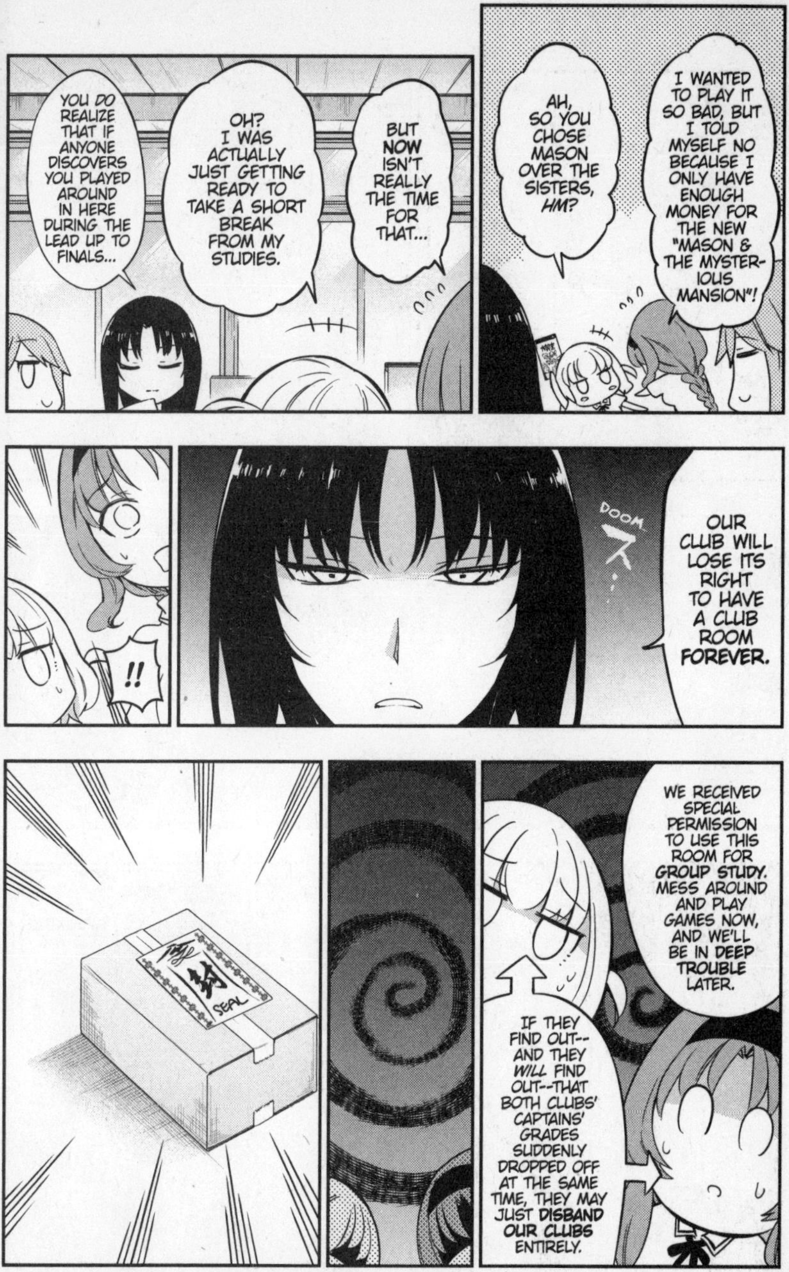
I WANTED TO PLAY IT SO BAD, BUT I TOLD MYSELF NO BECAUSE I ONLY HAVE ENOUGH MONEY FOR THE NEW "MASON & THE MYSTERIOUS MANSION"!
AH, SO YOU CHOSE MASON OVER THE SISTERS, *HM?*
BUT **NOW** ISN'T REALLY THE TIME FOR THAT...
OH? I WAS ACTUALLY JUST GETTING READY TO TAKE A SHORT BREAK FROM MY STUDIES.
YOU *DO* REALIZE THAT IF ANYONE DISCOVERS YOU PLAYED AROUND IN HERE DURING THE LEAD UP TO FINALS...
DOOM
OUR CLUB WILL LOSE ITS RIGHT TO HAVE A CLUB ROOM **FOREVER.**
!!
WE RECEIVED SPECIAL PERMISSION TO USE THIS ROOM FOR **GROUP STUDY.** MESS AROUND AND PLAY GAMES NOW, AND WE'LL BE IN DEEP TROUBLE LATER.
IF THEY FIND OUT--AND THEY *WILL* FIND OUT--THAT BOTH CLUBS' CAPTAINS' GRADES SUDDENLY DROPPED OFF AT THE SAME TIME, THEY MAY JUST **DISBAND OUR CLUBS** ENTIRELY.
SEAL

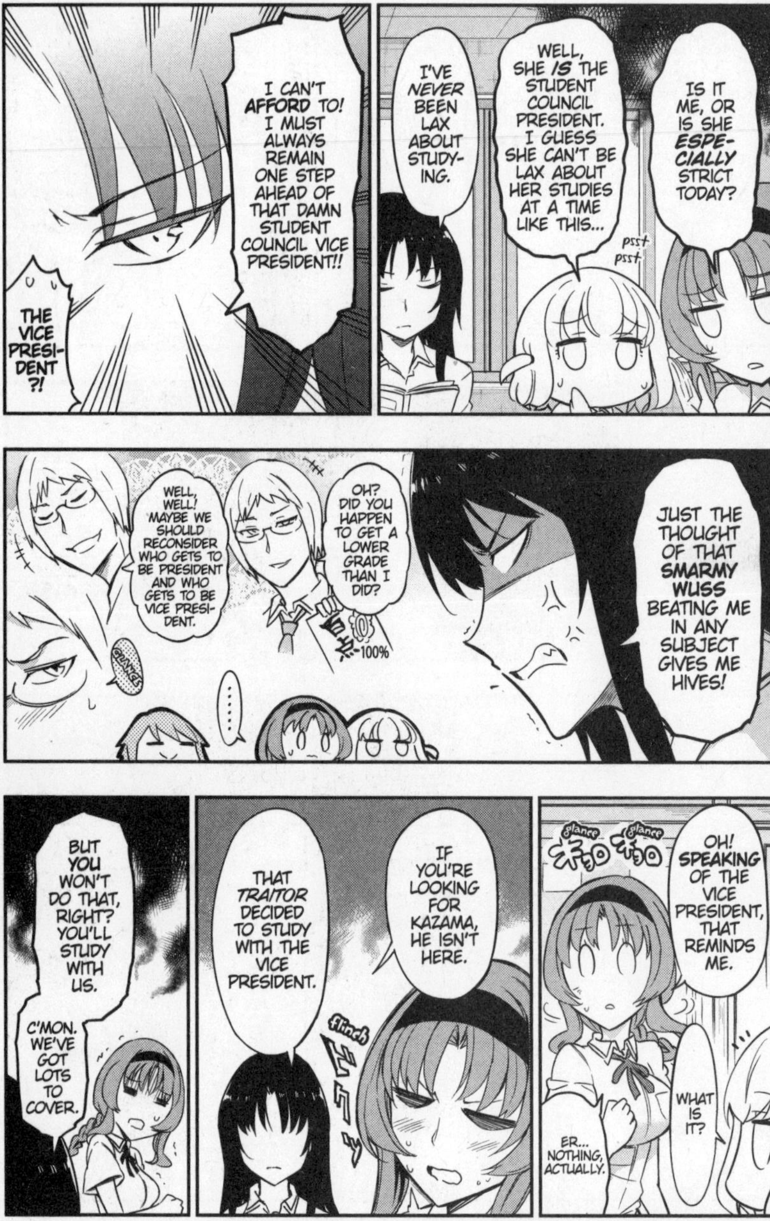
IS IT ME, OR IS SHE ESPECIALLY STRICT TODAY?
WELL, SHE IS THE STUDENT COUNCIL PRESIDENT. I GUESS SHE CAN'T BE LAX ABOUT HER STUDIES AT A TIME LIKE THIS...
psst psst
I'VE NEVER BEEN LAX ABOUT STUDYING.
I CAN'T AFFORD TO! I MUST ALWAYS REMAIN ONE STEP AHEAD OF THAT DAMN STUDENT COUNCIL VICE PRESIDENT!!
THE VICE PRESIDENT ?!
JUST THE THOUGHT OF THAT SMARMY WUSS BEATING ME IN ANY SUBJECT GIVES ME HIVES!
OH? DID YOU HAPPEN TO GET A LOWER GRADE THAN I DID?
100%
WELL, WELL! MAYBE WE SHOULD RECONSIDER WHO GETS TO BE PRESIDENT AND WHO GETS TO BE VICE PRESIDENT.
GLANCE
......
glance glance
OH! SPEAKING OF THE VICE PRESIDENT, THAT REMINDS ME.
WHAT IS IT?
ER... NOTHING, ACTUALLY.
IF YOU'RE LOOKING FOR KAZAMA, HE ISN'T HERE.
flinch
THAT TRAITOR DECIDED TO STUDY WITH THE VICE PRESIDENT.
BUT YOU WON'T DO THAT, RIGHT? YOU'LL STUDY WITH US.
C'MON. WE'VE GOT LOTS TO COVER.

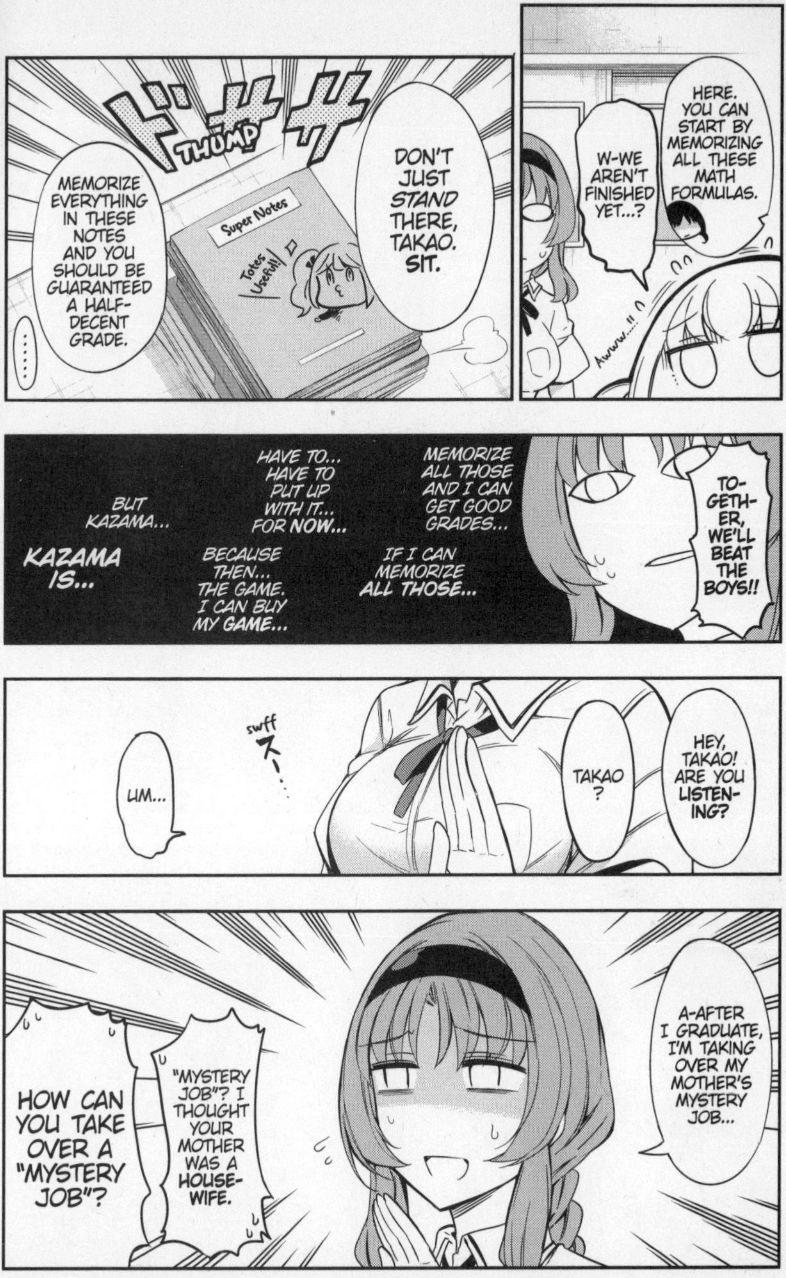
HERE. YOU CAN START BY MEMORIZING ALL THESE MATH FORMULAS.
W-WE AREN'T FINISHED YET...?
Awww...!!
DON'T JUST STAND THERE, TAKAO. SIT.
THUMP
Super Notes
Totes Useful!
MEMORIZE EVERYTHING IN THESE NOTES AND YOU SHOULD BE GUARANTEED A HALF-DECENT GRADE.
......
TO-GETH-ER, WE'LL BEAT THE BOYS!!
MEMORIZE ALL THOSE AND I CAN GET GOOD GRADES...
HAVE TO... HAVE TO PUT UP WITH IT... FOR NOW...
BUT KAZAMA...
IF I CAN MEMORIZE ALL THOSE...
BECAUSE THEN... THE GAME. I CAN BUY MY GAME...
KAZAMA IS...
HEY, TAKAO! ARE YOU LISTEN-ING?
TAKAO?
swff
UM...
A-AFTER I GRADUATE, I'M TAKING OVER MY MOTHER'S MYSTERY JOB...
"MYSTERY JOB"? I THOUGHT YOUR MOTHER WAS A HOUSE-WIFE.
HOW CAN YOU TAKE OVER A "MYSTERY JOB"?

Why yes,
I am a
housewife.
Honest!

D-FRAGMENTS

ディーふらぐ!

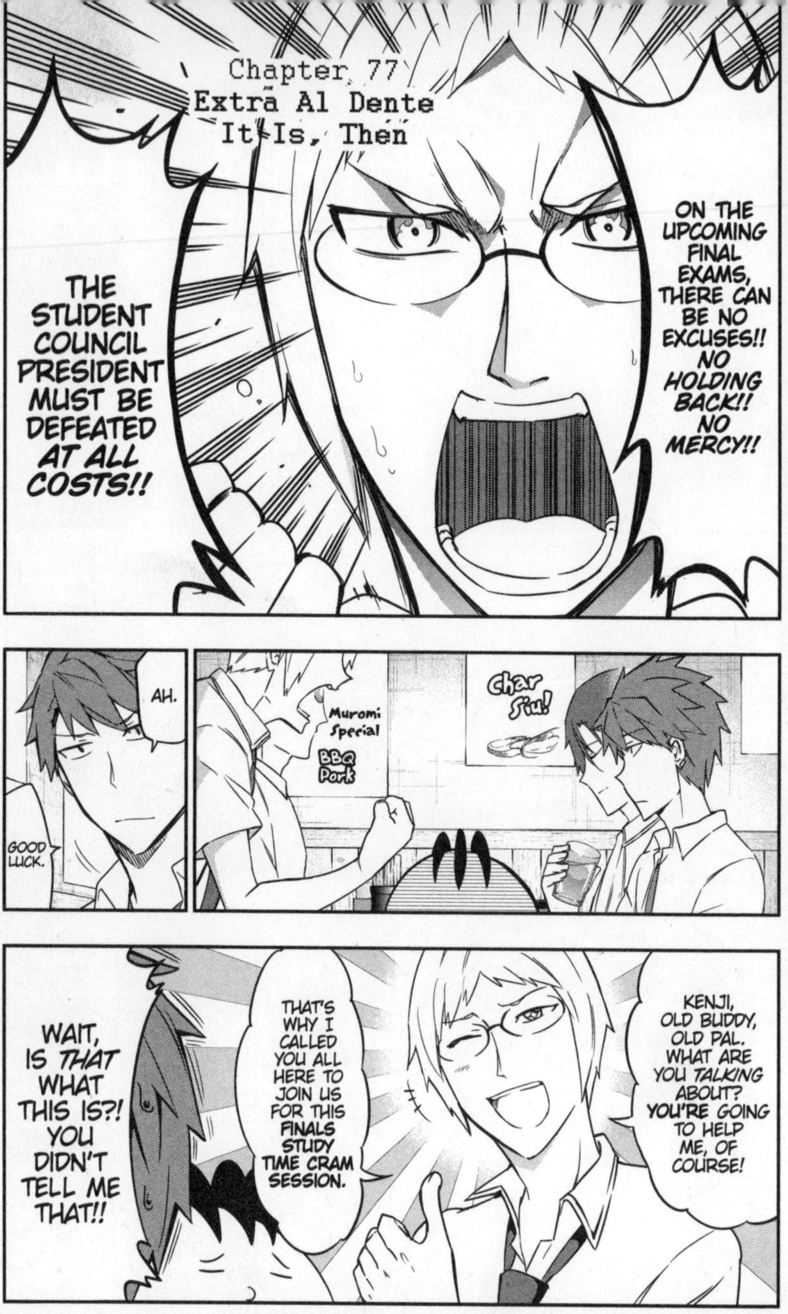
Chapter 77 Extra Al Dente It Is, Then
ON THE UPCOMING FINAL EXAMS, THERE CAN BE NO EXCUSES!! NO HOLDING BACK!! NO MERCY!!
THE STUDENT COUNCIL PRESIDENT MUST BE DEFEATED AT ALL COSTS!!
Char Siu!
Muromi Special
BBQ Pork
AH.
GOOD LUCK.
KENJI, OLD BUDDY, OLD PAL. WHAT ARE YOU TALKING ABOUT? YOU'RE GOING TO HELP ME, OF COURSE!
THAT'S WHY I CALLED YOU ALL HERE TO JOIN US FOR THIS FINALS STUDY TIME CRAM SESSION.
WAIT, IS THAT WHAT THIS IS?! YOU DIDN'T TELL ME THAT!!

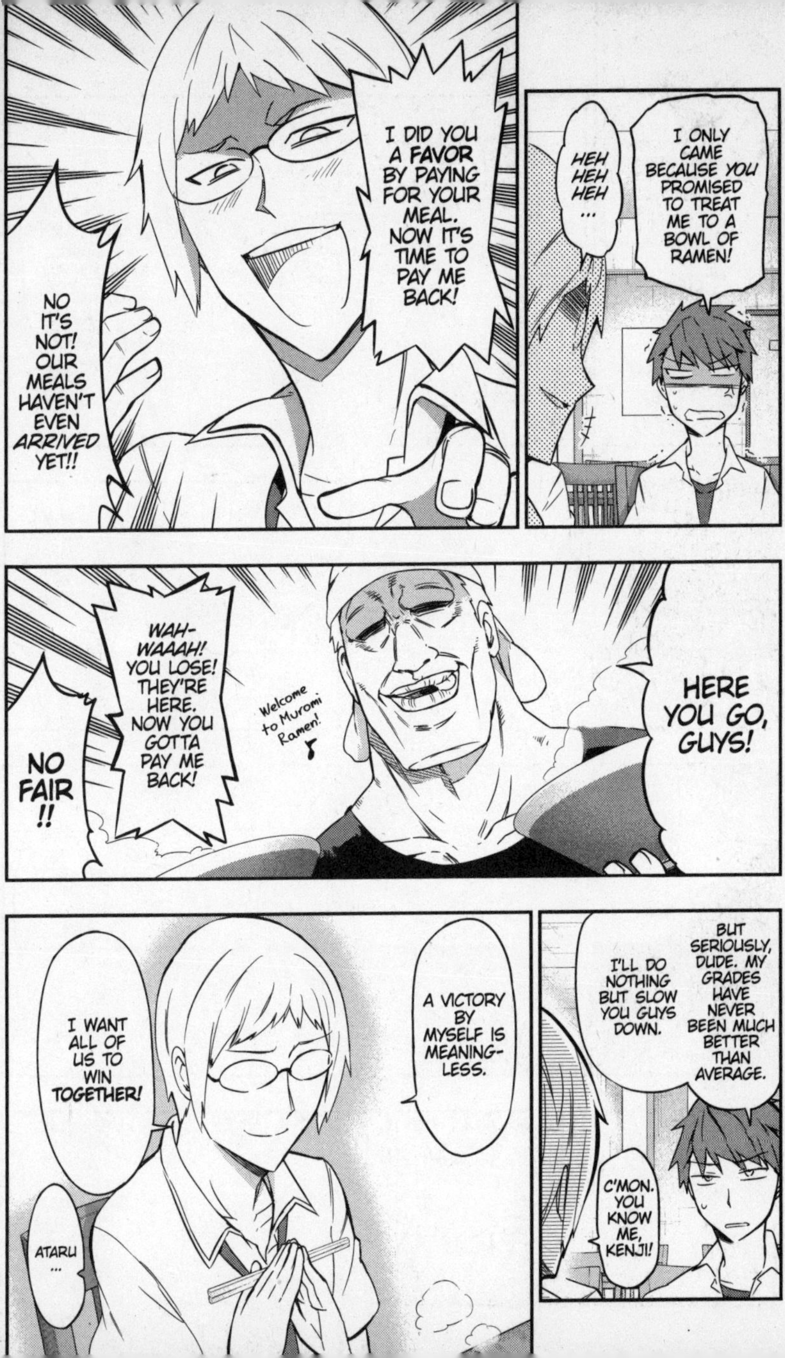
I ONLY CAME BECAUSE *YOU* PROMISED TO TREAT ME TO A BOWL OF RAMEN!
HEH HEH HEH ...
I DID YOU A **FAVOR** BY PAYING FOR YOUR MEAL. NOW IT'S TIME TO PAY ME BACK!
NO IT'S NOT! OUR MEALS HAVEN'T EVEN *ARRIVED* YET!!
HERE YOU GO, GUYS!
Welcome to Muromi Ramen! ♪
WAH-WAAAH! YOU LOSE! THEY'RE HERE. NOW YOU GOTTA PAY ME BACK!
NO FAIR!!
BUT SERIOUSLY, DUDE. MY GRADES HAVE NEVER BEEN MUCH BETTER THAN AVERAGE.
I'LL DO NOTHING BUT SLOW YOU GUYS DOWN.
C'MON. YOU KNOW ME, KENJI!
A VICTORY BY MYSELF IS MEANING-LESS.
I WANT ALL OF US TO WIN TOGETHER!
ATARU ...

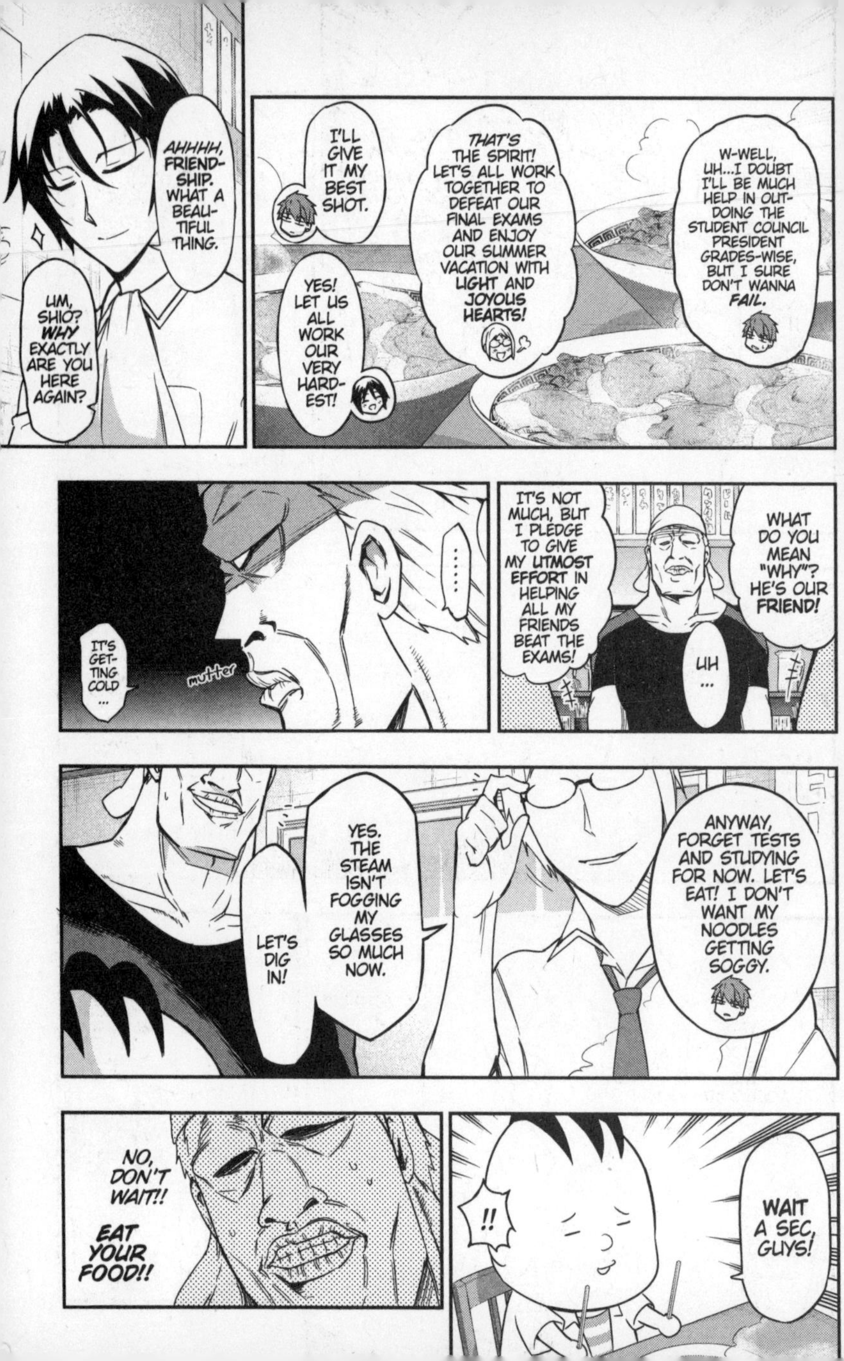
W-WELL, UH...I DOUBT I'LL BE MUCH HELP IN OUT-DOING THE STUDENT COUNCIL PRESIDENT GRADES-WISE, BUT I SURE DON'T WANNA FAIL.
THAT'S THE SPIRIT! LET'S ALL WORK TOGETHER TO DEFEAT OUR FINAL EXAMS AND ENJOY OUR SUMMER VACATION WITH LIGHT AND JOYOUS HEARTS!
I'LL GIVE IT MY BEST SHOT.
YES! LET US ALL WORK OUR VERY HARD-EST!
AHHHH, FRIEND-SHIP. WHAT A BEAU-TIFUL THING.
UM, SHIO? WHY EXACTLY ARE YOU HERE AGAIN?
WHAT DO YOU MEAN "WHY"? HE'S OUR FRIEND!
IT'S NOT MUCH, BUT I PLEDGE TO GIVE MY UTMOST EFFORT IN HELPING ALL MY FRIENDS BEAT THE EXAMS!
UH ...
......
mutter
IT'S GET-TING COLD ...
ANYWAY, FORGET TESTS AND STUDYING FOR NOW. LET'S EAT! I DON'T WANT MY NOODLES GETTING SOGGY.
YES. THE STEAM ISN'T FOGGING MY GLASSES SO MUCH NOW.
LET'S DIG IN!
WAIT A SEC, GUYS!
!!
NO, DON'T WAIT!!
EAT YOUR FOOD!!

WELL... IT ISN'T AS IF YOKOSHIMA HAS ANY NEED TO BE HERE IF YOKOSHIMA HAS NO DESIRE TO STAY...

TRUE... HE'S RIGHT... HE HASN'T...

AND BOY ARE THEY REALLY DRAGGING OUT THEIR SENTENCES!

AS THE NOTORIOUS LITTLE FOOT, ONE OF THE KAZAMA GANG'S FOUNDING MEMBERS, I, LITTLEFOOT YOKOSHIMA, HAVE NOT YET GIVEN MY APPROVAL OF THIS FINALS STUDY TIME CRAM SESSION IN WHICH ATARU, ANOTHER FOUNDING MEMBER OF THE KAZAMA GANG, HAS DECLARED HIS ATTEMPT TO OUTDO CURRENT STUDENT COUNCIL PRESIDENT KARASUNO CHITOSE GRADE-WISE DURING OUR UPCOMING FINAL EXAMS...

COULD YOU DRAG THIS OUT ANY LONGER?! YOUR FOOD IS GOING COLD!!

YOU MIGHT HAVE ACCEPTED THINGS, KEN-CHAN, BUT I STILL HAVE MY DOUBTS!

STOP PROLONGING THIS!! YOU'VE ALL KNOWN EACH OTHER SINCE YOU WERE LITTLE, RIGHT?! HOW IS ANY OF THIS NEW INFORMATION?!

YOU NEVER EVEN BOTHER TO STUDY AND YOU STILL END UP ONE OF THE TOP SCORERS IN OUR ENTIRE CLASS, YOU LUCKY JERK!!

AFTER ALL...

YEAH. WE'VE ALWAYS LEANED TOO HEAVILY ON YOKOSHIMA TO CARRY US...

WHOA, HOLD IT! I KNOW THAT LOOK! YOU BETTER NOT BE DRIFTING INTO A FLASHBACK!

MID TERM EXAMS

597pts	Dai Mejiro
595pts	Yokoshima
	Shio Hachi

OY, YOU!! DON'T KEEP JAWIN'! BITE INTO YOUR FOOD INSTEAD!

COME TO THINK OF IT, I DO RECALL SEEING YOKOSHIMA'S NAME HIGH ON THE LIST OF MID-TERM RESULTS.

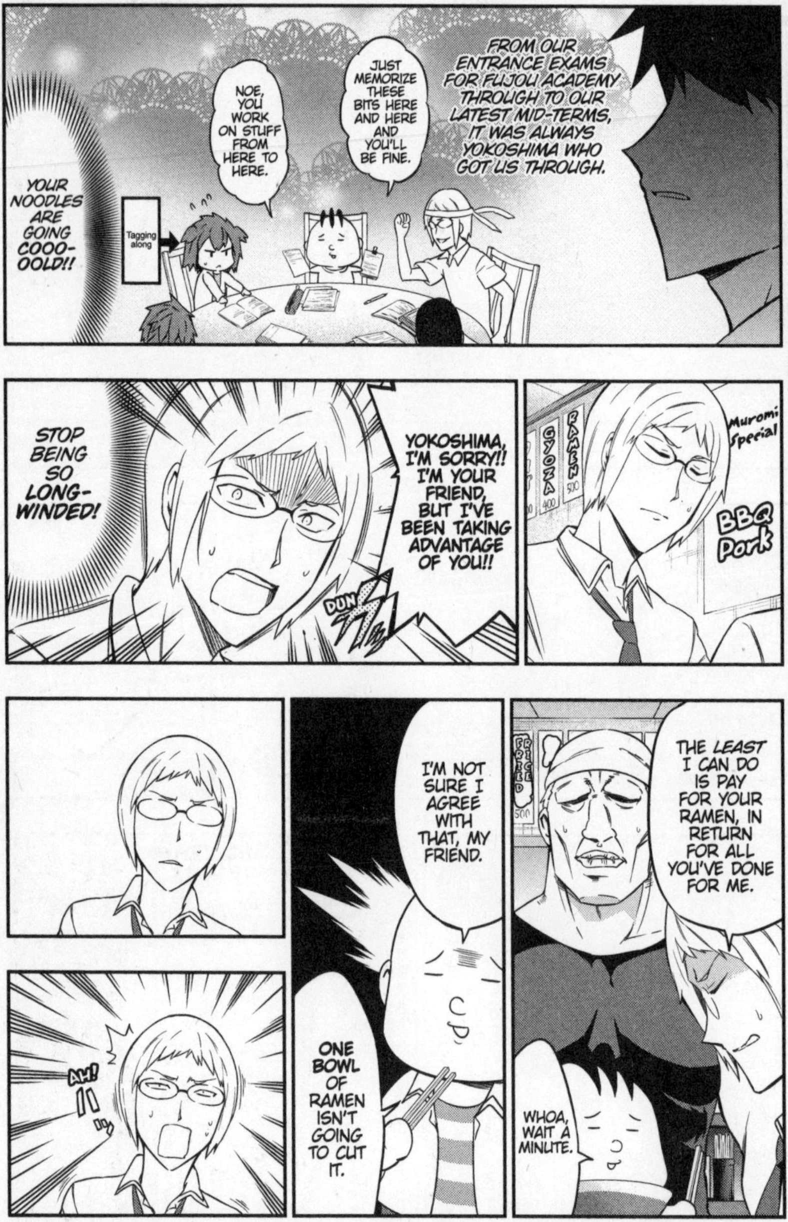
FROM OUR ENTRANCE EXAMS FOR FUJOU ACADEMY THROUGH TO OUR LATEST MID-TERMS, IT WAS ALWAYS YOKOSHIMA WHO GOT US THROUGH.
JUST MEMORIZE THESE BITS HERE AND HERE AND YOU'LL BE FINE.
NOE, YOU WORK ON STUFF FROM HERE TO HERE.
Tagging along
YOUR NOODLES ARE GOING COOOOOLD!!
Muromi Special
RAMEN 500
GYOZA 400
BBQ Pork
YOKOSHIMA, I'M SORRY!! I'M YOUR FRIEND, BUT I'VE BEEN TAKING ADVANTAGE OF YOU!!
DUN
STOP BEING SO LONG-WINDED!
THE LEAST I CAN DO IS PAY FOR YOUR RAMEN, IN RETURN FOR ALL YOU'VE DONE FOR ME.
FRIED RICE
500
WHOA, WAIT A MINUTE.
I'M NOT SURE I AGREE WITH THAT, MY FRIEND.
ONE BOWL OF RAMEN ISN'T GOING TO CUT IT.
AH!!

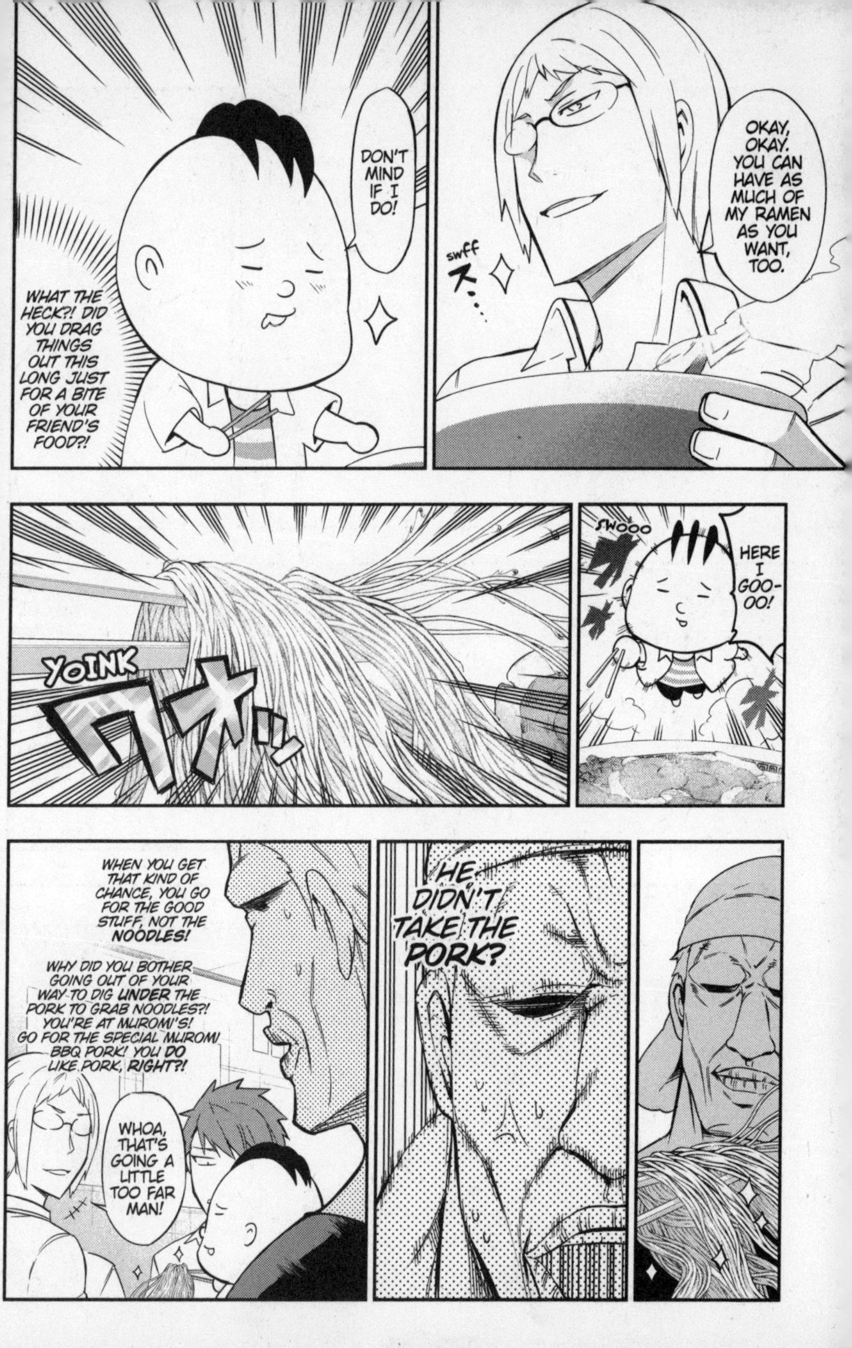
OKAY, OKAY. YOU CAN HAVE AS MUCH OF MY RAMEN AS YOU WANT, TOO.
swff
DON'T MIND IF I DO!
WHAT THE HECK?! DID YOU DRAG THINGS OUT THIS LONG JUST FOR A BITE OF YOUR FRIEND'S FOOD?!
SWOOO
HERE I GOO-OO!
YOINK
HE DIDN'T TAKE THE PORK?
WHEN YOU GET THAT KIND OF CHANCE, YOU GO FOR THE GOOD STUFF, NOT THE NOODLES!
WHY DID YOU BOTHER GOING OUT OF YOUR WAY TO DIG UNDER THE PORK TO GRAB NOODLES?! YOU'RE AT MUROMI'S! GO FOR THE SPECIAL MUROMI BBQ PORK! YOU DO LIKE PORK, RIGHT?!
WHOA, THAT'S GOING A LITTLE TOO FAR MAN!

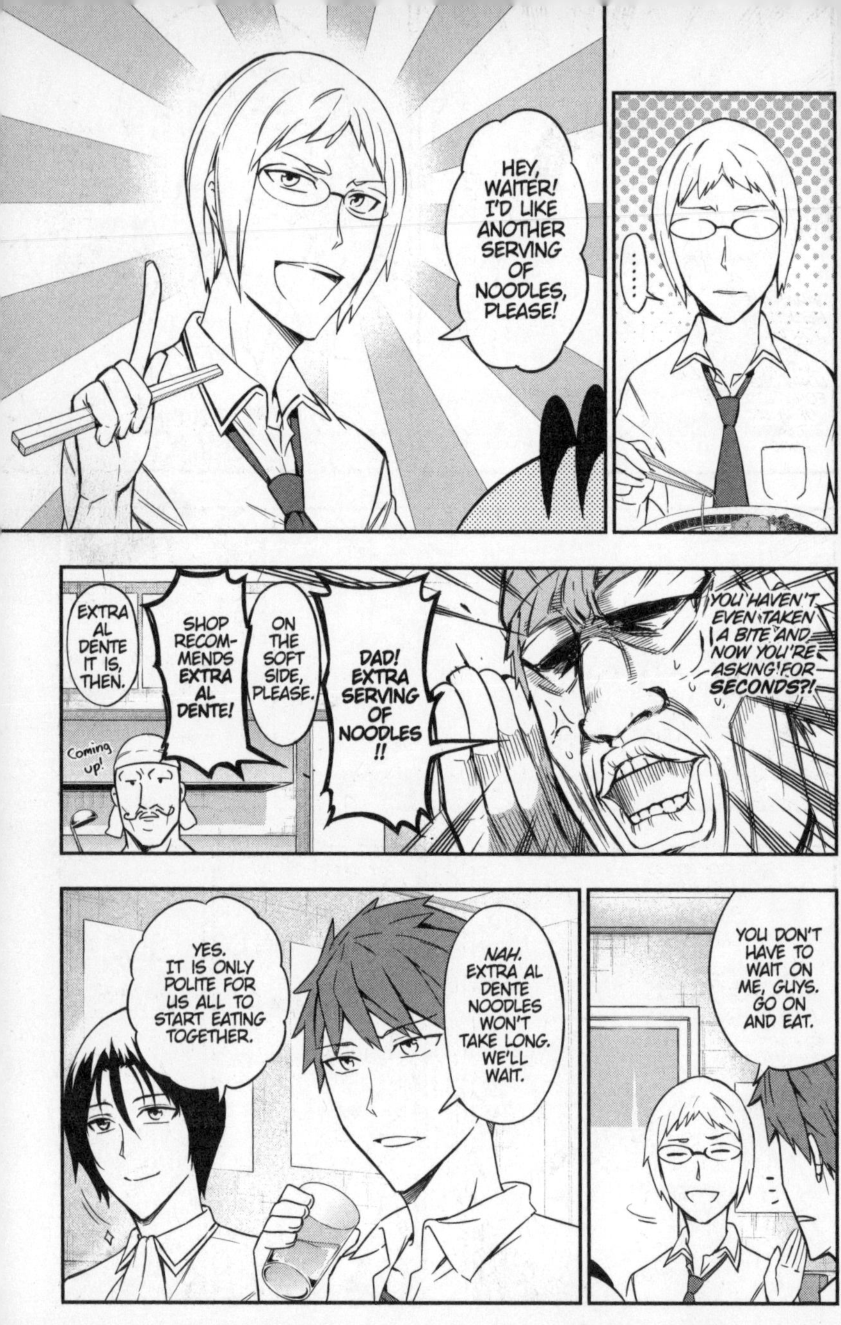
……
HEY, WAITER! I'D LIKE ANOTHER SERVING OF NOODLES, PLEASE!
YOU HAVEN'T EVEN TAKEN A BITE AND NOW YOU'RE ASKING FOR SECONDS?!
DAD! EXTRA SERVING OF NOODLES !!
ON THE SOFT SIDE, PLEASE.
SHOP RECOMMENDS EXTRA AL DENTE!
EXTRA AL DENTE IT IS, THEN.
Coming up!
YOU DON'T HAVE TO WAIT ON ME, GUYS. GO ON AND EAT.
NAH. EXTRA AL DENTE NOODLES WON'T TAKE LONG. WE'LL WAIT.
YES. IT IS ONLY POLITE FOR US ALL TO START EATING TOGETHER.

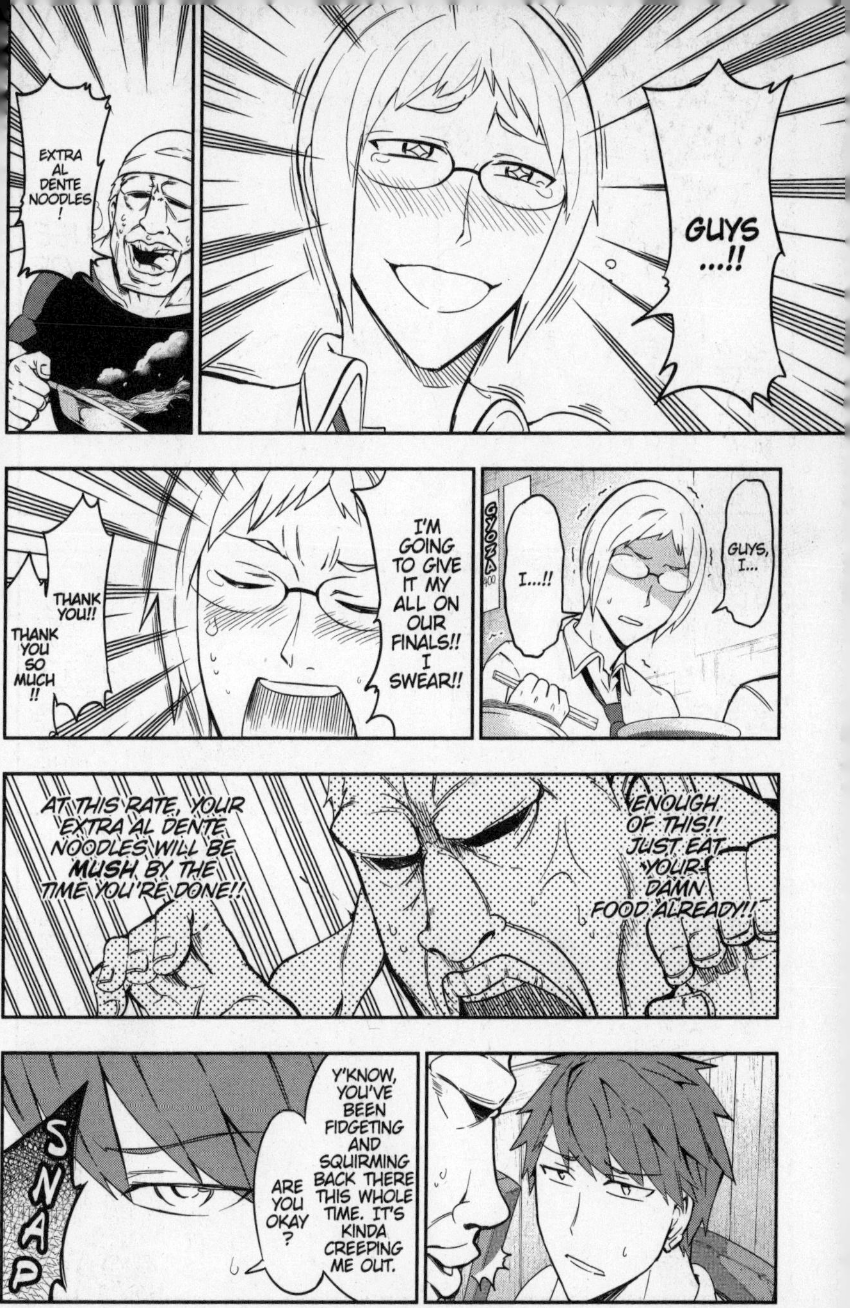
GUYS ...!!
EXTRA AL DENTE NOODLES !
GUYS, I...
GYOZA
I...!!
I'M GOING TO GIVE IT MY ALL ON OUR FINALS!! I SWEAR!!
THANK YOU!!
THANK YOU SO MUCH !!
ENOUGH OF THIS!! JUST EAT YOUR DAMN FOOD ALREADY!!
AT THIS RATE, YOUR EXTRA AL DENTE NOODLES WILL BE MUSH BY THE TIME YOU'RE DONE!!
Y'KNOW, YOU'VE BEEN FIDGETING AND SQUIRMING BACK THERE THIS WHOLE TIME. IT'S KINDA CREEPING ME OUT.
ARE YOU OKAY ?
SNAP

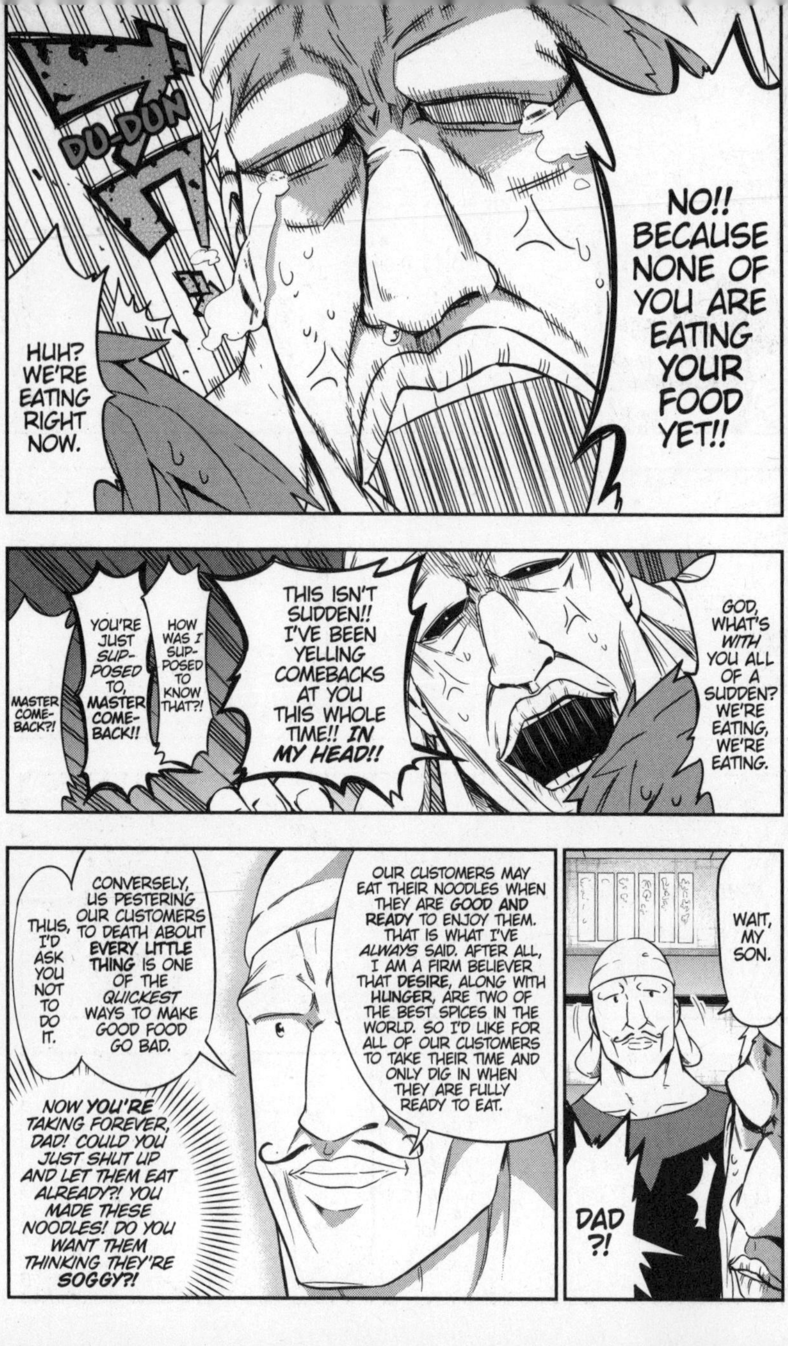
NO!! BECAUSE NONE OF YOU ARE EATING YOUR FOOD YET!!
DU-DUN
HUH? WE'RE EATING RIGHT NOW.
GOD, WHAT'S WITH YOU ALL OF A SUDDEN? WE'RE EATING, WE'RE EATING.
THIS ISN'T SUDDEN!! I'VE BEEN YELLING COMEBACKS AT YOU THIS WHOLE TIME!! IN MY HEAD!!
HOW WAS I SUPPOSED TO KNOW THAT?!
YOU'RE JUST SUPPOSED TO, MASTER COMEBACK!!
MASTER COMEBACK?!
WAIT, MY SON.
DAD?!
OUR CUSTOMERS MAY EAT THEIR NOODLES WHEN THEY ARE GOOD AND READY TO ENJOY THEM. THAT IS WHAT I'VE ALWAYS SAID. AFTER ALL, I AM A FIRM BELIEVER THAT DESIRE, ALONG WITH HUNGER, ARE TWO OF THE BEST SPICES IN THE WORLD. SO I'D LIKE FOR ALL OF OUR CUSTOMERS TO TAKE THEIR TIME AND ONLY DIG IN WHEN THEY ARE FULLY READY TO EAT.
CONVERSELY, US PESTERING OUR CUSTOMERS TO DEATH ABOUT EVERY LITTLE THING IS ONE OF THE QUICKEST WAYS TO MAKE GOOD FOOD GO BAD.
THUS, I'D ASK YOU NOT TO DO IT.
NOW YOU'RE TAKING FOREVER, DAD! COULD YOU JUST SHUT UP AND LET THEM EAT ALREADY?! YOU MADE THESE NOODLES! DO YOU WANT THEM THINKING THEY'RE SOGGY?!

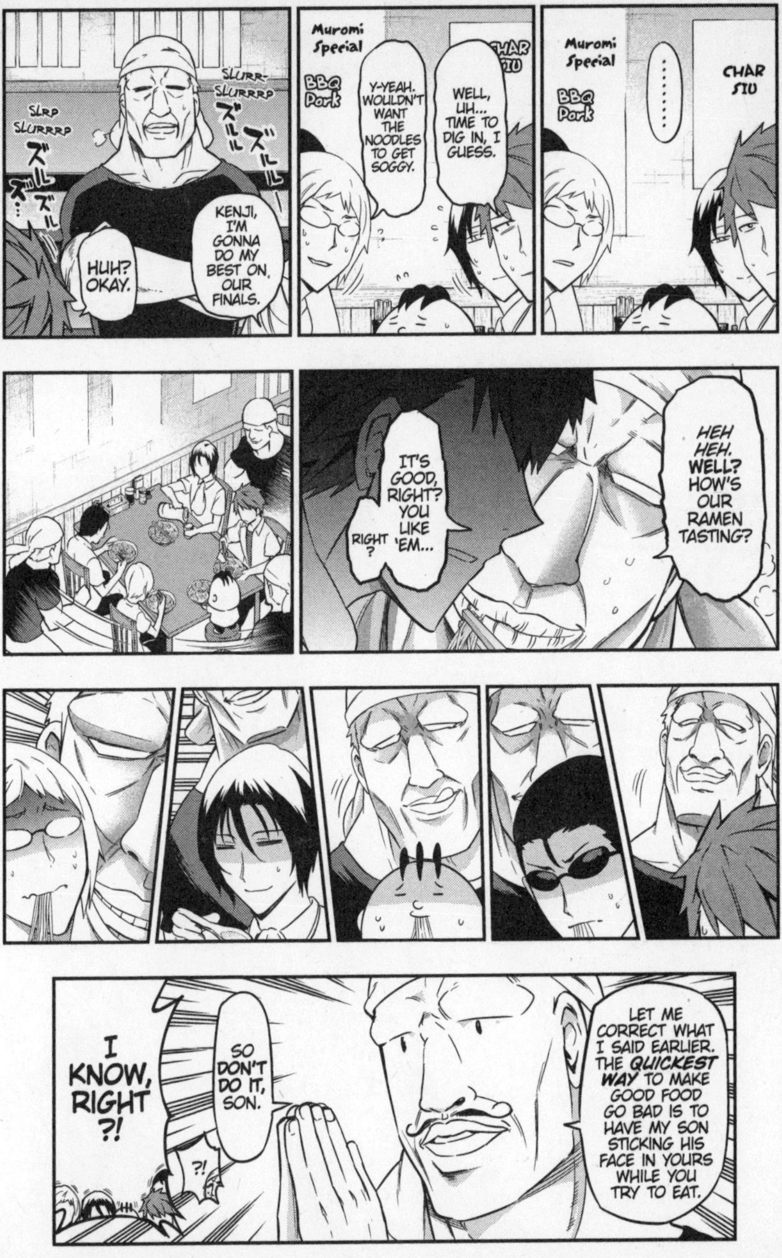
Muromi Special
BBQ Pork
CHAR SIU
......
Muromi Special
BBQ Pork
CHAR SIU
WELL, UH... TIME TO DIG IN, I GUESS.
Y-YEAH. WOULDN'T WANT THE NOODLES TO GET SOGGY.
SLURR-SLURRRP
ズルルー
KENJI, I'M GONNA DO MY BEST ON OUR FINALS.
HUH? OKAY.
SLRP SLURRRP
ズルズルズ…
HEH HEH. WELL? HOW'S OUR RAMEN TASTING?
IT'S GOOD, RIGHT? YOU LIKE 'EM...
RIGHT?
LET ME CORRECT WHAT I SAID EARLIER. THE QUICKEST WAY TO MAKE GOOD FOOD GO BAD IS TO HAVE MY SON STICKING HIS FACE IN YOURS WHILE YOU TRY TO EAT.
SO DON'T DO IT, SON.
?!
I KNOW, RIGHT?!

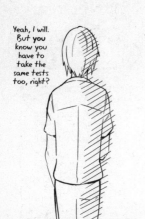

Ataru... give it your best on the final, okay?
Yeah, I will. But you know you have to take the same tests too, right?

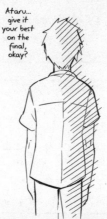

D-FRAGMENTS ディーふらぐめんつ！

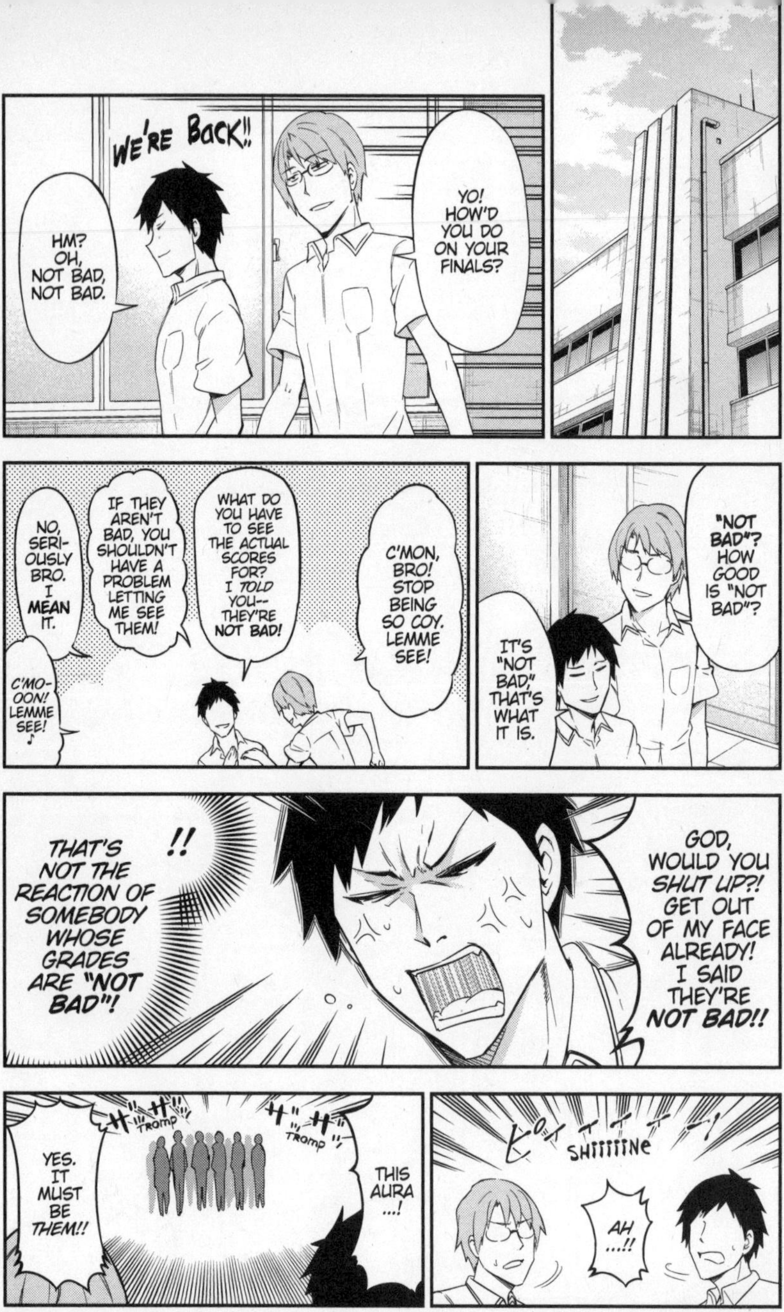
WE'RE BACK!!
YO! HOW'D YOU DO ON YOUR FINALS?
HM? OH, NOT BAD, NOT BAD.
"NOT BAD"? HOW GOOD IS "NOT BAD"?
IT'S "NOT BAD," THAT'S WHAT IT IS.
C'MON, BRO! STOP BEING SO COY. LEMME SEE!
WHAT DO YOU HAVE TO SEE THE ACTUAL SCORES FOR? I TOLD YOU-- THEY'RE NOT BAD!
IF THEY AREN'T BAD, YOU SHOULDN'T HAVE A PROBLEM LETTING ME SEE THEM!
NO, SERIOUSLY BRO. I MEAN IT.
C'MO-OON! LEMME SEE! ♪
GOD, WOULD YOU SHUT UP?! GET OUT OF MY FACE ALREADY! I SAID THEY'RE NOT BAD!!
!!
THAT'S NOT THE REACTION OF SOMEBODY WHOSE GRADES ARE "NOT BAD"!
SHIIIIIINE
AH ...!!
TRAMP
TRAMP
THIS AURA ...!
YES. IT MUST BE THEM!!

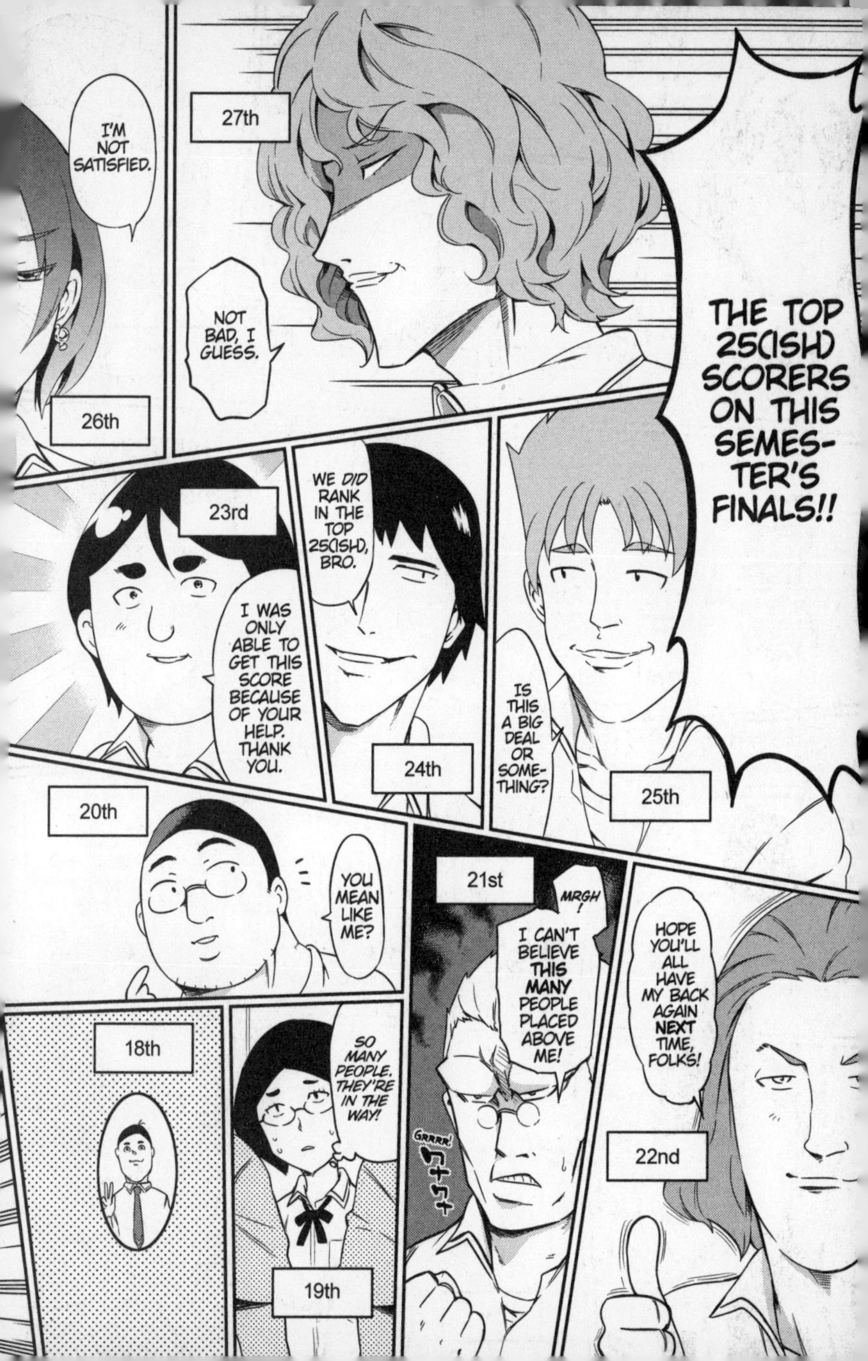
THE TOP 25(ISH) SCORERS ON THIS SEMES-TER'S FINALS!!
27th
NOT BAD, I GUESS.
I'M NOT SATISFIED.
26th
IS THIS A BIG DEAL OR SOME-THING?
25th
WE *DID* RANK IN THE TOP 25(ISH), BRO.
24th
23rd
I WAS ONLY ABLE TO GET THIS SCORE BECAUSE OF YOUR HELP. THANK YOU.
HOPE YOU'LL ALL HAVE MY BACK AGAIN NEXT TIME, FOLKS!
22nd
21st
MRGH!
I CAN'T BELIEVE THIS MANY PEOPLE PLACED ABOVE ME!
GRRRR!
20th
YOU MEAN LIKE ME?
SO MANY PEOPLE. THEY'RE IN THE WAY!
19th
18th

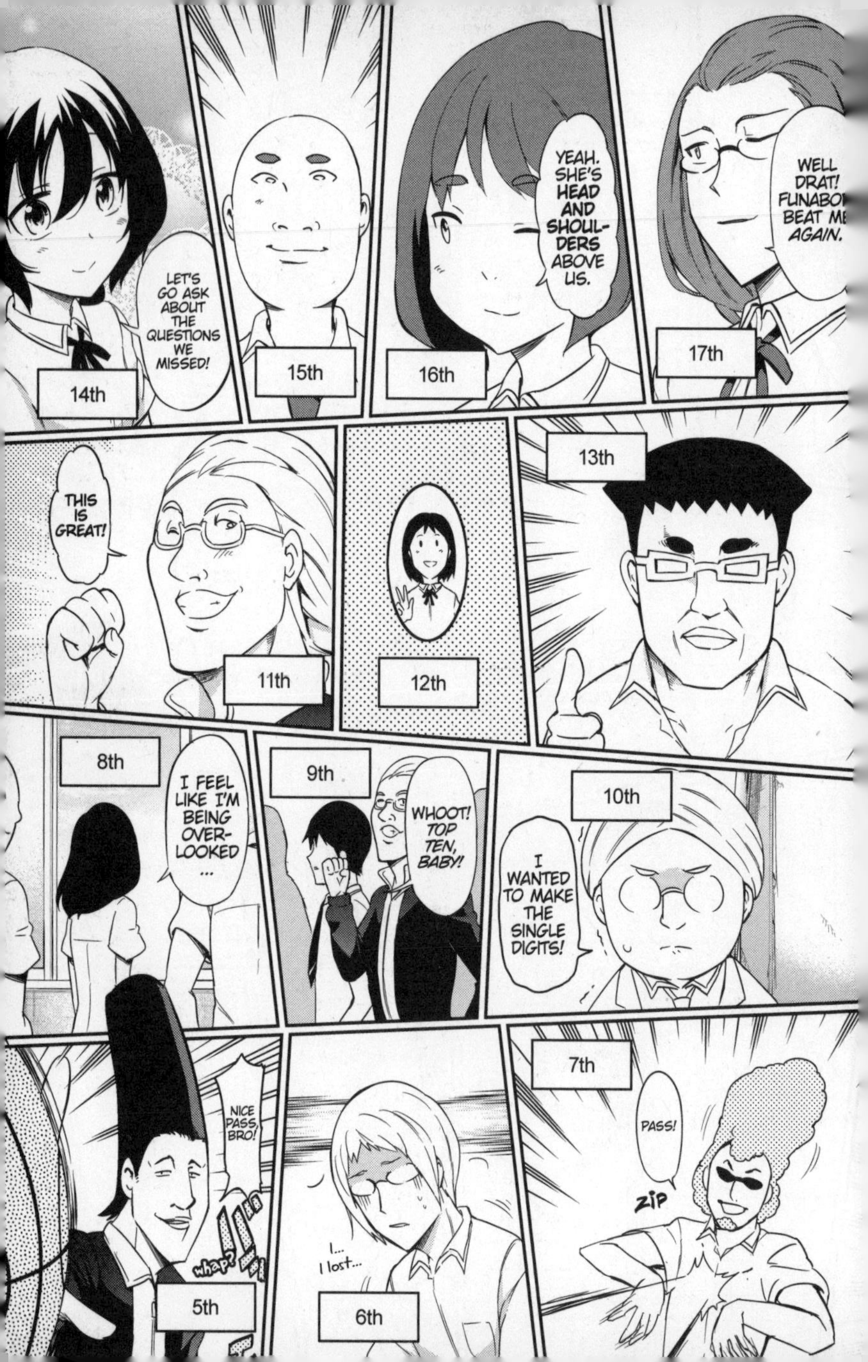
WELL DRAT! FUNABO BEAT ME AGAIN.
17th
YEAH. SHE'S HEAD AND SHOULDERS ABOVE US.
16th
15th
LET'S GO ASK ABOUT THE QUESTIONS WE MISSED!
14th
13th
12th
THIS IS GREAT!
11th
10th
I WANTED TO MAKE THE SINGLE DIGITS!
9th
WHOOT! TOP TEN, BABY!
8th
I FEEL LIKE I'M BEING OVERLOOKED ...
7th
PASS!
ZIP
I... I lost...
6th
NICE PASS BRO!
whap?
5th

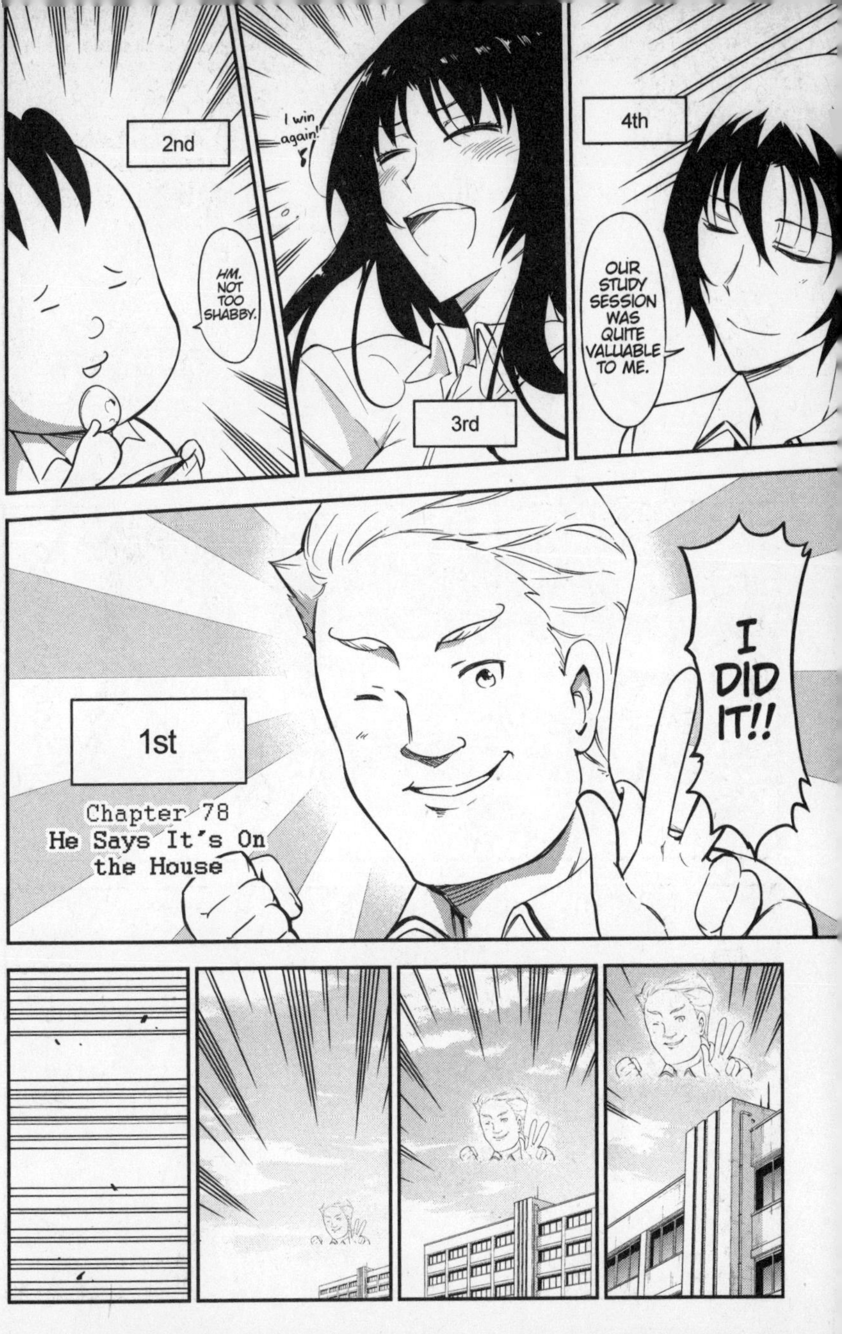
4th
OUR STUDY SESSION WAS QUITE VALUABLE TO ME.
I win again!
3rd
2nd
HM. NOT TOO SHABBY.
I DID IT!!
1st
Chapter 78
He Says It's On the House

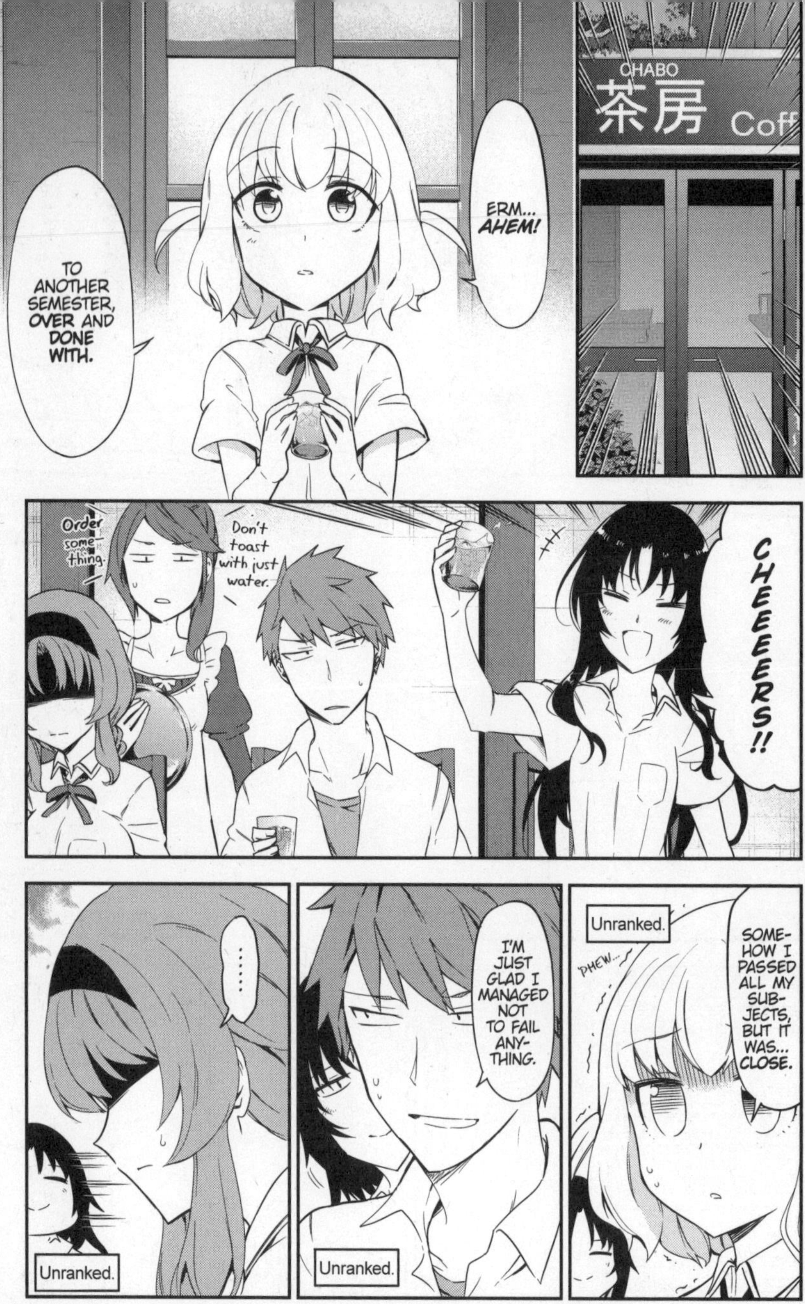

CHABO
茶房
Coff
ERM... AHEM!
TO ANOTHER SEMESTER, OVER AND DONE WITH.
CHEEEEERS!!
Don't toast with just water.
Order something.
SOMEHOW I PASSED ALL MY SUBJECTS, BUT IT WAS... CLOSE.
Unranked.
PHEW...
I'M JUST GLAD I MANAGED NOT TO FAIL ANYTHING.
Unranked.
......
Unranked.

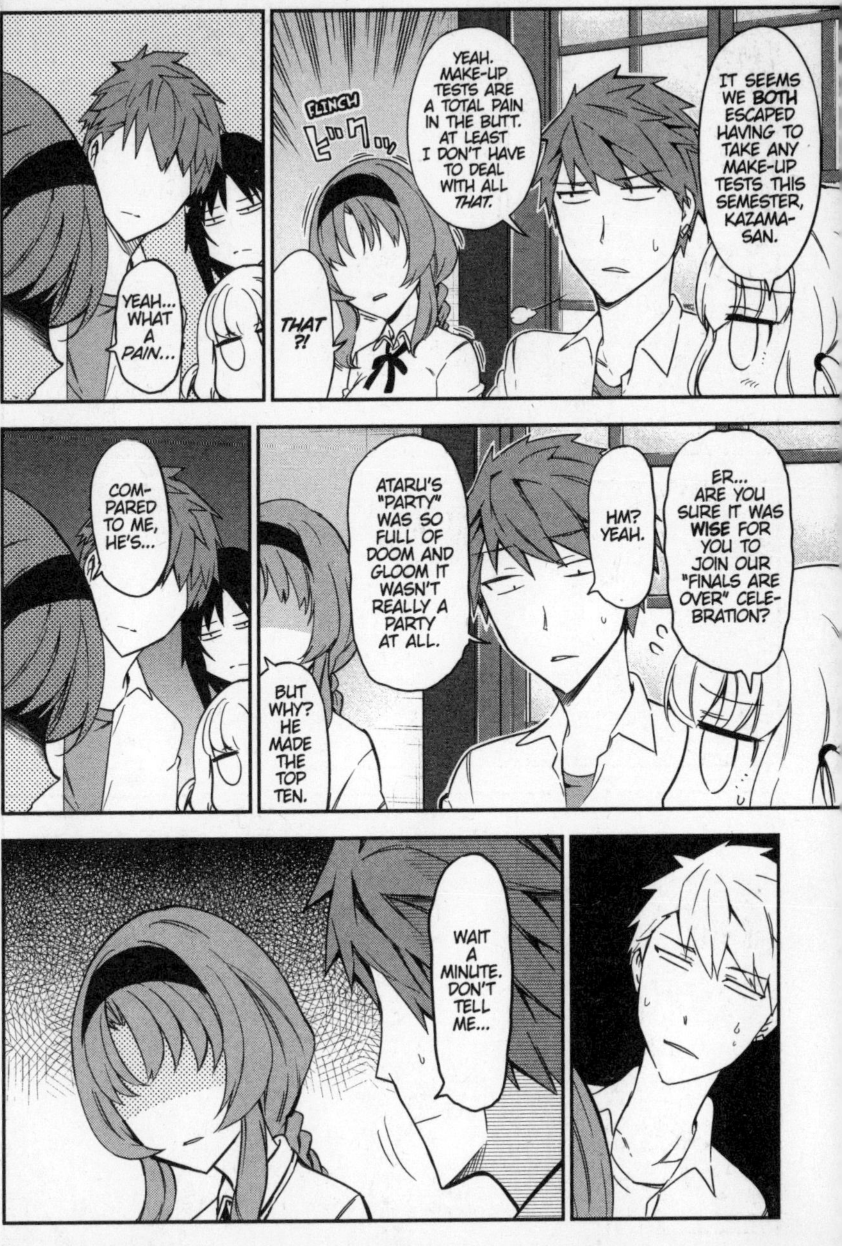
IT SEEMS WE BOTH ESCAPED HAVING TO TAKE ANY MAKE-UP TESTS THIS SEMESTER, KAZAMA-SAN.
YEAH. MAKE-UP TESTS ARE A TOTAL PAIN IN THE BUTT. AT LEAST I DON'T HAVE TO DEAL WITH ALL THAT.
FLINCH
THAT?!
YEAH... WHAT A PAIN...
ER... ARE YOU SURE IT WAS WISE FOR YOU TO JOIN OUR "FINALS ARE OVER" CELEBRATION?
HM? YEAH.
ATARU'S "PARTY" WAS SO FULL OF DOOM AND GLOOM IT WASN'T REALLY A PARTY AT ALL.
BUT WHY? HE MADE THE TOP TEN.
COMPARED TO ME, HE'S...
WAIT A MINUTE. DON'T TELL ME...

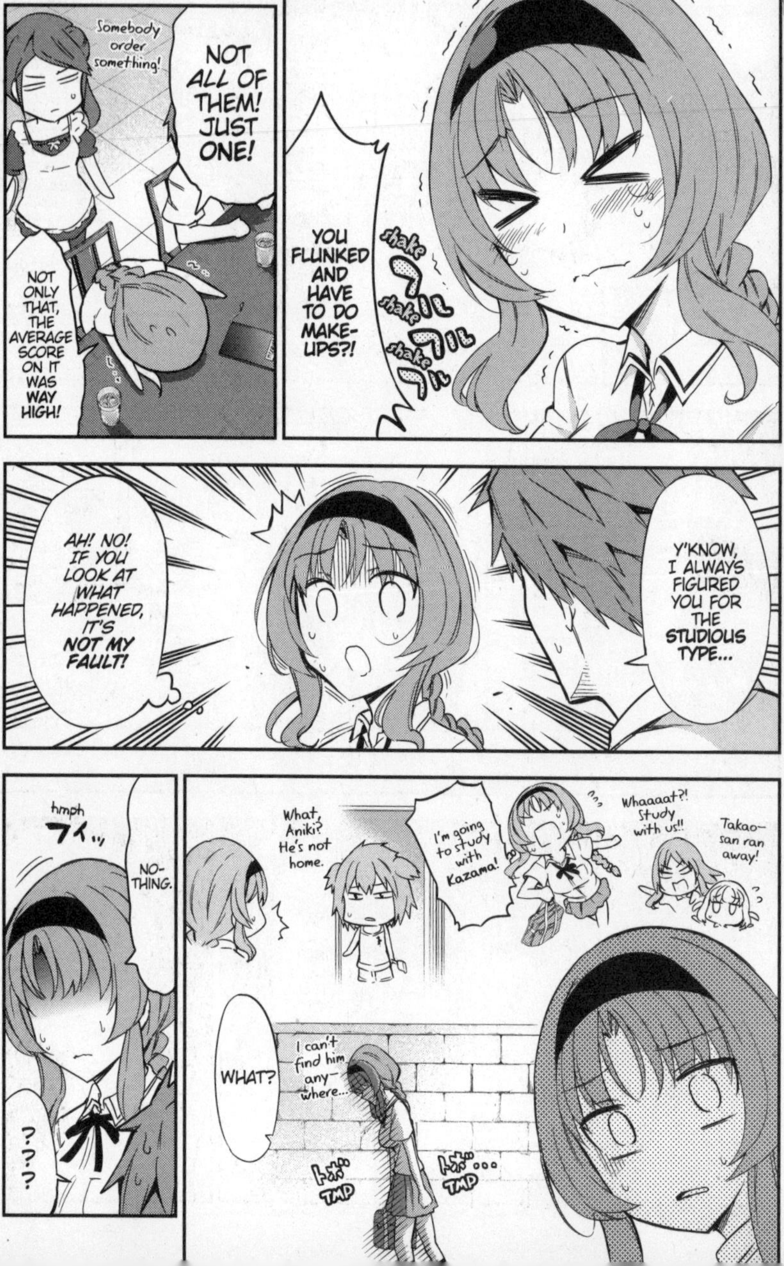
YOU FLUNKED AND HAVE TO DO MAKE-UPS?!
shake
shake
shake
NOT ALL OF THEM! JUST ONE!
Somebody order something!
NOT ONLY THAT, THE AVERAGE SCORE ON IT WAS WAY HIGH!
Y'KNOW, I ALWAYS FIGURED YOU FOR THE STUDIOUS TYPE...
AH! NO! IF YOU LOOK AT WHAT HAPPENED, IT'S NOT MY FAULT!
Takao-san ran away!
Whaaaat?! Study with us!!
I'm going to study with Kazama!
What, Aniki? He's not home.
TMP
TMP
I can't find him anywhere...
WHAT?
hmph
NO-THING.

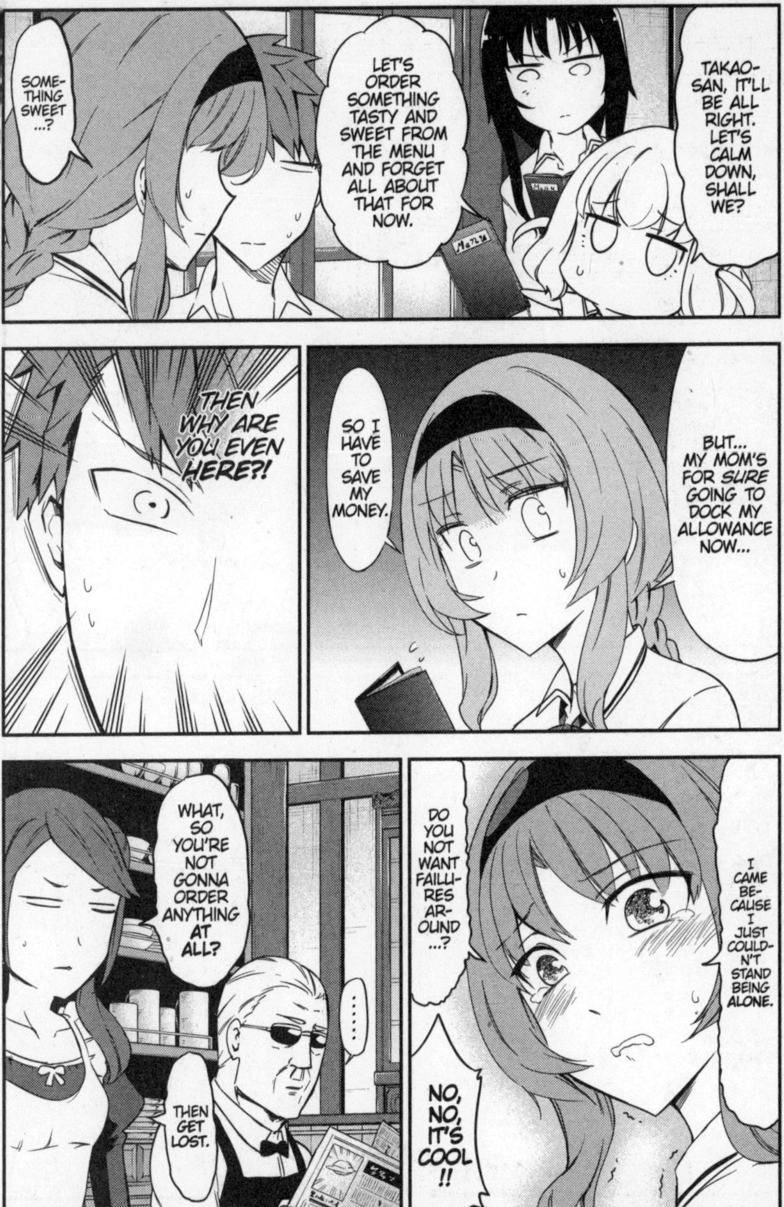
TAKAO-SAN, IT'LL BE ALL RIGHT. LET'S CALM DOWN, SHALL WE?
LET'S ORDER SOMETHING TASTY AND SWEET FROM THE MENU AND FORGET ALL ABOUT THAT FOR NOW.
SOMETHING SWEET ...?
BUT... MY MOM'S FOR *SURE* GOING TO DOCK MY ALLOWANCE NOW...
SO I HAVE TO SAVE MY MONEY.
THEN WHY ARE YOU EVEN HERE?!
I CAME BECAUSE I JUST COULDN'T STAND BEING ALONE.
DO YOU NOT WANT FAILURES AROUND ...?
NO, NO, IT'S COOL !!
WHAT, SO YOU'RE NOT GONNA ORDER ANYTHING **AT** ALL?
......
THEN GET LOST.

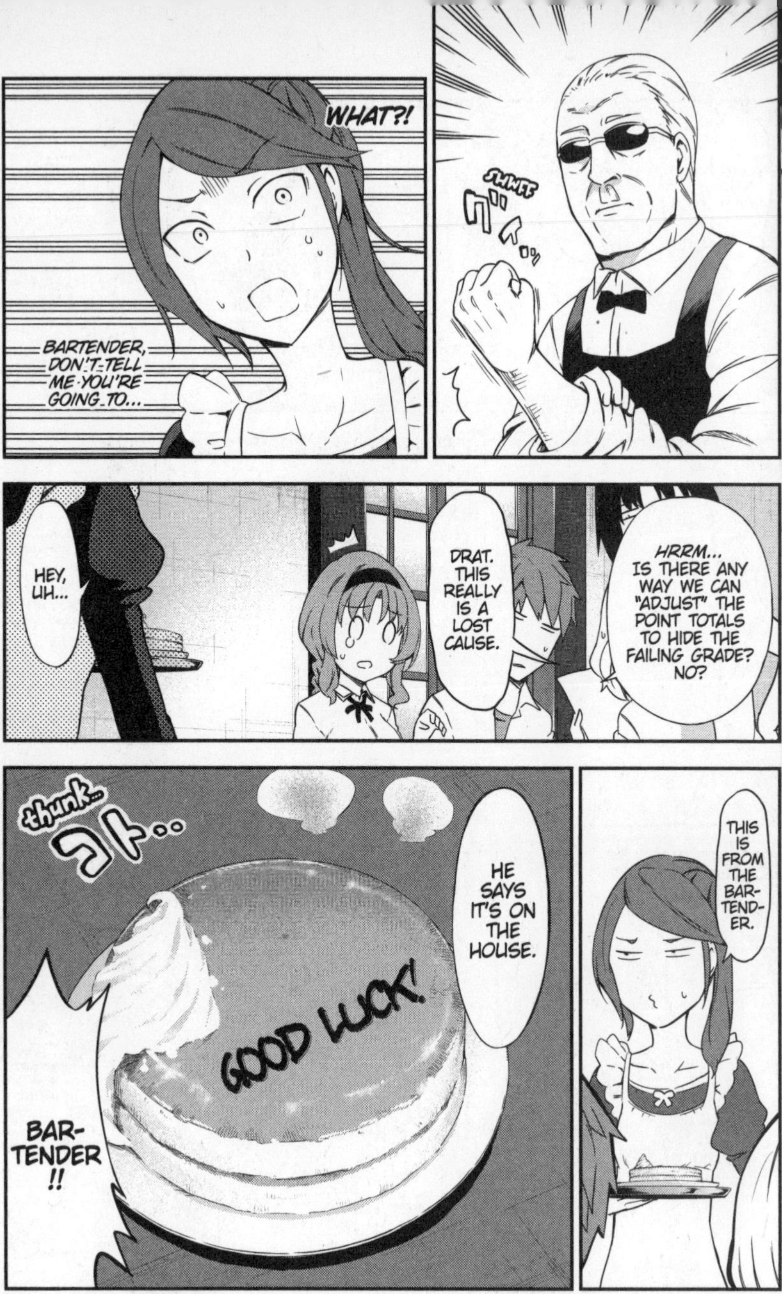
SHWFF
グッ..
WHAT?!
BARTENDER, DON'T TELL ME YOU'RE GOING TO...
HRRM... IS THERE ANY WAY WE CAN "ADJUST" THE POINT TOTALS TO HIDE THE FAILING GRADE? NO?
DRAT. THIS REALLY IS A LOST CAUSE.
HEY, UH...
THIS IS FROM THE BAR-TENDER.
HE SAYS IT'S ON THE HOUSE.
thunk...
コト..
GOOD LUCK!
BAR-TENDER !!

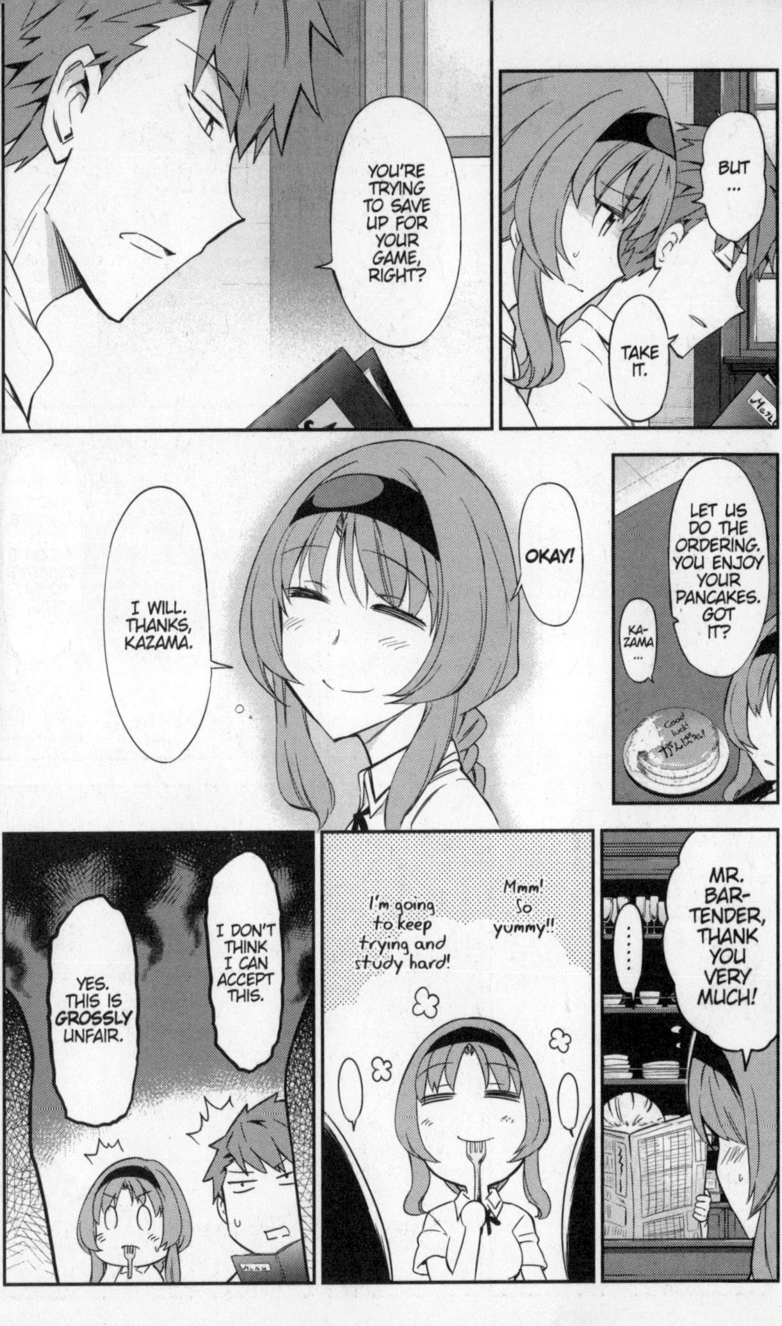
BUT ...
TAKE IT.
YOU'RE TRYING TO SAVE UP FOR YOUR GAME, RIGHT?
LET US DO THE ORDERING. YOU ENJOY YOUR PANCAKES. GOT IT?
KA-ZAMA ...
OKAY!
I WILL. THANKS, KAZAMA.
MR. BAR-TENDER, THANK YOU VERY MUCH!
......
Mmm! So yummy!!
I'm going to keep trying and study hard!
I DON'T THINK I CAN ACCEPT THIS.
YES. THIS IS GROSSLY UNFAIR.

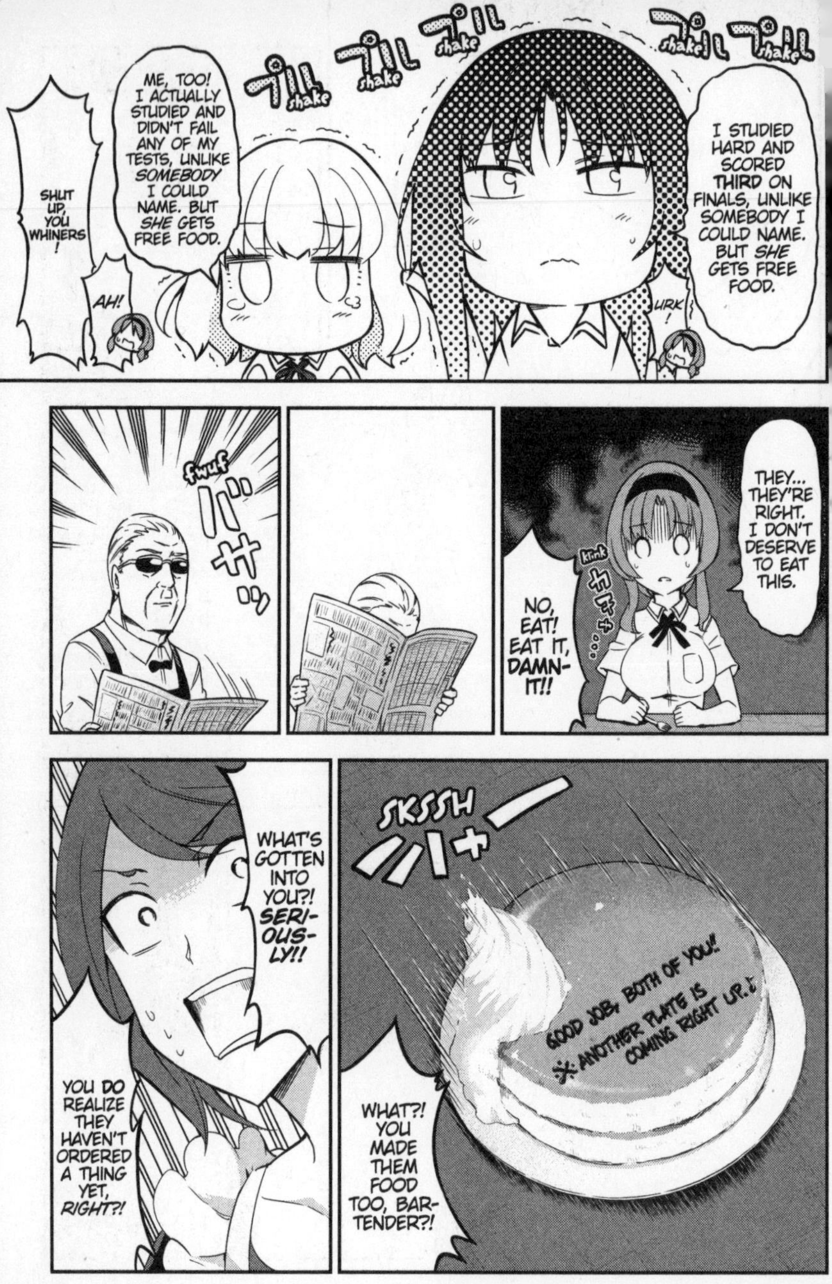
プルプル shake
プルプル shake
I STUDIED HARD AND SCORED THIRD ON FINALS, UNLIKE SOMEBODY I COULD NAME. BUT SHE GETS FREE FOOD.
URK!
プルプル shake
プルプル shake
ME, TOO! I ACTUALLY STUDIED AND DIDN'T FAIL ANY OF MY TESTS, UNLIKE SOMEBODY I COULD NAME. BUT SHE GETS FREE FOOD.
AH!
SHUT UP, YOU WHINERS!
THEY... THEY'RE RIGHT. I DON'T DESERVE TO EAT THIS.
klink カチャ
NO, EAT! EAT IT, DAMN-IT!!
fwuf バサッ
SKSSH シャー
GOOD JOB, BOTH OF YOU!
※ANOTHER PLATE IS COMING RIGHT UP.
WHAT?! YOU MADE THEM FOOD TOO, BAR-TENDER?!
WHAT'S GOTTEN INTO YOU?! SERI-OUS-LY!!
YOU DO REALIZE THEY HAVEN'T ORDERED A THING YET, RIGHT?!

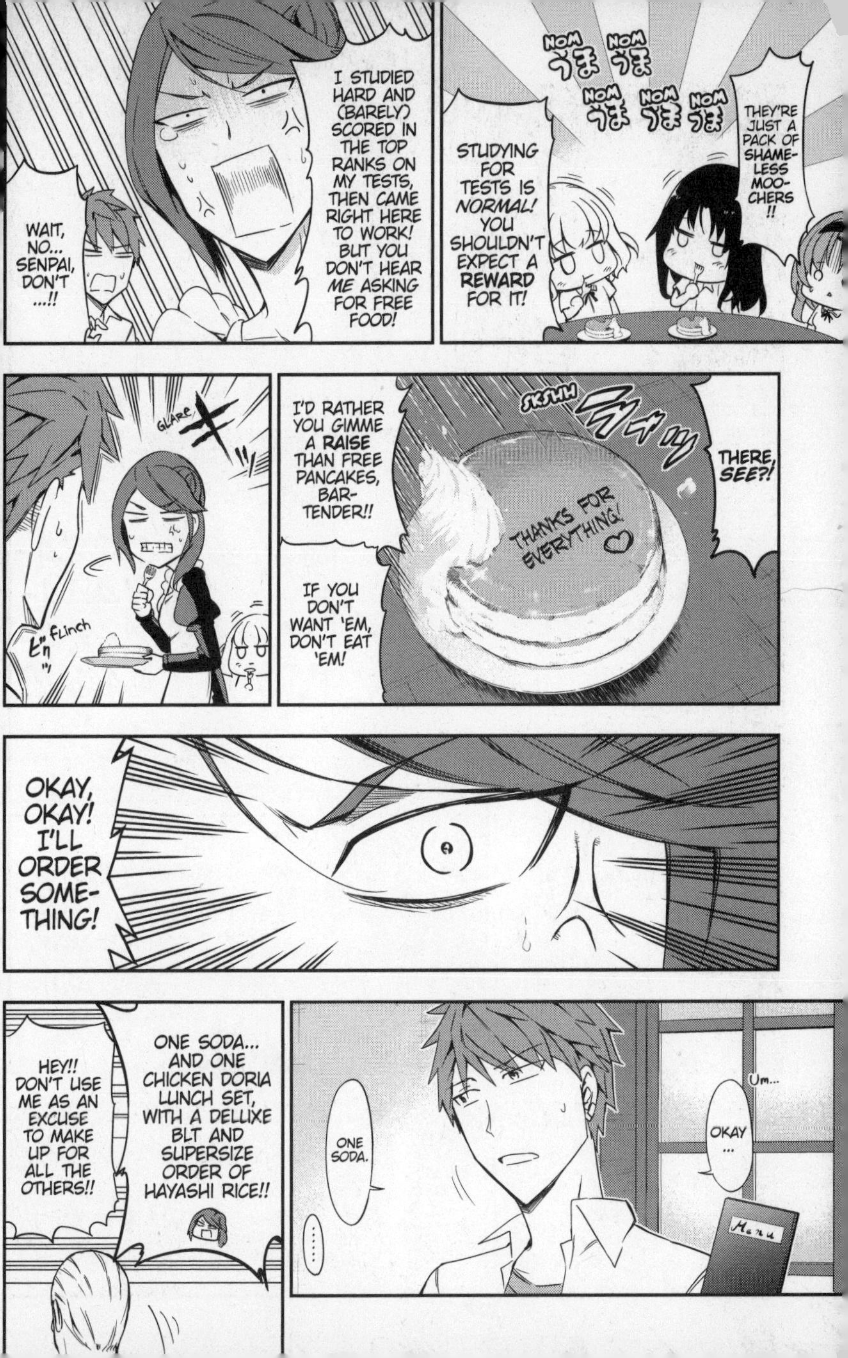
NOM NOM
うま うま
NOM NOM NOM
うま うま うま
THEY'RE JUST A PACK OF SHAME-LESS MOO-CHERS!!
STUDYING FOR TESTS IS NORMAL! YOU SHOULDN'T EXPECT A REWARD FOR IT!
I STUDIED HARD AND (BARELY) SCORED IN THE TOP RANKS ON MY TESTS, THEN CAME RIGHT HERE TO WORK! BUT YOU DON'T HEAR ME ASKING FOR FREE FOOD!
WAIT, NO... SENPAI, DON'T ...!!
SKSHH
THERE, SEE?!
THANKS FOR EVERYTHING!
I'D RATHER YOU GIMME A RAISE THAN FREE PANCAKES, BAR-TENDER!!
IF YOU DON'T WANT 'EM, DON'T EAT 'EM!
GLARE
FLINCH
OKAY, OKAY! I'LL ORDER SOME-THING!
Um...
OKAY ...
ONE SODA.
......
Menu
ONE SODA... AND ONE CHICKEN DORIA LUNCH SET, WITH A DELUXE BLT AND SUPERSIZE ORDER OF HAYASHI RICE!!
HEY!! DON'T USE ME AS AN EXCUSE TO MAKE UP FOR ALL THE OTHERS!!

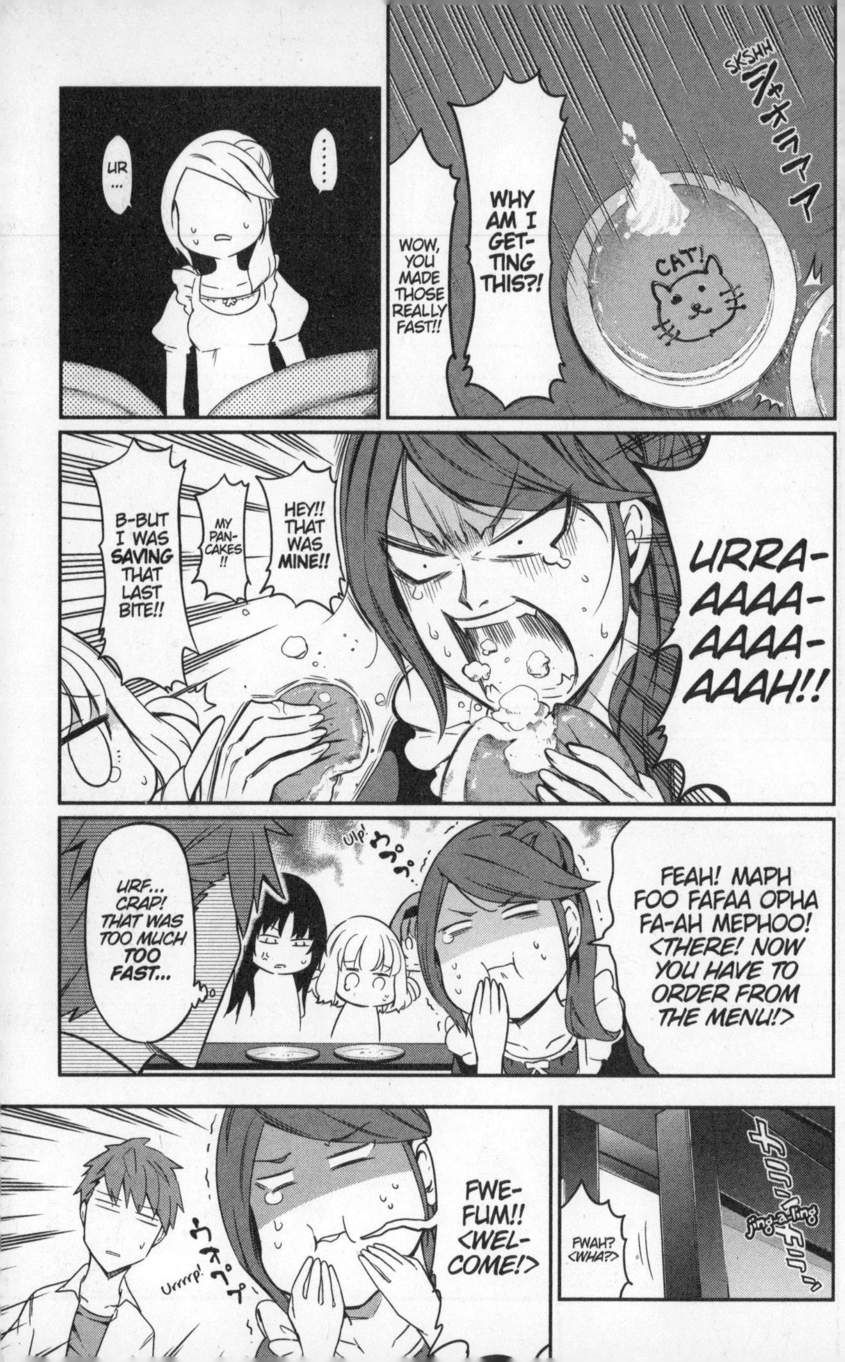
SKSHH
WHY AM I GET-TING THIS?!
WOW, YOU MADE THOSE REALLY FAST!!
CAT!
......
UR ...
URRA-AAAA-AAAA-AAAH!!
HEY!! THAT WAS MINE!!
MY PAN-CAKES!!
B-BUT I WAS SAVING THAT LAST BITE!!
FEAH! MAPH FOO FAFAA OPHA FA-AH MEPHOO! <THERE! NOW YOU HAVE TO ORDER FROM THE MENU!>
Ulp!
URF... CRAP! THAT WAS TOO MUCH TOO FAST...
jing-a-ling
FWAH? <WHA?>
FWE-FUM!! <WEL-COME!>
Urrrp!

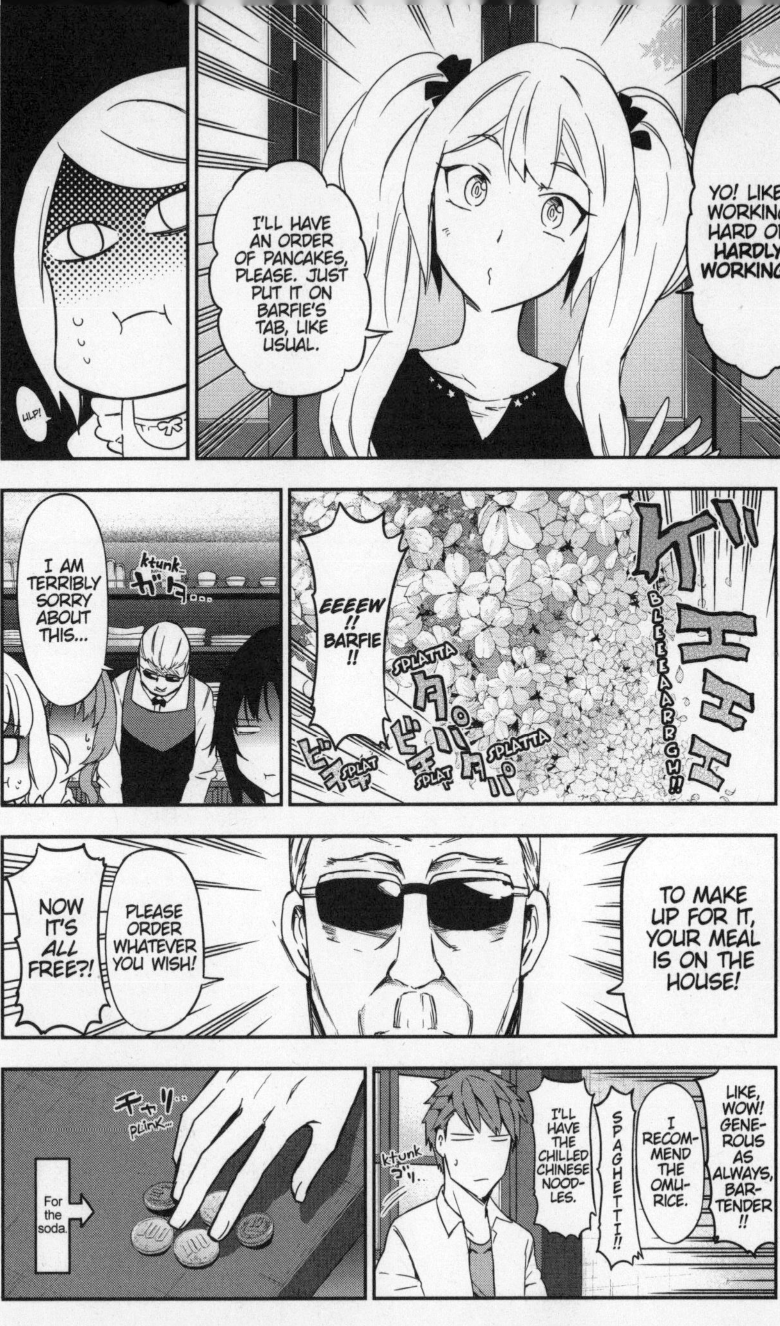
YO! LIKE, WORKING HARD OR HARDLY WORKING?
I'LL HAVE AN ORDER OF PANCAKES, PLEASE. JUST PUT IT ON BARFIE'S TAB, LIKE USUAL.
ULP!
BLEEEAARRGH!!
EEEEW!! BARFIE!!
SPLATTA
SPLAT
SPLATTA
SPLAT
ktunk...
I AM TERRIBLY SORRY ABOUT THIS...
TO MAKE UP FOR IT, YOUR MEAL IS ON THE HOUSE!
PLEASE ORDER WHATEVER YOU WISH!
NOW IT'S ALL FREE?!
LIKE, WOW! GENEROUS AS ALWAYS, BARTENDER!!
I RECOMMEND THE OMURICE.
SPAGHETTI!!
I'LL HAVE THE CHILLED CHINESE NOODLES.
ktunk
plink...
For the soda.

D-FRAGMENTS

ディーふらぐ！

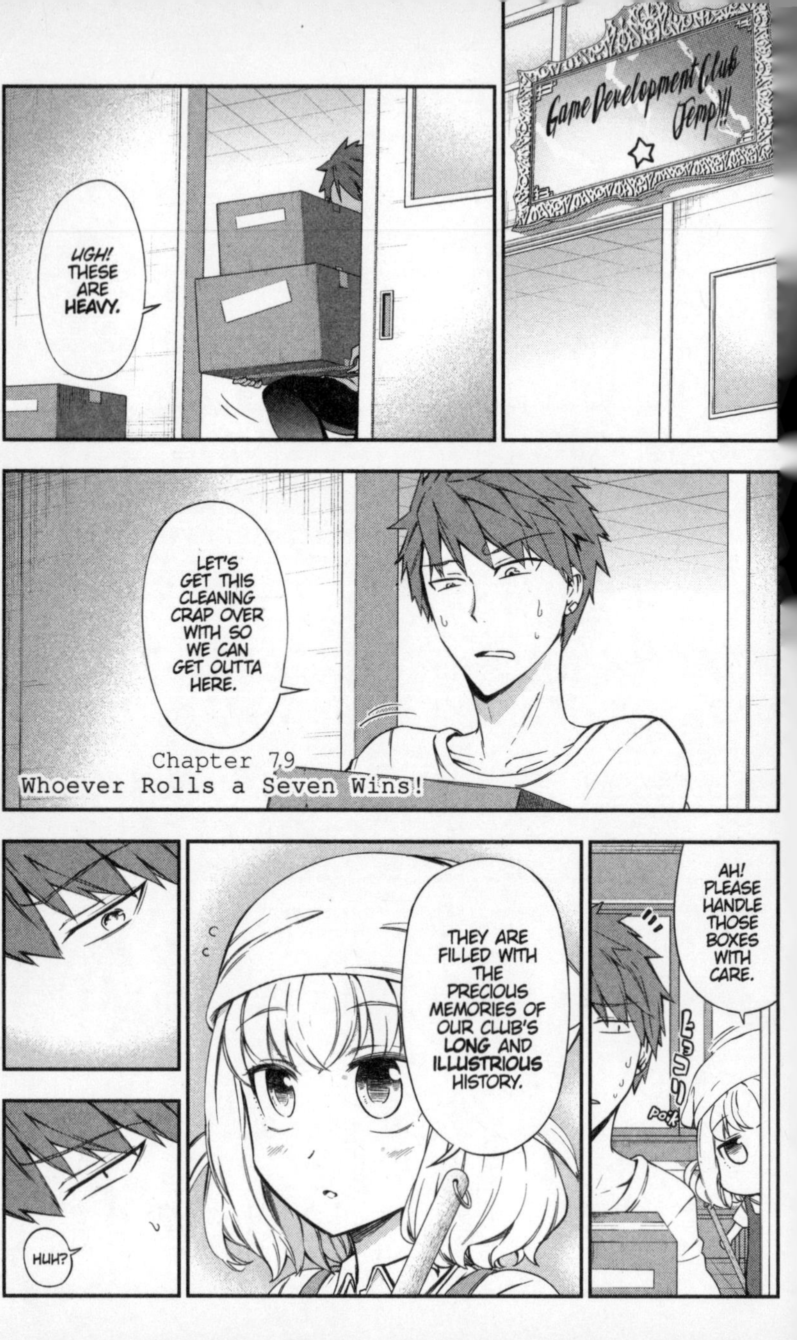
Game Development Club (Temp)!!!
UGH! THESE ARE HEAVY.
LET'S GET THIS CLEANING CRAP OVER WITH SO WE CAN GET OUTTA HERE.
Chapter 7.9
Whoever Rolls a Seven Wins!
AH! PLEASE HANDLE THOSE BOXES WITH CARE.
THEY ARE FILLED WITH THE PRECIOUS MEMORIES OF OUR CLUB'S LONG AND ILLUSTRIOUS HISTORY.
HUH?

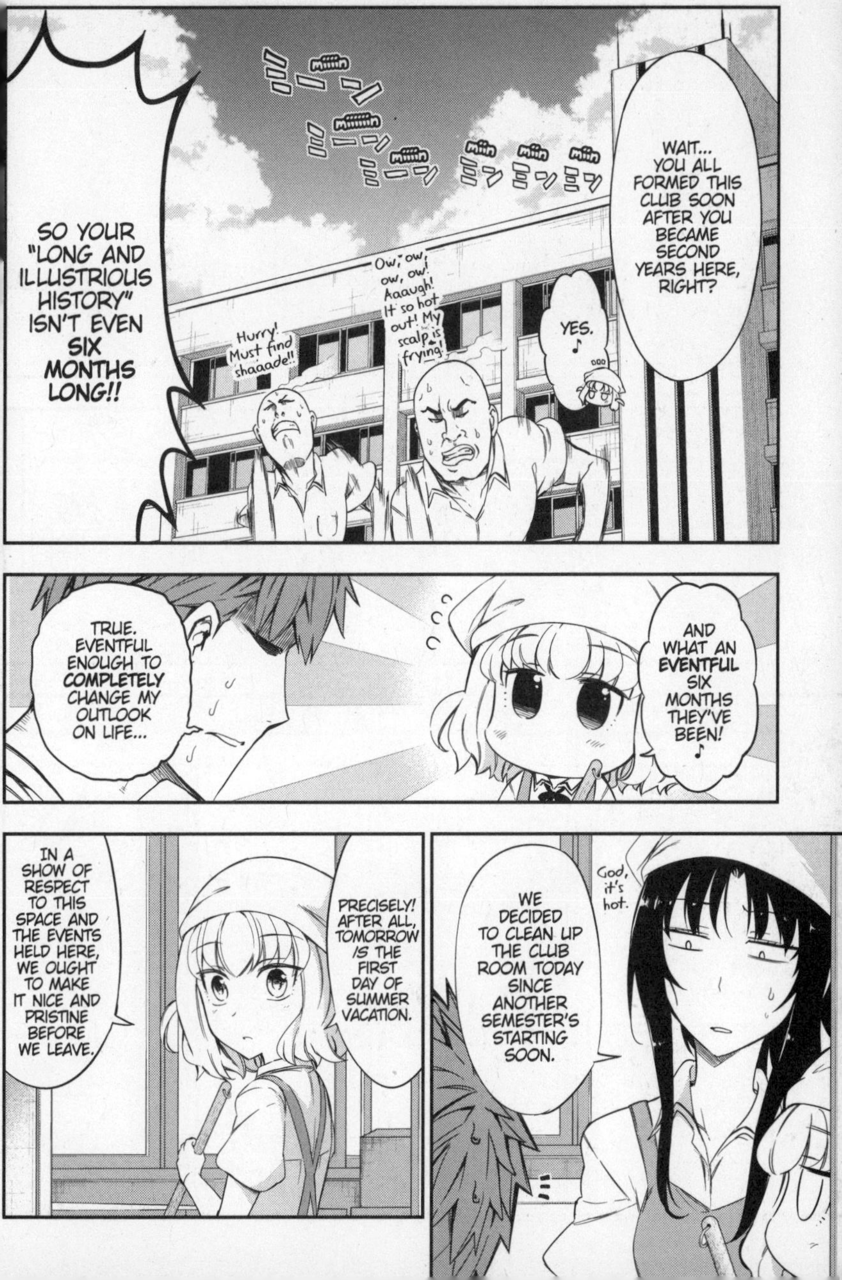
WAIT... YOU ALL FORMED THIS CLUB SOON AFTER YOU BECAME SECOND YEARS HERE, RIGHT?
YES. ♪
miiin
miiiiin
miiin
miin miin miin
Ow, ow, ow, ow! Aaaugh! It so hot out! My scalp is frying!
Hurry! Must find shaaade!!
SO YOUR "LONG AND ILLUSTRIOUS HISTORY" ISN'T EVEN SIX MONTHS LONG!!
AND WHAT AN EVENTFUL SIX MONTHS THEY'VE BEEN! ♪
TRUE. EVENTFUL ENOUGH TO COMPLETELY CHANGE MY OUTLOOK ON LIFE...
God, it's hot.
WE DECIDED TO CLEAN UP THE CLUB ROOM TODAY SINCE ANOTHER SEMESTER'S STARTING SOON.
PRECISELY! AFTER ALL, TOMORROW IS THE FIRST DAY OF SUMMER VACATION.
IN A SHOW OF RESPECT TO THIS SPACE AND THE EVENTS HELD HERE, WE OUGHT TO MAKE IT NICE AND PRISTINE BEFORE WE LEAVE.

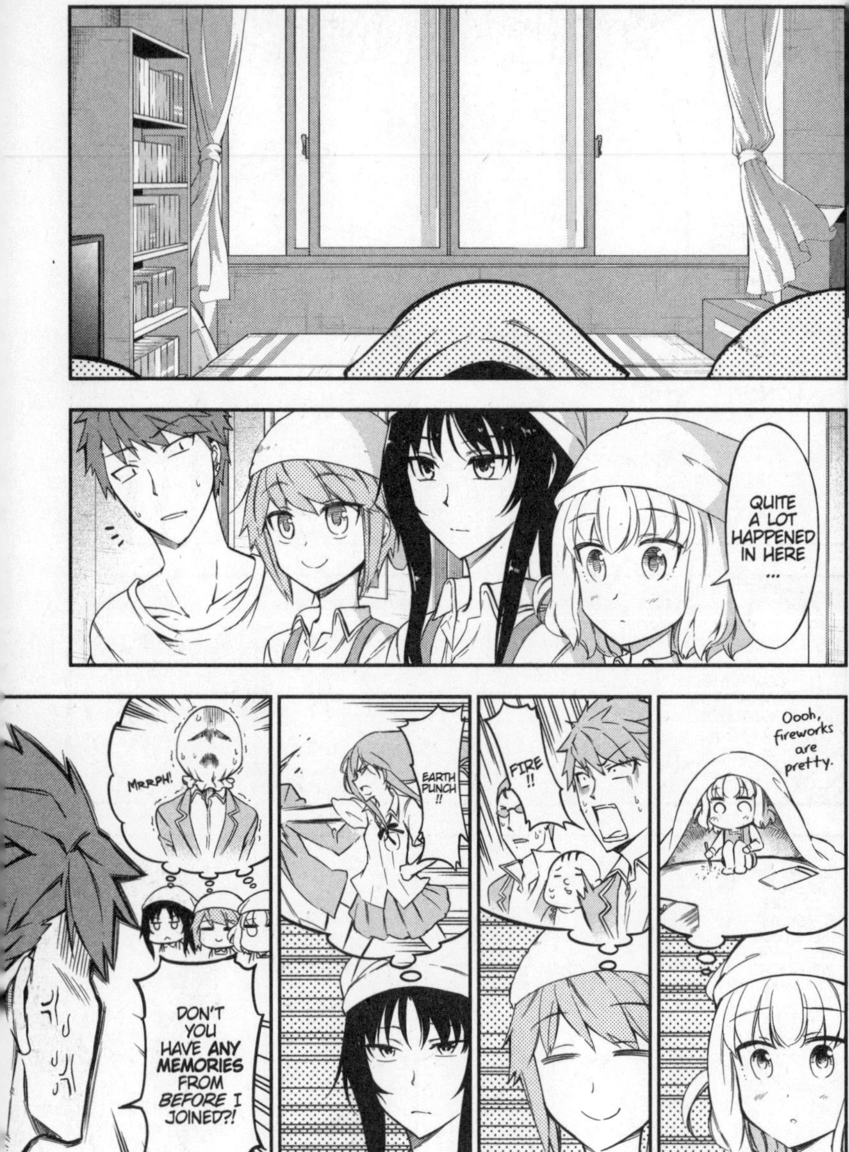

QUITE A LOT HAPPENED IN HERE ...
Oooh, fireworks are pretty.
FIRE !!
EARTH PUNCH !!
MRRPH!
DON'T YOU HAVE ANY MEMORIES FROM *BEFORE* I JOINED?!

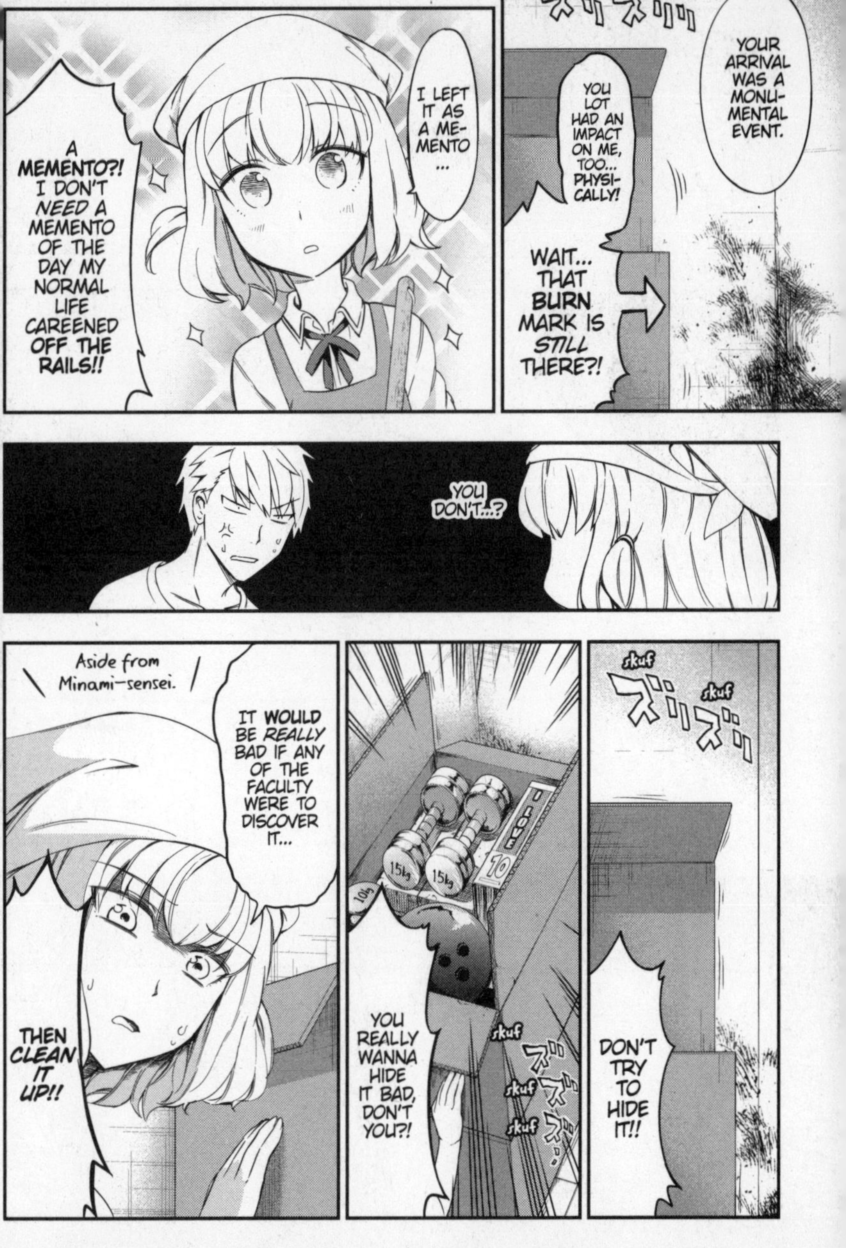
skuf skuf skuf
YOUR ARRIVAL WAS A MONUMENTAL EVENT.
YOU LOT HAD AN IMPACT ON ME, TOO... PHYSICALLY!
WAIT... THAT BURN MARK IS STILL THERE?!
I LEFT IT AS A MEMENTO...
A MEMENTO?! I DON'T NEED A MEMENTO OF THE DAY MY NORMAL LIFE CAREENED OFF THE RAILS!!
YOU DON'T...?
skuf skuf
DON'T TRY TO HIDE IT!!
skuf skuf skuf
YOU REALLY WANNA HIDE IT BAD, DON'T YOU?!
IT WOULD BE REALLY BAD IF ANY OF THE FACULTY WERE TO DISCOVER IT...
Aside from Minami-sensei.
THEN CLEAN IT UP!!

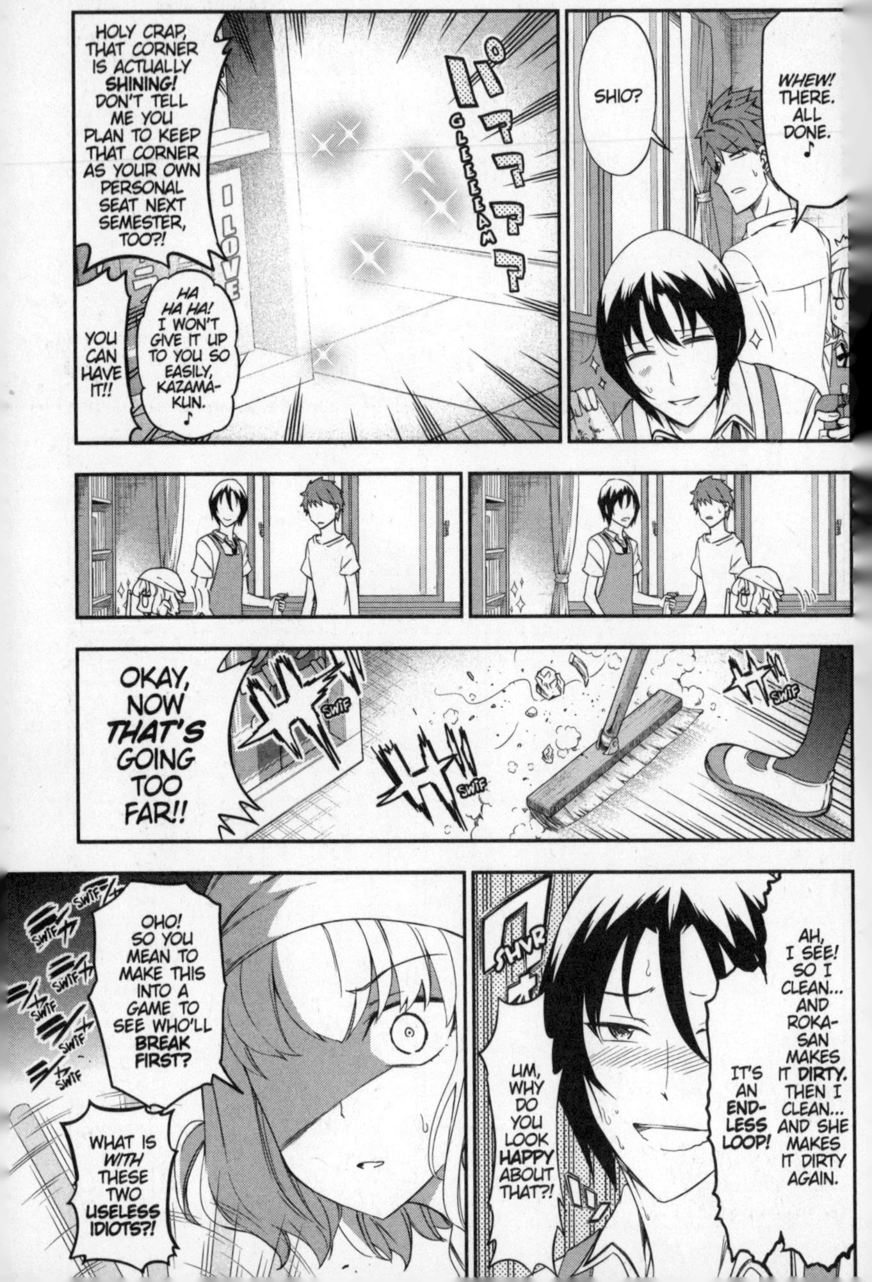
WHEW! THERE. ALL DONE. ♪
SHIO?
GLEEEEAM
HOLY CRAP, THAT CORNER IS ACTUALLY SHINING! DON'T TELL ME YOU PLAN TO KEEP THAT CORNER AS YOUR OWN PERSONAL SEAT NEXT SEMESTER, TOO?!
HA HA HA! I WON'T GIVE IT UP TO YOU SO EASILY, KAZAMA-KUN. ♪
YOU CAN HAVE IT!!
I LOVE
SWIF
OKAY, NOW THAT'S GOING TOO FAR!!
SWIF
SWIF
SHVR
AH, I SEE! SO I CLEAN... AND ROKA-SAN MAKES IT DIRTY. THEN I CLEAN... AND SHE MAKES IT DIRTY AGAIN.
IT'S AN END-LESS LOOP!
UM, WHY DO YOU LOOK HAPPY ABOUT THAT?!
SWIF
OHO! SO YOU MEAN TO MAKE THIS INTO A GAME TO SEE WHO'LL BREAK FIRST?
SWIF
SWIF
SWIF
SWIF
WHAT IS WITH THESE TWO USELESS IDIOTS?!

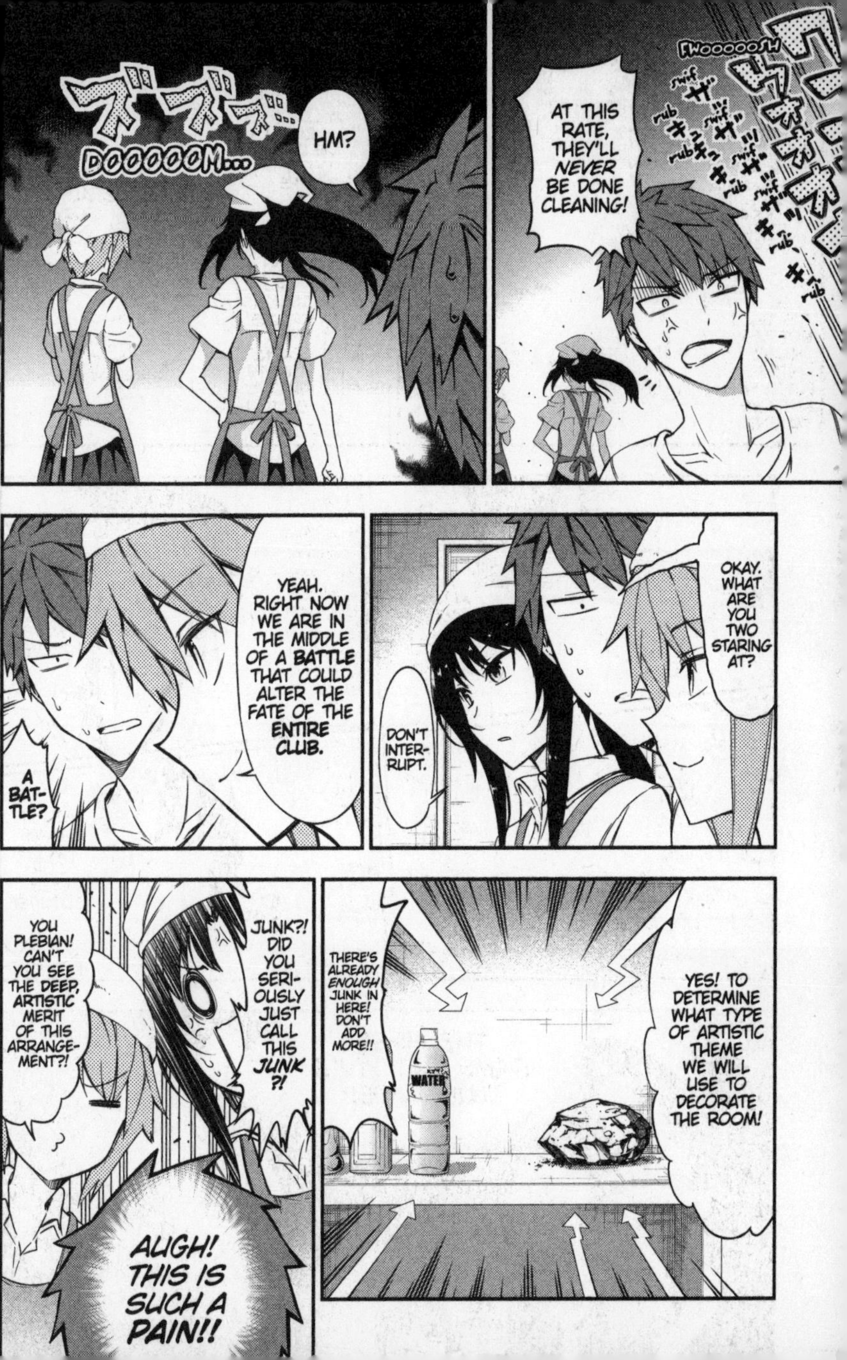
WHOOOOOSH
AT THIS RATE, THEY'LL NEVER BE DONE CLEANING!
DOOOOOM...
HM?
OKAY. WHAT ARE YOU TWO STARING AT?
DON'T INTERRUPT.
YEAH. RIGHT NOW WE ARE IN THE MIDDLE OF A BATTLE THAT COULD ALTER THE FATE OF THE ENTIRE CLUB.
A BATTLE?
YES! TO DETERMINE WHAT TYPE OF ARTISTIC THEME WE WILL USE TO DECORATE THE ROOM!
WATER
THERE'S ALREADY ENOUGH JUNK IN HERE! DON'T ADD MORE!!
JUNK?! DID YOU SERIOUSLY JUST CALL THIS JUNK?!
YOU PLEBIAN! CAN'T YOU SEE THE DEEP, ARTISTIC MERIT OF THIS ARRANGEMENT?!
AUGH! THIS IS SUCH A PAIN!!

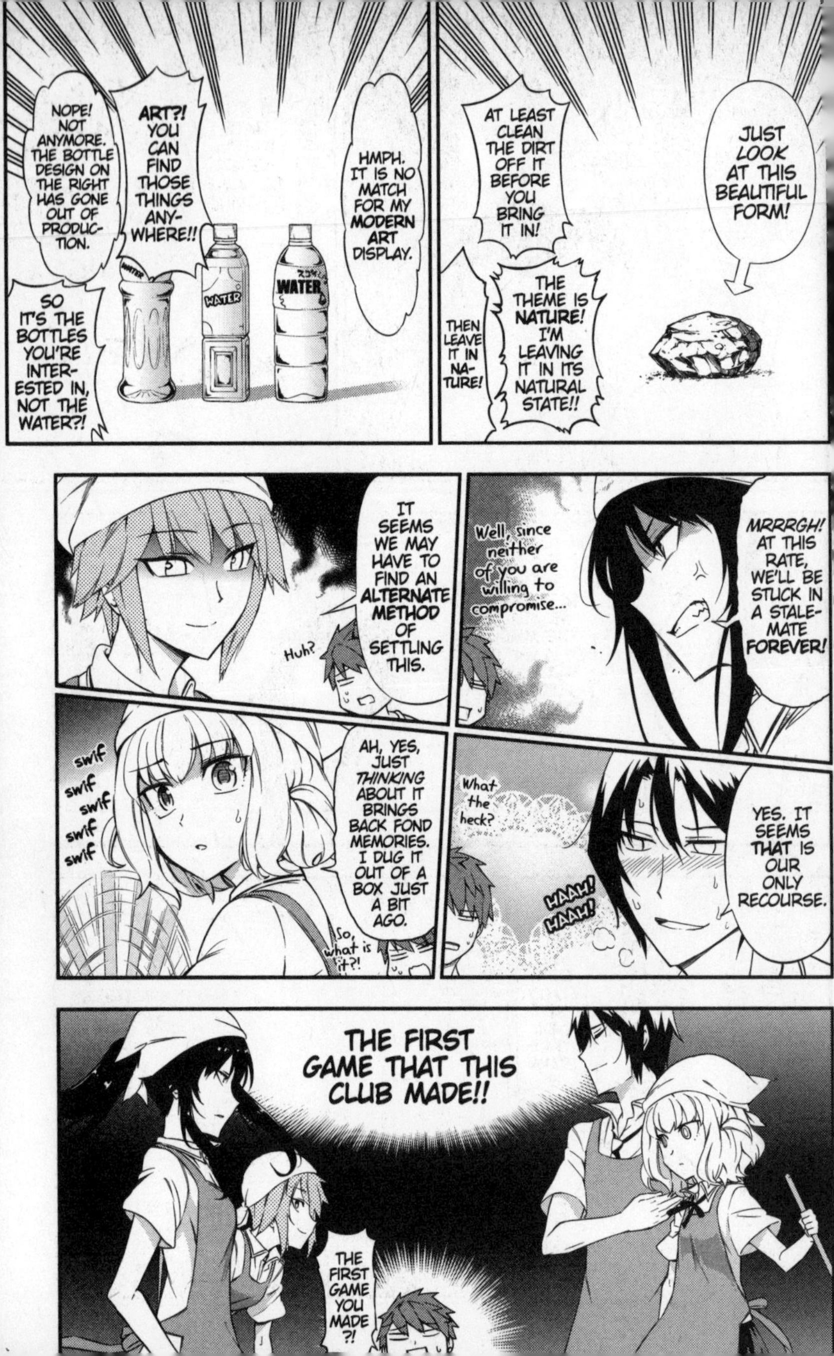
JUST LOOK AT THIS BEAUTIFUL FORM!
AT LEAST CLEAN THE DIRT OFF IT BEFORE YOU BRING IT IN!
THE THEME IS NATURE! I'M LEAVING IT IN ITS NATURAL STATE!!
THEN LEAVE IT IN NATURE!
HMPH. IT IS NO MATCH FOR MY MODERN ART DISPLAY.
ART?! YOU CAN FIND THOSE THINGS ANYWHERE!!
NOPE! NOT ANYMORE. THE BOTTLE DESIGN ON THE RIGHT HAS GONE OUT OF PRODUCTION.
WATER
WATER
SO IT'S THE BOTTLES YOU'RE INTERESTED IN, NOT THE WATER?!
MRRRGH! AT THIS RATE, WE'LL BE STUCK IN A STALEMATE FOREVER!
Well, since neither of you are willing to compromise...
IT SEEMS WE MAY HAVE TO FIND AN ALTERNATE METHOD OF SETTLING THIS.
Huh?
YES. IT SEEMS THAT IS OUR ONLY RECOURSE.
What the heck?
HAAH! HAAH!
AH, YES, JUST THINKING ABOUT IT BRINGS BACK FOND MEMORIES. I DUG IT OUT OF A BOX JUST A BIT AGO.
swif swif swif swif swif
So, what is it?!
THE FIRST GAME THAT THIS CLUB MADE!!
THE FIRST GAME YOU MADE?!

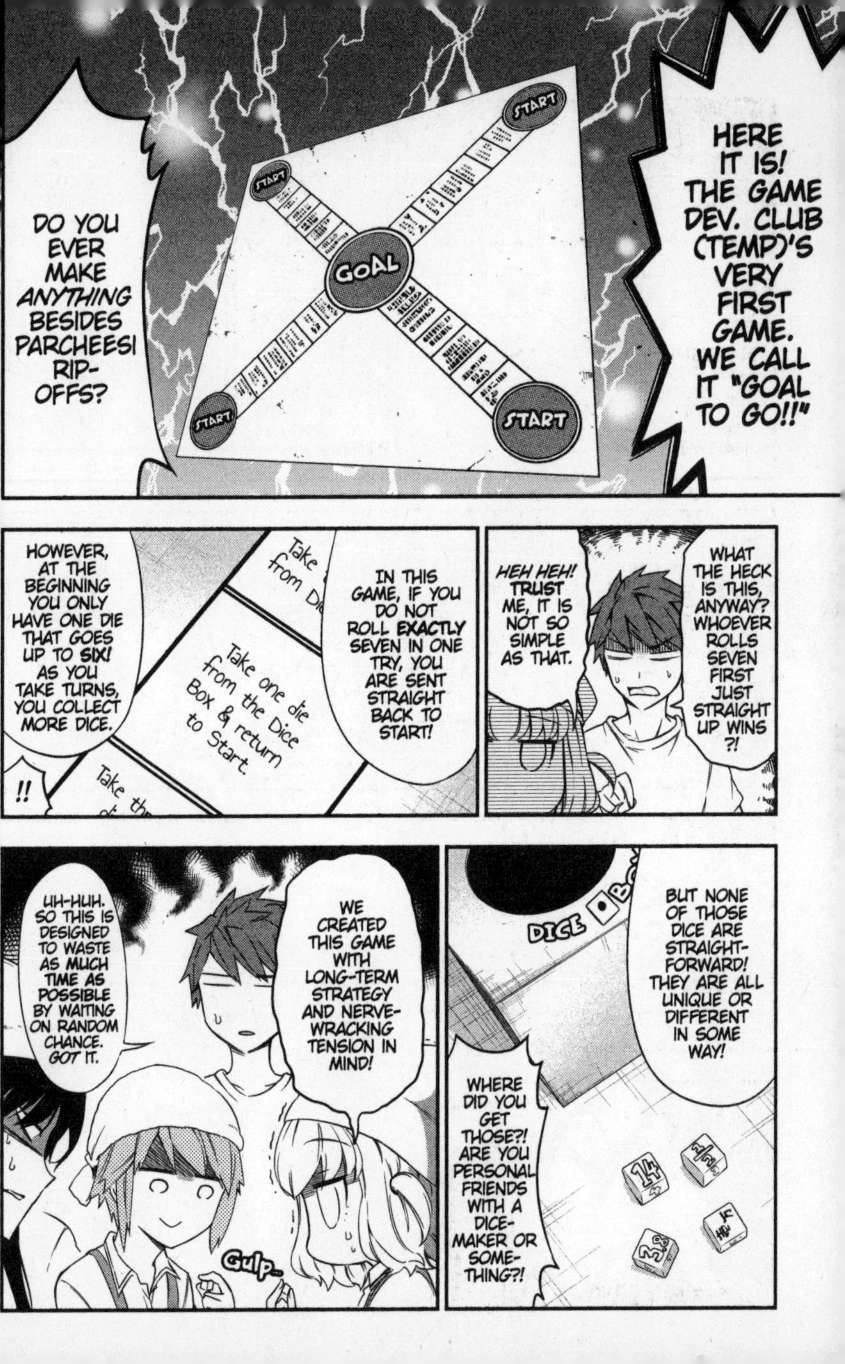
HERE IT IS! THE GAME DEV. CLUB (TEMP)'S VERY FIRST GAME. WE CALL IT "GOAL TO GO!!"
START
START
GOAL
START
START
DO YOU EVER MAKE *ANYTHING* BESIDES PARCHEESI RIP-OFFS?
WHAT THE HECK IS THIS, ANYWAY? WHOEVER ROLLS SEVEN FIRST JUST STRAIGHT UP WINS?!
HEH HEH! **TRUST** ME, IT IS NOT SO SIMPLE AS THAT.
IN THIS GAME, IF YOU DO NOT ROLL **EXACTLY** SEVEN IN ONE TRY, YOU ARE SENT STRAIGHT BACK TO START!
Take one die from the Dice Box & return to Start.
HOWEVER, AT THE BEGINNING YOU ONLY HAVE ONE DIE THAT GOES UP TO **SIX!** AS YOU TAKE TURNS, YOU COLLECT MORE DICE.
!!
BUT NONE OF THOSE DICE ARE STRAIGHT-FORWARD! THEY ARE ALL UNIQUE OR DIFFERENT IN SOME WAY!
DICE
WHERE DID YOU GET THOSE?! ARE YOU PERSONAL FRIENDS WITH A DICE-MAKER OR SOME-THING?!
WE CREATED THIS GAME WITH LONG-TERM STRATEGY AND NERVE-WRACKING TENSION IN MIND!
UH-HUH. SO THIS IS DESIGNED TO WASTE AS MUCH TIME AS POSSIBLE BY WAITING ON RANDOM CHANCE. *GOT* IT.
Gulp...

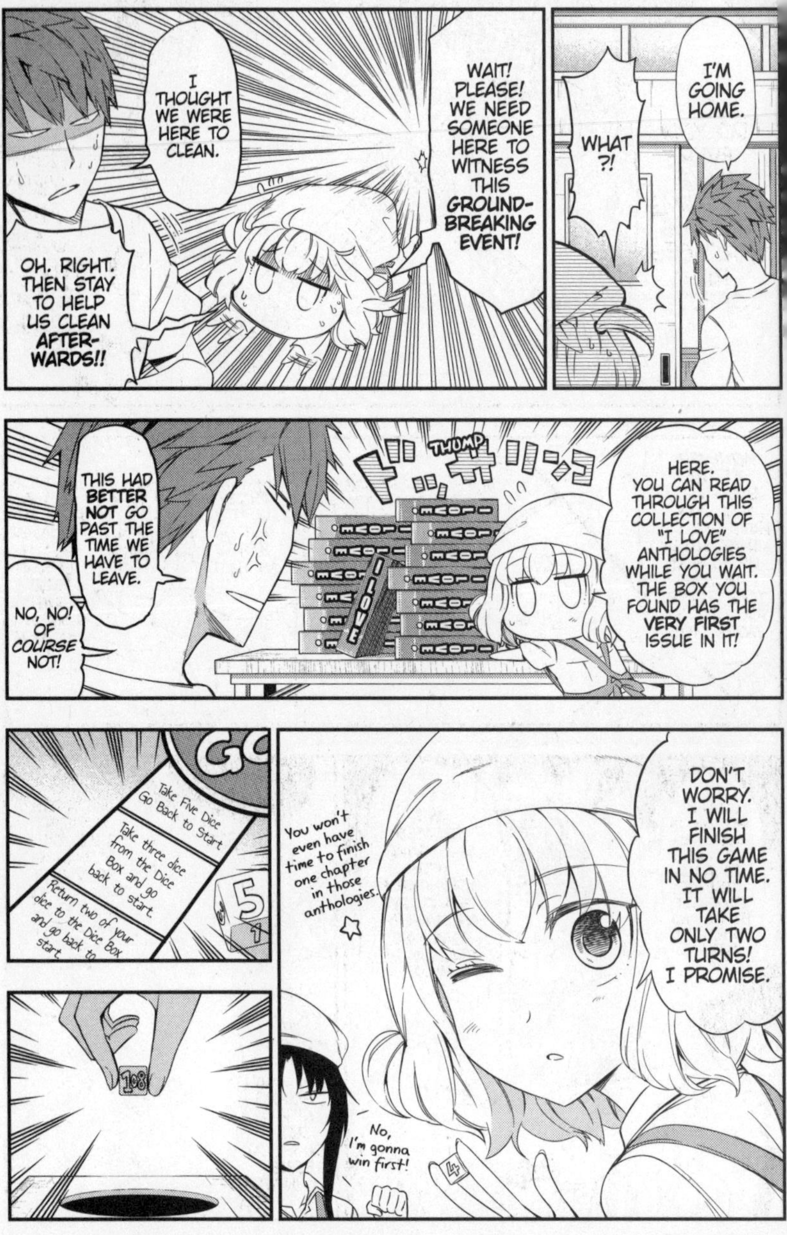
I'M GOING HOME.
WHAT?!
WAIT! PLEASE! WE NEED SOMEONE HERE TO WITNESS THIS GROUND-BREAKING EVENT!
I THOUGHT WE WERE HERE TO CLEAN.
OH. RIGHT. THEN STAY TO HELP US CLEAN AFTER-WARDS!!
THUMP
HERE. YOU CAN READ THROUGH THIS COLLECTION OF "I LOVE" ANTHOLOGIES WHILE YOU WAIT. THE BOX YOU FOUND HAS THE VERY FIRST ISSUE IN IT!
I LOVE
THIS HAD BETTER NOT GO PAST THE TIME WE HAVE TO LEAVE.
NO, NO! OF COURSE NOT!
DON'T WORRY. I WILL FINISH THIS GAME IN NO TIME. IT WILL TAKE ONLY TWO TURNS! I PROMISE.
You won't even have time to finish one chapter in those anthologies.
No, I'm gonna win first!
GO
Take Five Dice Go Back to Start
Take three dice from the Dice Box and go back to start.
Return two of your dice to the Dice Box and go back to start.
5
108

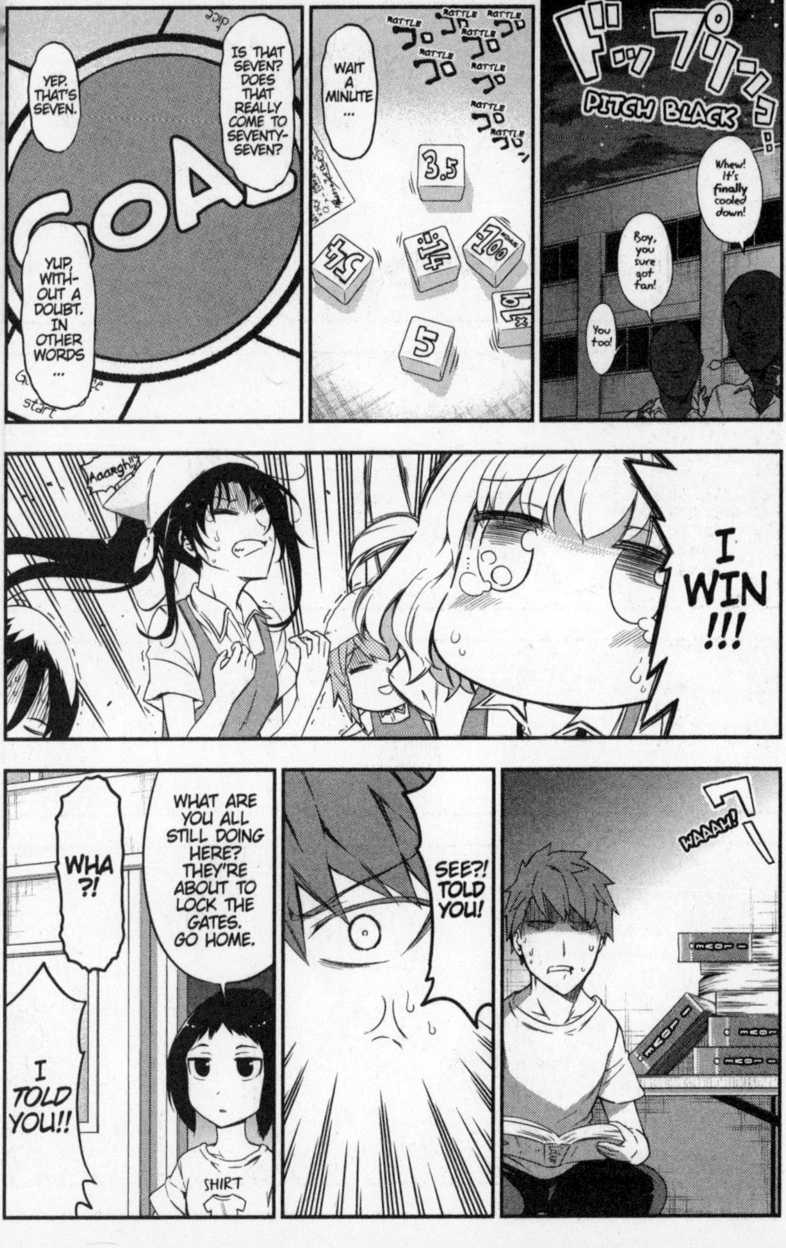
PITCH BLACK
Whew! It's finally cooled down!
Boy, you sure got tan!
You too!
RATTLE RATTLE RATTLE RATTLE RATTLE RATTLE RATTLE
WAIT A MINUTE ...
IS THAT SEVEN? DOES THAT REALLY COME TO SEVENTY-SEVEN?
YEP. THAT'S SEVEN.
YUP, WITH-OUT A DOUBT. IN OTHER WORDS ...
I WIN !!!
Aaaargh!!
WAAAH!
SEE?! TOLD YOU!
WHAT ARE YOU ALL STILL DOING HERE? THEY'RE ABOUT TO LOCK THE GATES. GO HOME.
WHA ?!
I TOLD YOU!!
SHIRT

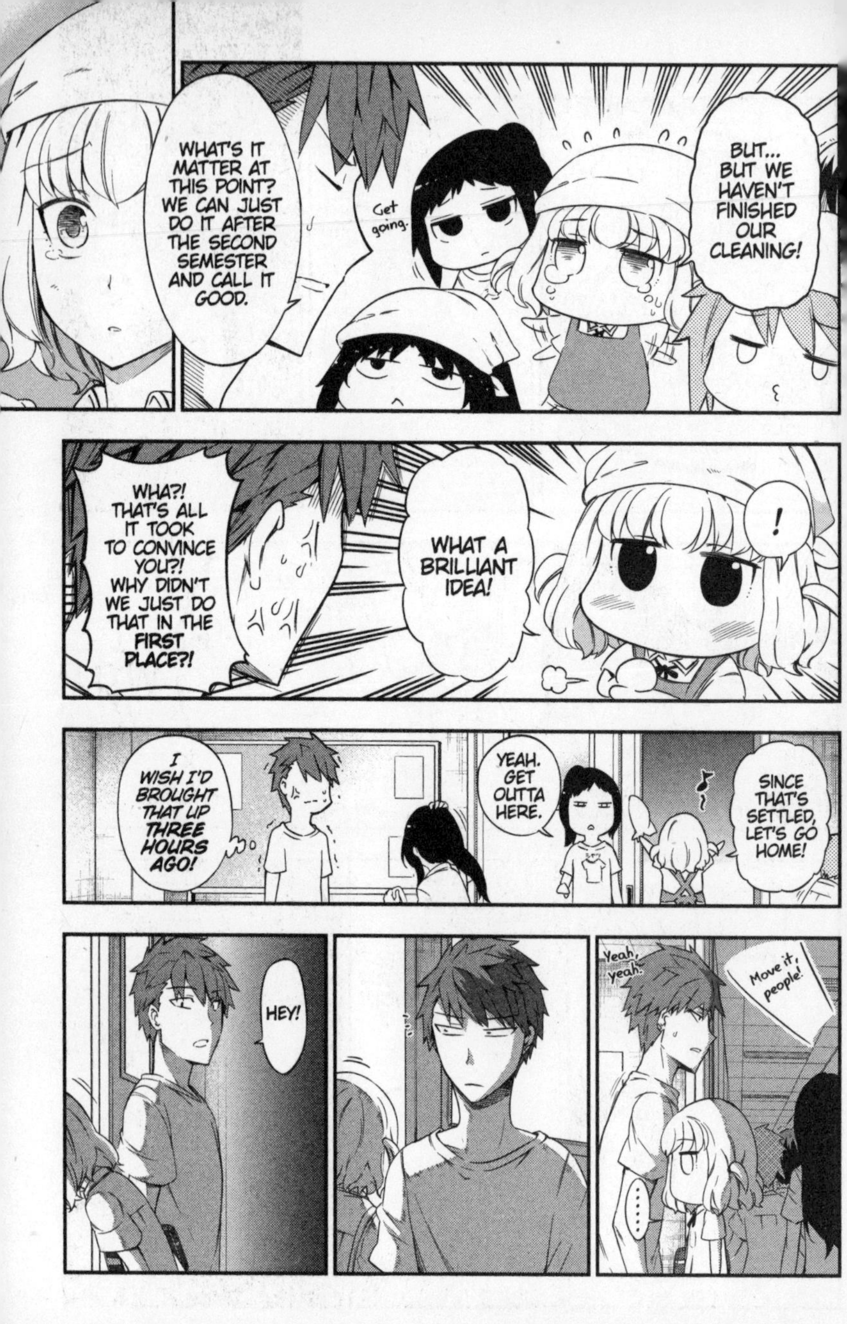
BUT... BUT WE HAVEN'T FINISHED OUR CLEANING!
Get going.
WHAT'S IT MATTER AT THIS POINT? WE CAN JUST DO IT AFTER THE SECOND SEMESTER AND CALL IT GOOD.
!
WHAT A BRILLIANT IDEA!
WHA?! THAT'S ALL IT TOOK TO CONVINCE YOU?! WHY DIDN'T WE JUST DO THAT IN THE FIRST PLACE?!
SINCE THAT'S SETTLED, LET'S GO HOME!
YEAH. GET OUTTA HERE.
I WISH I'D BROUGHT THAT UP THREE HOURS AGO!
Move it, people!
Yeah, yeah.
......
HEY!

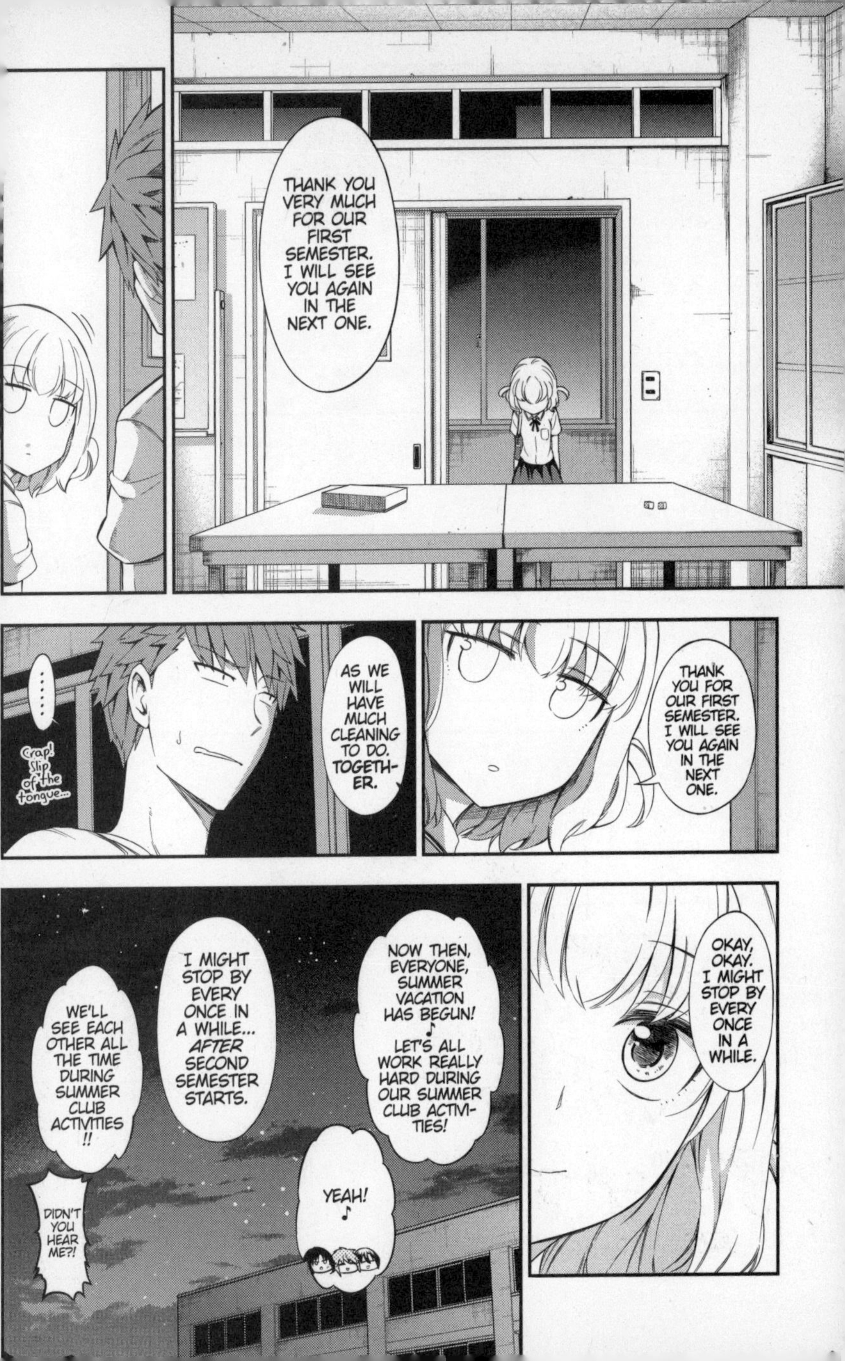
THANK YOU VERY MUCH FOR OUR FIRST SEMESTER. I WILL SEE YOU AGAIN IN THE NEXT ONE.
THANK YOU FOR OUR FIRST SEMESTER. I WILL SEE YOU AGAIN IN THE NEXT ONE.
AS WE WILL HAVE MUCH CLEANING TO DO. TOGETHER.
……
Crap! Slip of the tongue...
OKAY, OKAY. I MIGHT STOP BY EVERY ONCE IN A WHILE.
NOW THEN, EVERYONE, SUMMER VACATION HAS BEGUN! ♪
LET'S ALL WORK REALLY HARD DURING OUR SUMMER CLUB ACTIVITIES!
YEAH! ♪
I MIGHT STOP BY EVERY ONCE IN A WHILE... *AFTER* SECOND SEMESTER STARTS.
WE'LL SEE EACH OTHER ALL THE TIME DURING SUMMER CLUB ACTIVITIES!!
DIDN'T YOU HEAR ME?!

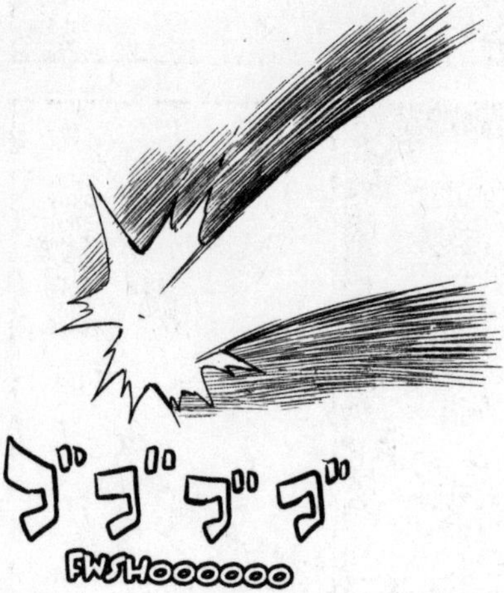
ゴゴゴゴ
FWSHOOOOOOO

D-FRAGMENTS

ディーふらぐ!

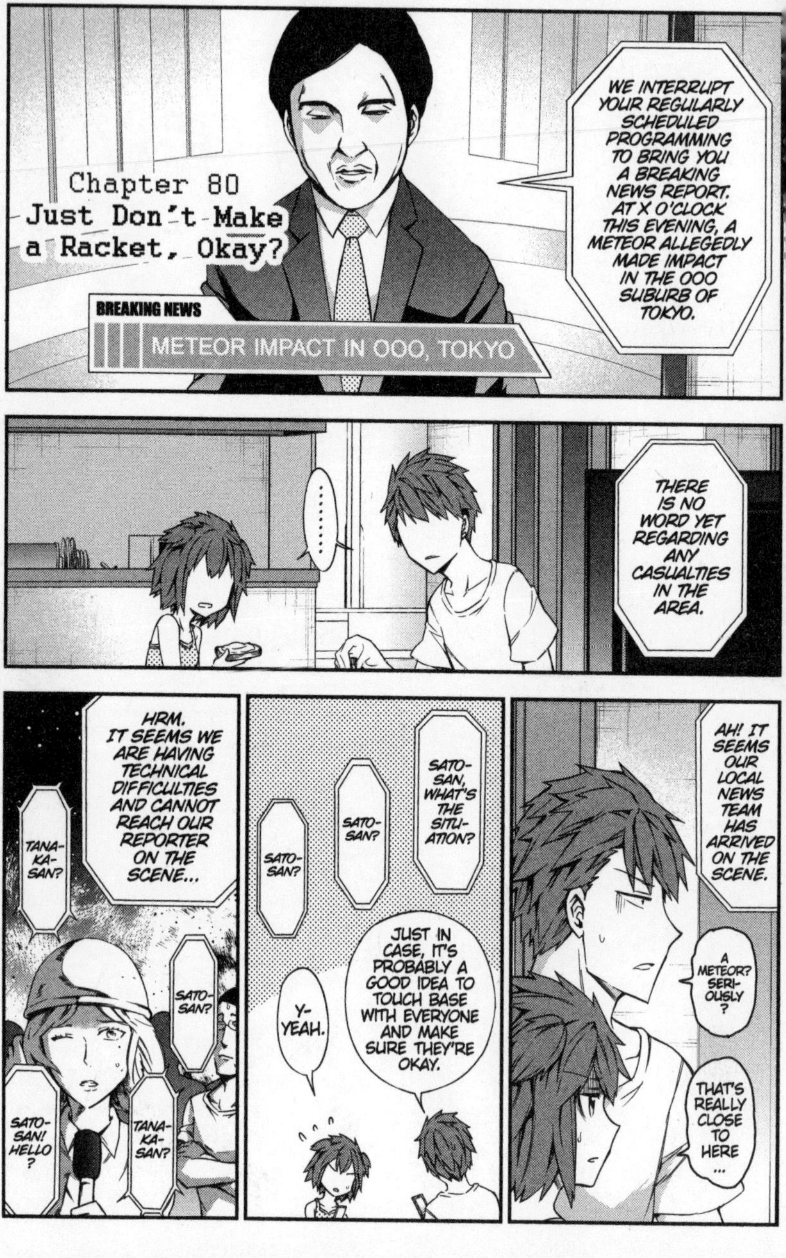
WE INTERRUPT YOUR REGULARLY SCHEDULED PROGRAMMING TO BRING YOU A BREAKING NEWS REPORT. AT X O'CLOCK THIS EVENING, A METEOR ALLEGEDLY MADE IMPACT IN THE OOO SUBURB OF TOKYO.
Chapter 80 Just Don't Make a Racket, Okay?
BREAKING NEWS
METEOR IMPACT IN OOO, TOKYO
THERE IS NO WORD YET REGARDING ANY CASUALTIES IN THE AREA.
....
AH! IT SEEMS OUR LOCAL NEWS TEAM HAS ARRIVED ON THE SCENE.
A METEOR? SERIOUSLY?
THAT'S REALLY CLOSE TO HERE...
SATO-SAN, WHAT'S THE SITUATION?
SATO-SAN?
SATO-SAN?
JUST IN CASE, IT'S PROBABLY A GOOD IDEA TO TOUCH BASE WITH EVERYONE AND MAKE SURE THEY'RE OKAY.
Y-YEAH.
HRM. IT SEEMS WE ARE HAVING TECHNICAL DIFFICULTIES AND CANNOT REACH OUR REPORTER ON THE SCENE...
TANAKA-SAN?
SATO-SAN?
TANA-KA-SAN?
SATO-SAN! HELLO?

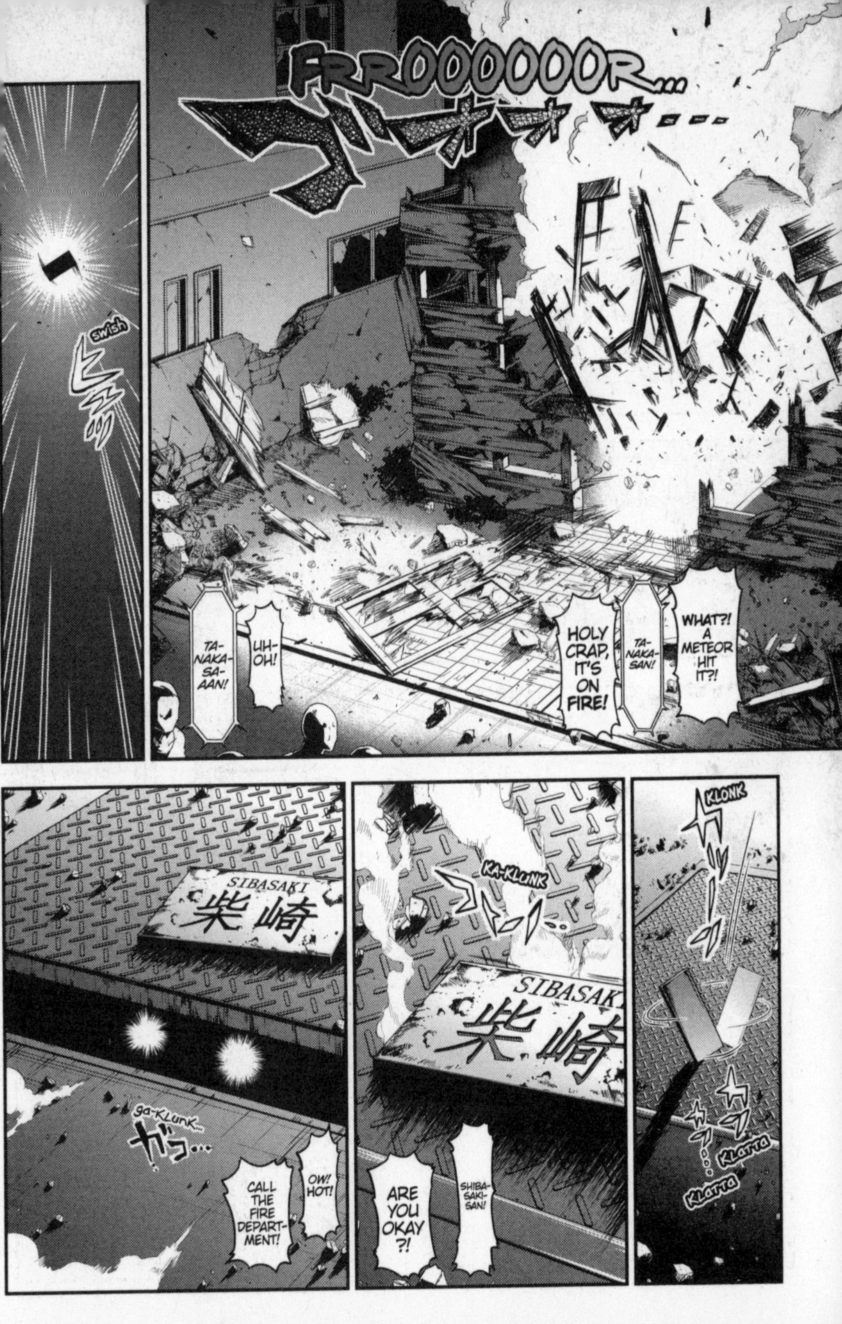
FRROOOOOOR...
WHAT?! A METEOR HIT IT?!
TA-NAKA-SAN!
HOLY CRAP, IT'S ON FIRE!
UH-OH!
TA-NAKA-SAAAN!
swish
KLONK
Klatta
Klatta
KA-KLUNK
SIBASAKI
柴崎
SHIBA-SAKI-SAN!
ARE YOU OKAY?!
SIBASAKI
柴崎
ga-klunk...
OW! HOT!
CALL THE FIRE DEPART-MENT!

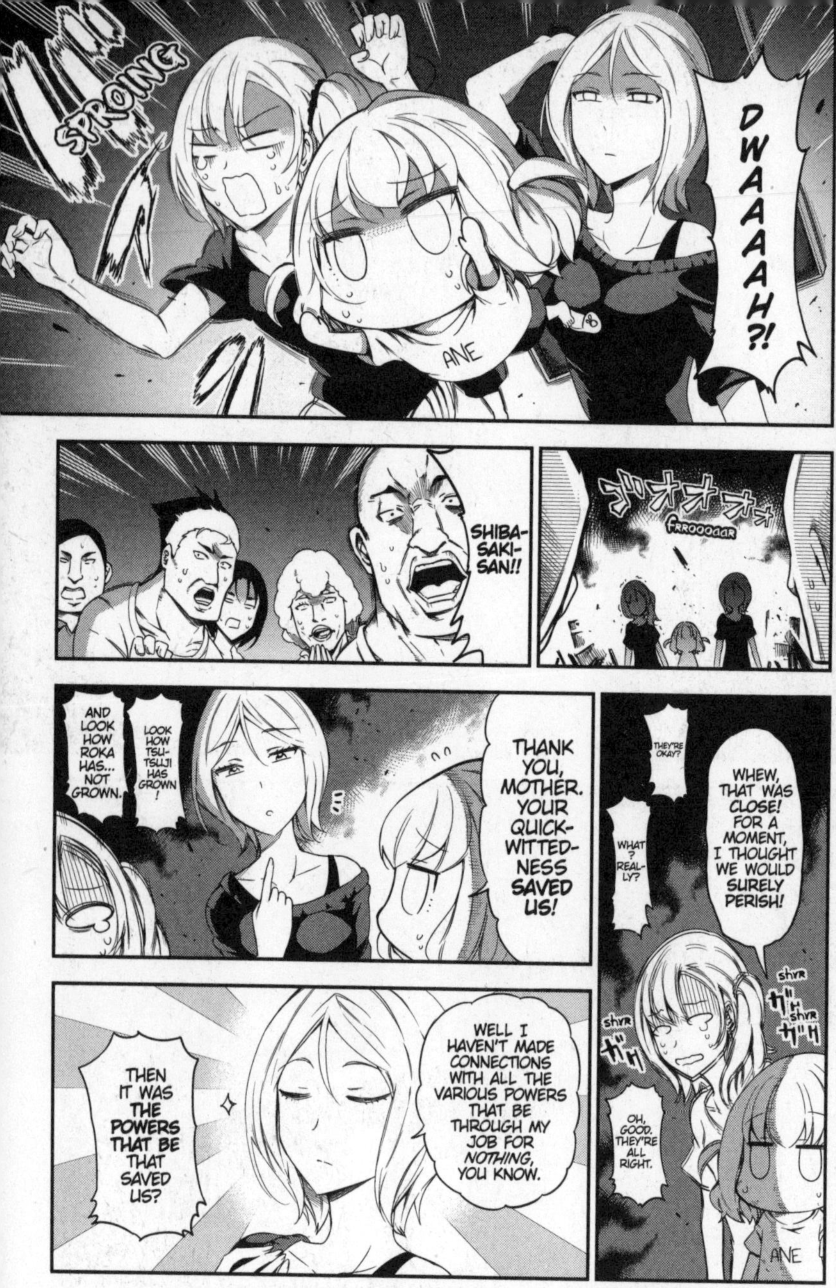
DWAAAAAH?!
SPROING
ANE
ゴオオオオ
FRROOOOAR
SHIBA-SAKI-SAN!!
WHEW, THAT WAS CLOSE! FOR A MOMENT, I THOUGHT WE WOULD SURELY PERISH!
THEY'RE OKAY?
WHAT? REALLY?
shvr
shvr
shvr
OH, GOOD. THEY'RE ALL RIGHT.
ANE
THANK YOU, MOTHER. YOUR QUICK-WITTED-NESS SAVED US!
LOOK HOW TSUTSUJI HAS GROWN!
AND LOOK HOW ROKA HAS... NOT GROWN.
WELL I HAVEN'T MADE CONNECTIONS WITH ALL THE VARIOUS POWERS THAT BE THROUGH MY JOB FOR NOTHING, YOU KNOW.
THEN IT WAS THE POWERS THAT BE THAT SAVED US?

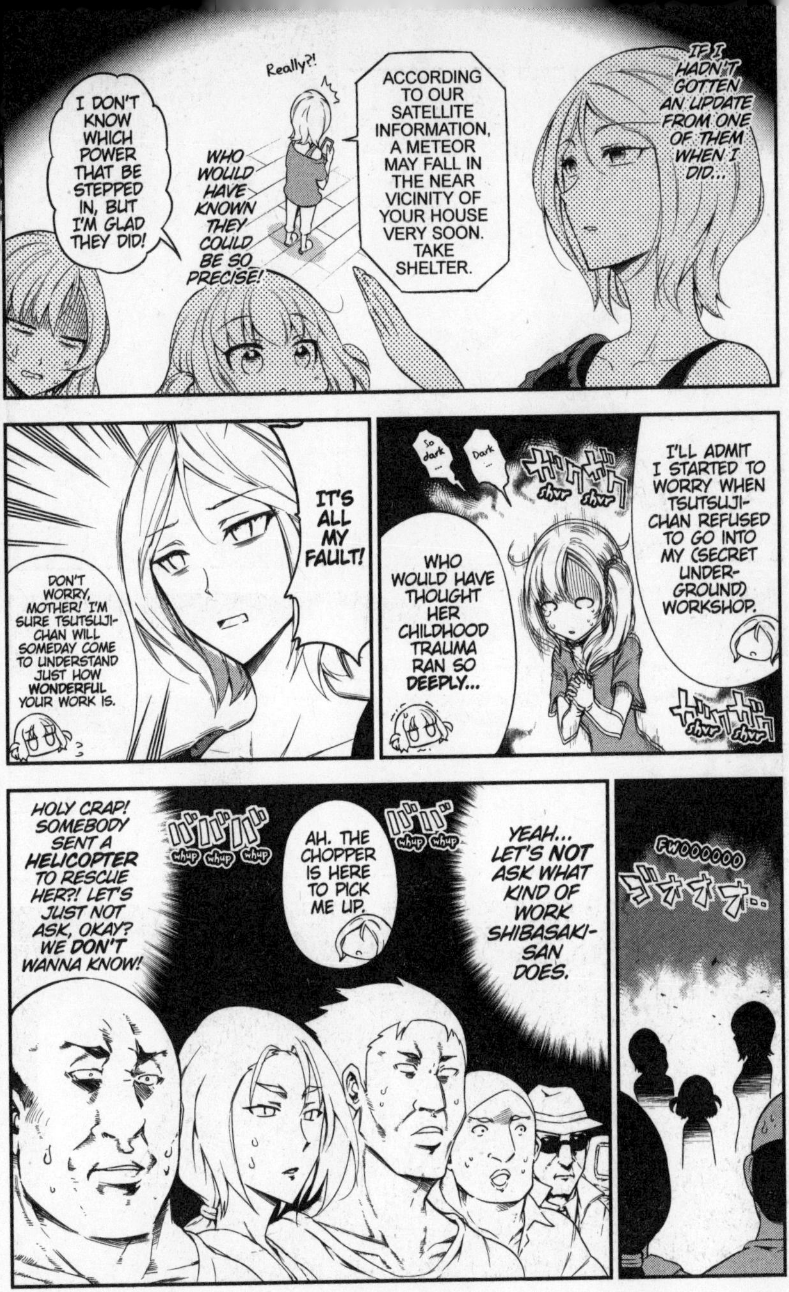
IF I HADN'T GOTTEN AN UPDATE FROM ONE OF THEM WHEN I DID...
ACCORDING TO OUR SATELLITE INFORMATION, A METEOR MAY FALL IN THE NEAR VICINITY OF YOUR HOUSE VERY SOON. TAKE SHELTER.
Really?!
WHO WOULD HAVE KNOWN THEY COULD BE SO PRECISE!
I DON'T KNOW WHICH POWER THAT BE STEPPED IN, BUT I'M GLAD THEY DID!
I'LL ADMIT I STARTED TO WORRY WHEN TSUTSUJI-CHAN REFUSED TO GO INTO MY (SECRET UNDERGROUND) WORKSHOP.
shvr shvr
So dark...
Dark...
WHO WOULD HAVE THOUGHT HER CHILDHOOD TRAUMA RAN SO DEEPLY...
shvr shvr
IT'S ALL MY FAULT!
DON'T WORRY, MOTHER! I'M SURE TSUTSUJI-CHAN WILL SOMEDAY COME TO UNDERSTAND JUST HOW WONDERFUL YOUR WORK IS.
FWOOOOOO
YEAH... LET'S NOT ASK WHAT KIND OF WORK SHIBASAKI-SAN DOES.
whup whup
AH. THE CHOPPER IS HERE TO PICK ME UP.
whup whup whup
HOLY CRAP! SOMEBODY SENT A HELICOPTER TO RESCUE HER?! LET'S JUST NOT ASK, OKAY? WE DON'T WANNA KNOW!

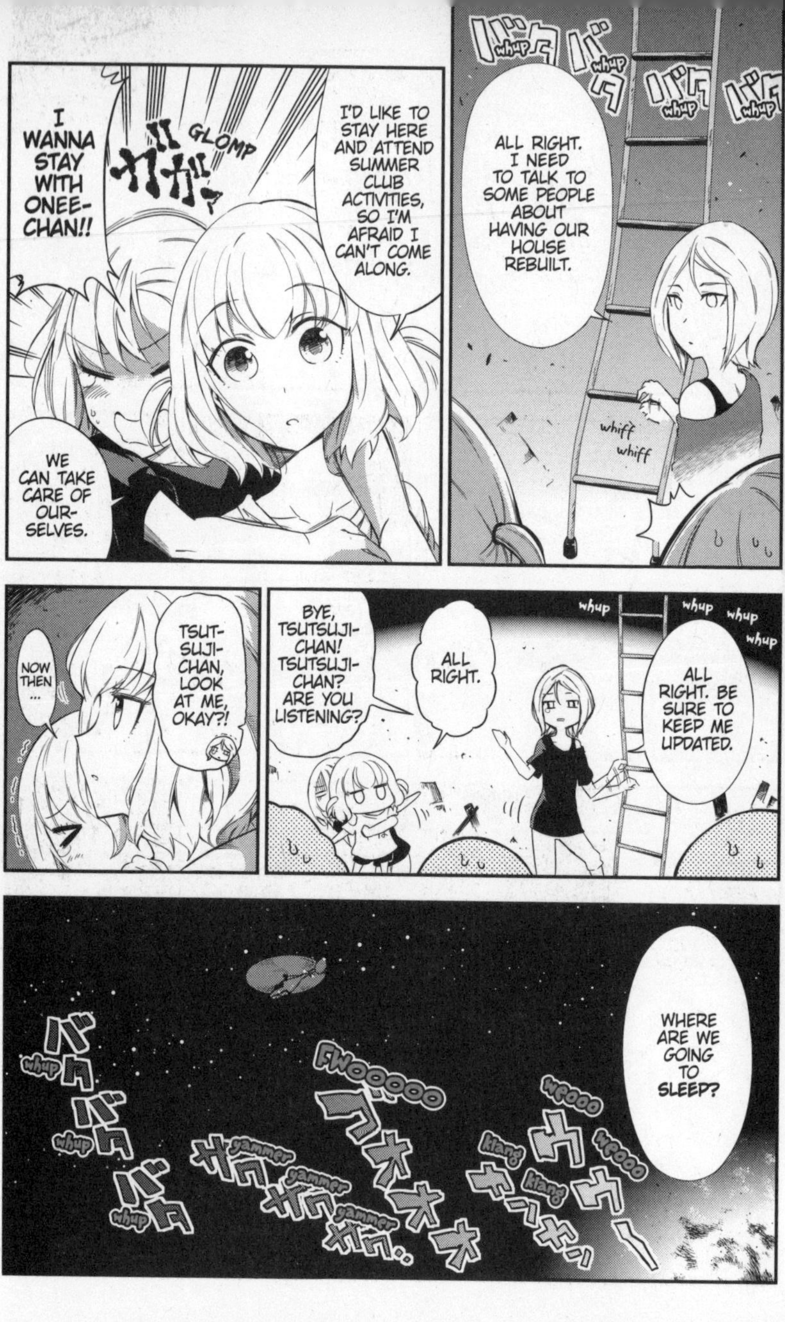
whup
whup
whup
whup
ALL RIGHT. I NEED TO TALK TO SOME PEOPLE ABOUT HAVING OUR HOUSE REBUILT.
whiff whiff
I'D LIKE TO STAY HERE AND ATTEND SUMMER CLUB ACTIVITIES, SO I'M AFRAID I CAN'T COME ALONG.
GLOMP
I WANNA STAY WITH ONEE-CHAN!!
WE CAN TAKE CARE OF OUR-SELVES.
whup whup whup whup
ALL RIGHT. BE SURE TO KEEP ME UPDATED.
ALL RIGHT.
BYE, TSUTSUJI-CHAN! TSUTSUJI-CHAN? ARE YOU LISTENING?
TSUT-SUJI-CHAN, LOOK AT ME, OKAY?!
NOW THEN ...
WHERE ARE WE GOING TO SLEEP?
WEOOO
WEOOO
klang klang
FWOOOOO
gammer gammer gammer
whup
whup
whup

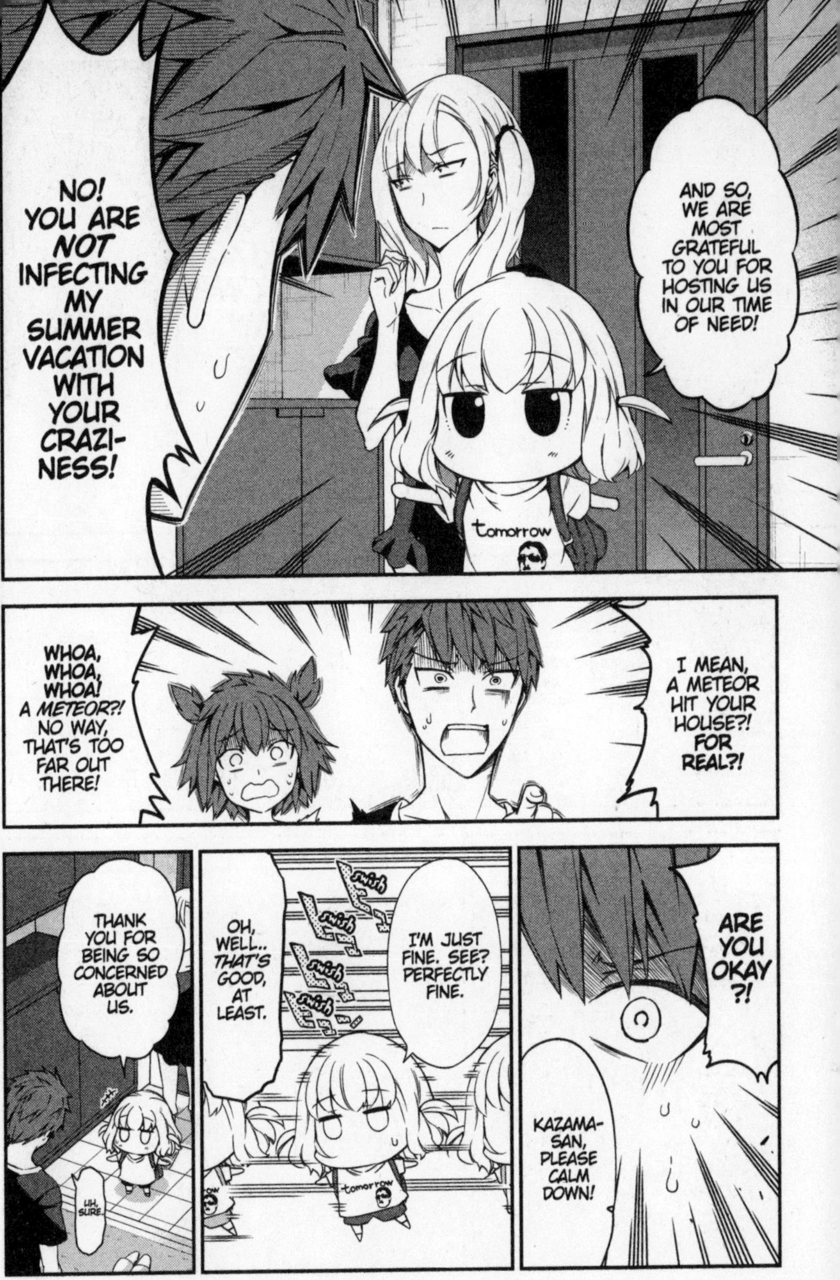
AND SO, WE ARE MOST GRATEFUL TO YOU FOR HOSTING US IN OUR TIME OF NEED!
NO! YOU ARE *NOT* INFECTING MY SUMMER VACATION WITH YOUR CRAZI- NESS!
tomorrow
I MEAN, A METEOR HIT YOUR HOUSE?! FOR REAL?!
WHOA, WHOA, WHOA! A *METEOR?!* NO WAY, THAT'S TOO FAR OUT THERE!
ARE YOU OKAY ?!
KAZAMA- SAN, PLEASE CALM DOWN!
I'M JUST FINE. SEE? PERFECTLY FINE.
swish
swish
swish
swish
tomorrow
OH, WELL.. *THAT'S* GOOD, AT LEAST.
THANK YOU FOR BEING SO CONCERNED ABOUT US.
UH, SURE.

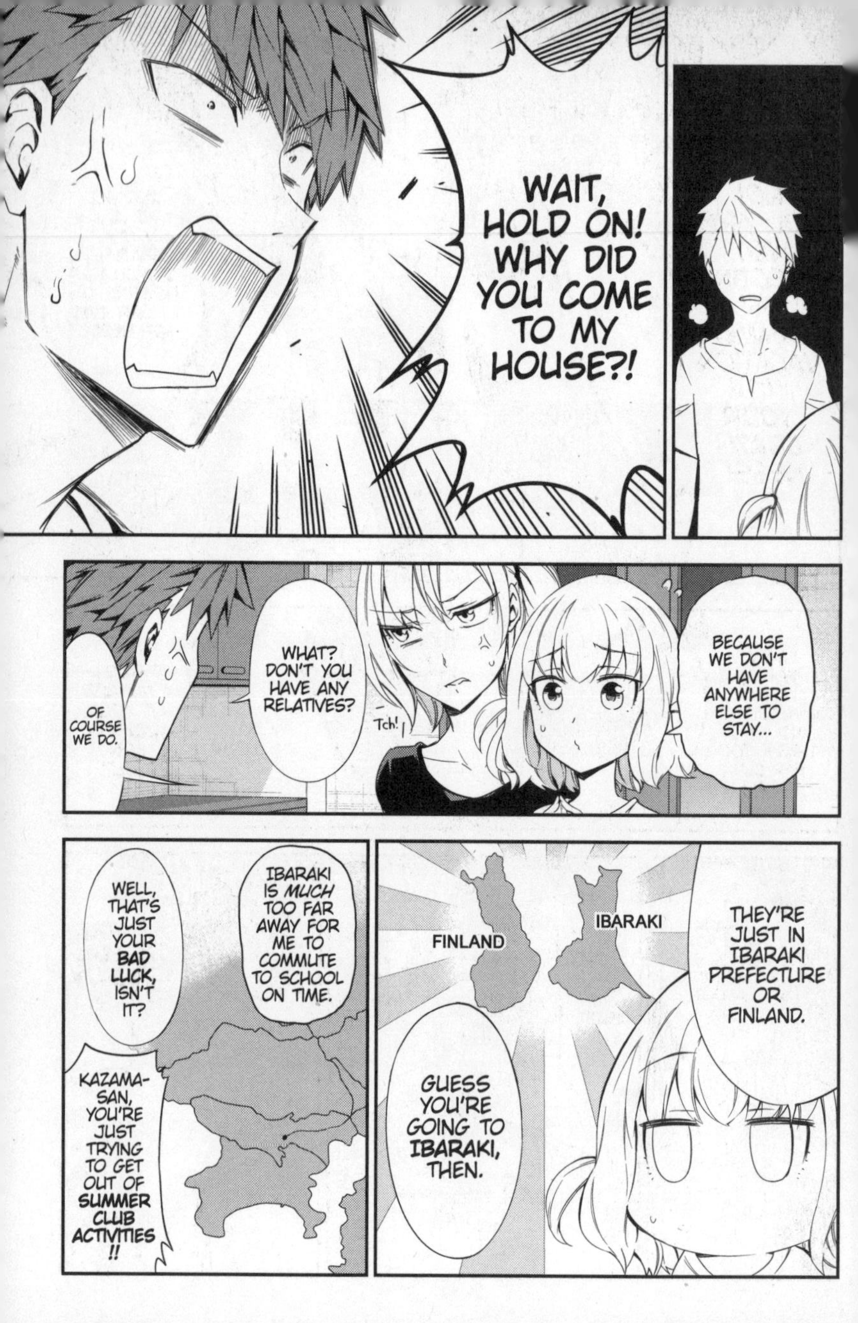
WAIT, HOLD ON! WHY DID YOU COME TO MY HOUSE?!
BECAUSE WE DON'T HAVE ANYWHERE ELSE TO STAY...
Tch!
WHAT? DON'T YOU HAVE ANY RELATIVES?
OF COURSE WE DO.
THEY'RE JUST IN IBARAKI PREFECTURE OR FINLAND.
IBARAKI
FINLAND
GUESS YOU'RE GOING TO IBARAKI, THEN.
IBARAKI IS *MUCH* TOO FAR AWAY FOR ME TO COMMUTE TO SCHOOL ON TIME.
WELL, THAT'S JUST YOUR **BAD LUCK**, ISN'T IT?
KAZAMA-SAN, YOU'RE JUST TRYING TO GET OUT OF **SUMMER CLUB ACTIVITIES**!!

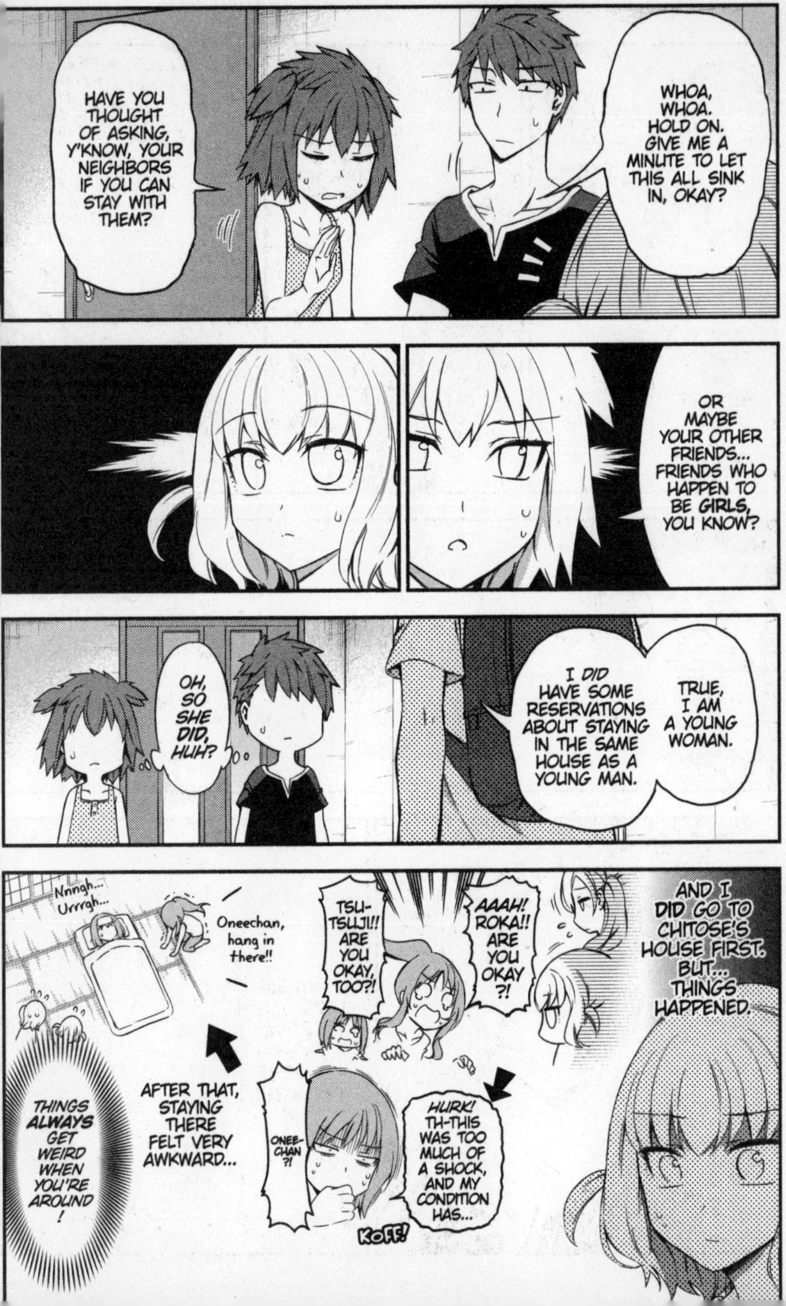
WHOA, WHOA. HOLD ON. GIVE ME A MINUTE TO LET THIS ALL SINK IN, OKAY?
HAVE YOU THOUGHT OF ASKING, Y'KNOW, YOUR NEIGHBORS IF YOU CAN STAY WITH THEM?
OR MAYBE YOUR OTHER FRIENDS... FRIENDS WHO HAPPEN TO BE GIRLS, YOU KNOW?
TRUE, I AM A YOUNG WOMAN.
I DID HAVE SOME RESERVATIONS ABOUT STAYING IN THE SAME HOUSE AS A YOUNG MAN.
OH, SO SHE DID, HUH?
AND I DID GO TO CHITOSE'S HOUSE FIRST. BUT... THINGS HAPPENED.
AAAH! ROKA!! ARE YOU OKAY?!
TSU-TSUJI!! ARE YOU OKAY, TOO?!
Oneechan, hang in there!!
Nnngh... Urrrgh...
HURK! TH-THIS WAS TOO MUCH OF A SHOCK, AND MY CONDITION HAS...
KOFF!
ONEE-CHAN?!
AFTER THAT, STAYING THERE FELT VERY AWKWARD...
THINGS ALWAYS GET WEIRD WHEN YOU'RE AROUND!

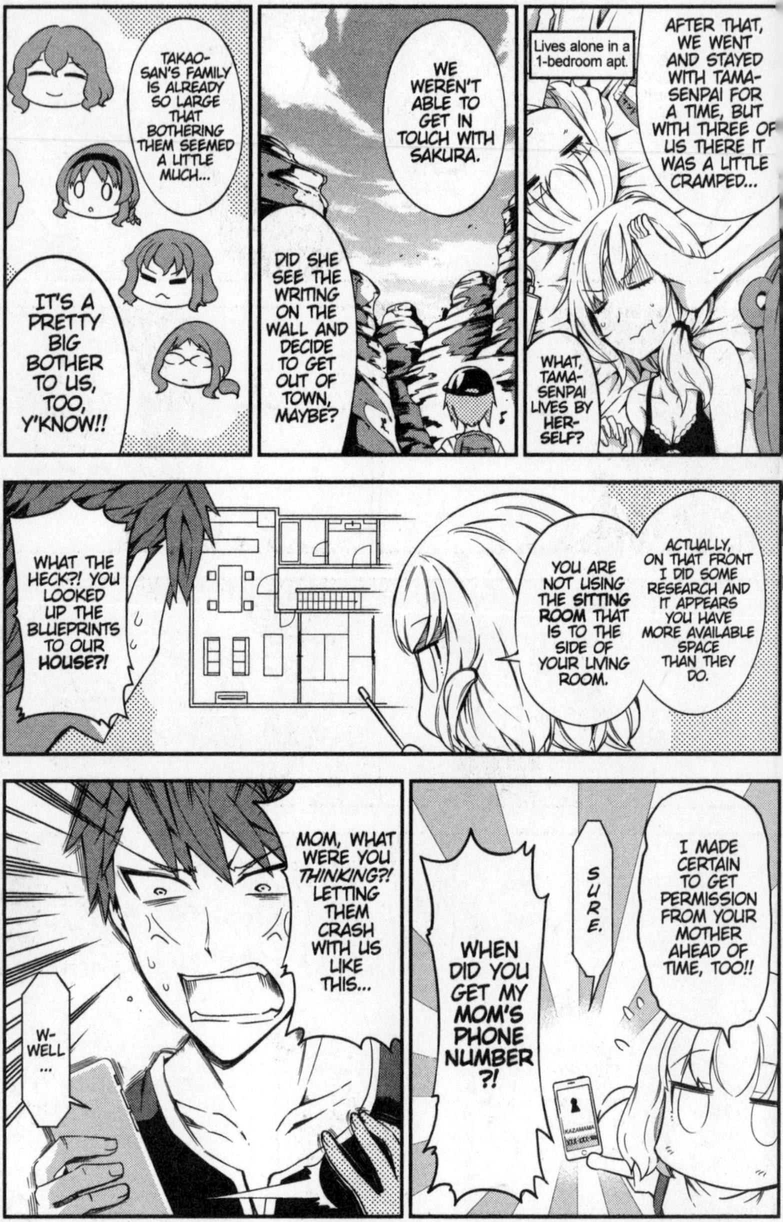
AFTER THAT, WE WENT AND STAYED WITH TAMA-SENPAI FOR A TIME, BUT WITH THREE OF US THERE IT WAS A LITTLE CRAMPED...
Lives alone in a 1-bedroom apt.
WHAT, TAMA-SENPAI LIVES BY HER-SELF?
WE WEREN'T ABLE TO GET IN TOUCH WITH SAKURA.
DID SHE SEE THE WRITING ON THE WALL AND DECIDE TO GET OUT OF TOWN, MAYBE?
TAKAO-SAN'S FAMILY IS ALREADY SO LARGE THAT BOTHERING THEM SEEMED A LITTLE MUCH...
IT'S A PRETTY BIG BOTHER TO US, TOO, Y'KNOW!!
ACTUALLY, ON THAT FRONT I DID SOME RESEARCH AND IT APPEARS YOU HAVE MORE AVAILABLE SPACE THAN THEY DO.
YOU ARE NOT USING THE SITTING ROOM THAT IS TO THE SIDE OF YOUR LIVING ROOM.
WHAT THE HECK?! YOU LOOKED UP THE BLUEPRINTS TO OUR HOUSE?!
I MADE CERTAIN TO GET PERMISSION FROM YOUR MOTHER AHEAD OF TIME, TOO!!
SURE.
WHEN DID YOU GET MY MOM'S PHONE NUMBER?!
KAZAMAMA
MOM, WHAT WERE YOU THINKING?! LETTING THEM CRASH WITH US LIKE THIS...
W-WELL...

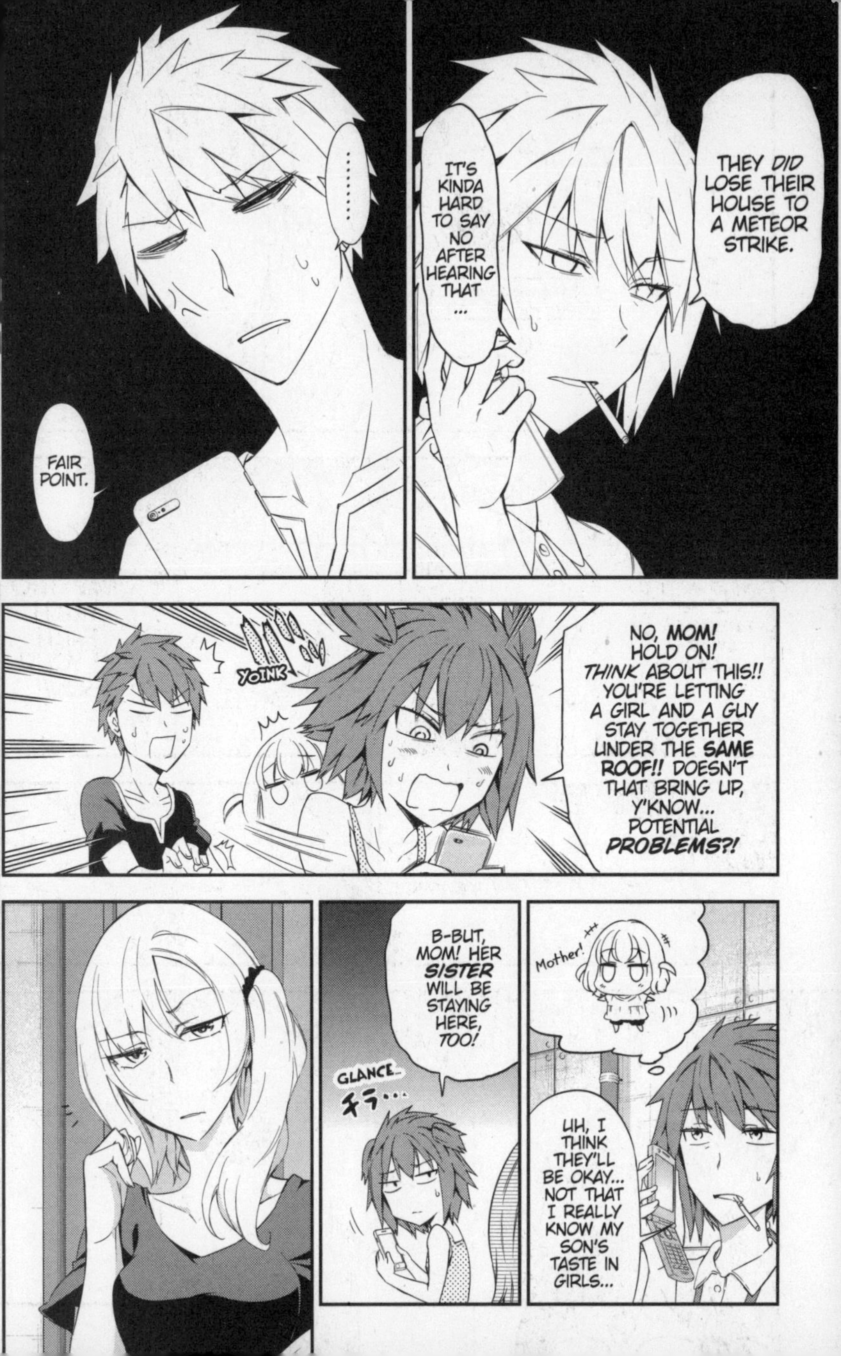
THEY DID LOSE THEIR HOUSE TO A METEOR STRIKE.
IT'S KINDA HARD TO SAY NO AFTER HEARING THAT ...
......
FAIR POINT.
NO, MOM! HOLD ON! THINK ABOUT THIS!! YOU'RE LETTING A GIRL AND A GUY STAY TOGETHER UNDER THE SAME ROOF!! DOESN'T THAT BRING UP, Y'KNOW... POTENTIAL PROBLEMS?!
YOINK
Mother!
UH, I THINK THEY'LL BE OKAY... NOT THAT I REALLY KNOW MY SON'S TASTE IN GIRLS...
B-BUT, MOM! HER SISTER WILL BE STAYING HERE, TOO!
GLANCE...
チラ...

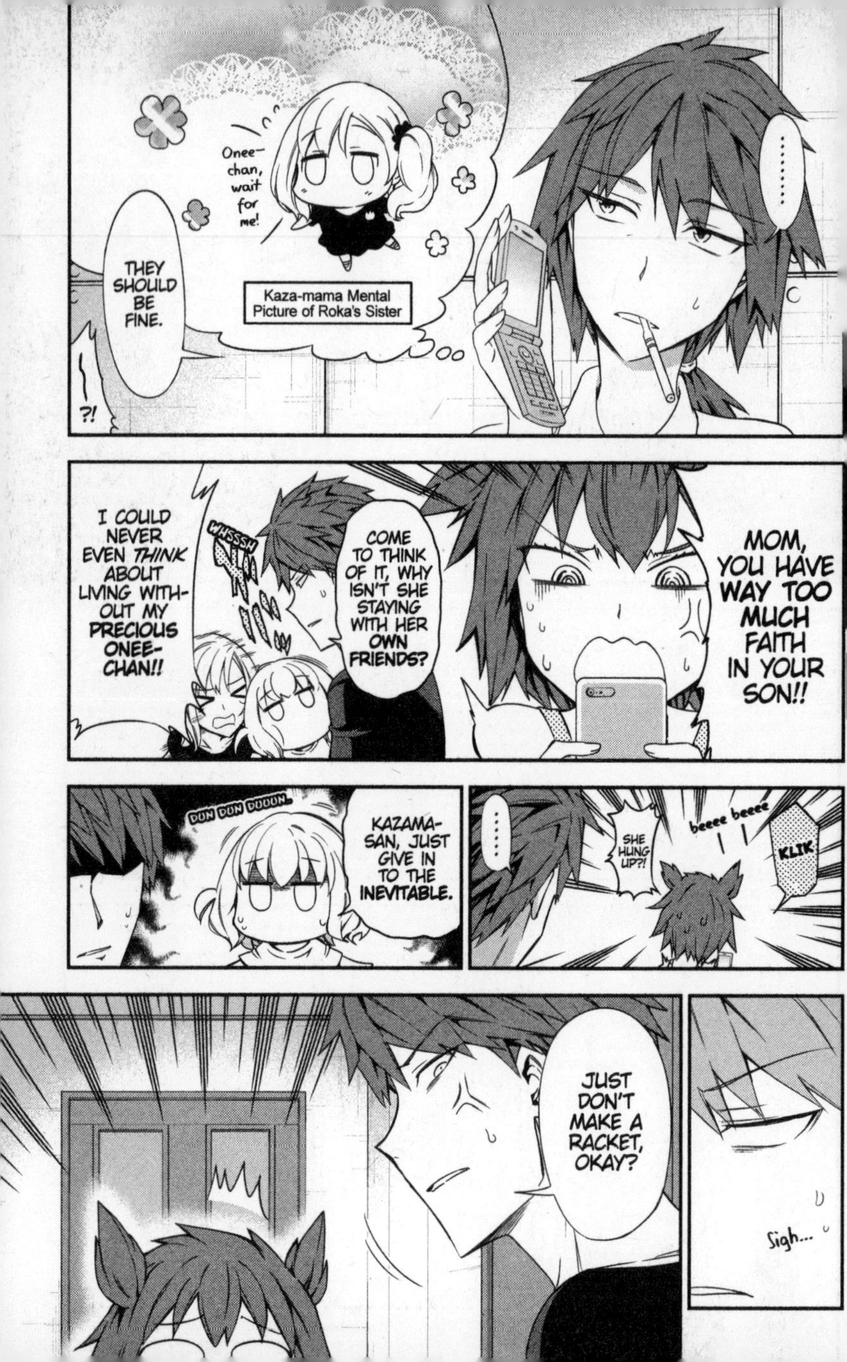
......
Onee-chan, wait for me!
Kaza-mama Mental Picture of Roka's Sister
THEY SHOULD BE FINE.
?!
MOM, YOU HAVE WAY TOO MUCH FAITH IN YOUR SON!!
COME TO THINK OF IT, WHY ISN'T SHE STAYING WITH HER OWN FRIENDS?
WHSSSH
I COULD NEVER EVEN *THINK* ABOUT LIVING WITH-OUT MY PRECIOUS ONEE-CHAN!!
KLIK
beeee beeee
SHE HUNG UP?!
......
KAZAMA-SAN, JUST GIVE IN TO THE INEVITABLE.
DUN DUN DUUUN.
Sigh...
JUST DON'T MAKE A RACKET, OKAY?

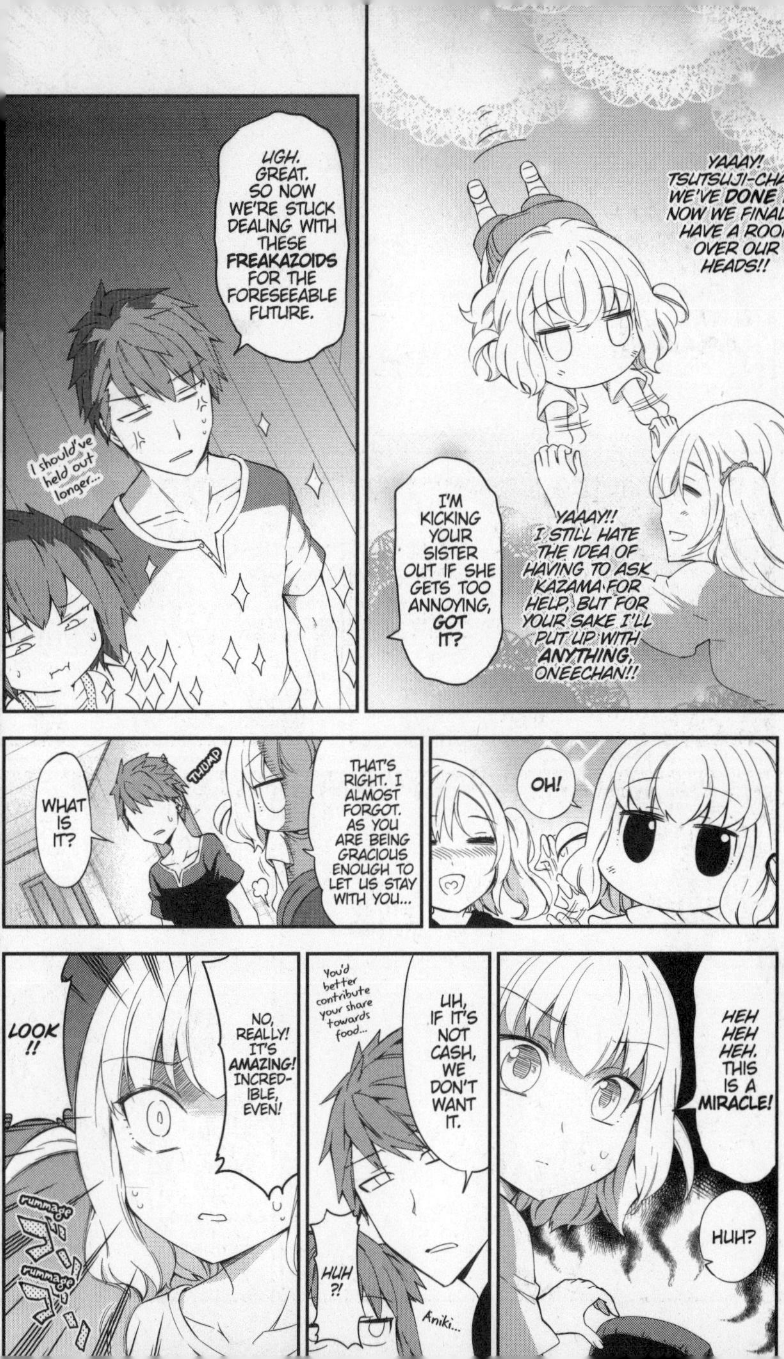
YAAAY! TSUTSUJI-CHAN, WE'VE DONE IT! NOW WE FINALLY HAVE A ROOF OVER OUR HEADS!!
YAAAY!! I STILL HATE THE IDEA OF HAVING TO ASK KAZAMA FOR HELP, BUT FOR YOUR SAKE I'LL PUT UP WITH ANYTHING, ONEECHAN!!
I'M KICKING YOUR SISTER OUT IF SHE GETS TOO ANNOYING, GOT IT?
UGH. GREAT. SO NOW WE'RE STUCK DEALING WITH THESE FREAKAZOIDS FOR THE FORESEEABLE FUTURE.
I should've held out longer...
OH!
THAT'S RIGHT. I ALMOST FORGOT. AS YOU ARE BEING GRACIOUS ENOUGH TO LET US STAY WITH YOU...
THUMP
WHAT IS IT?
HEH HEH HEH. THIS IS A MIRACLE!
HUH?
UH, IF IT'S NOT CASH, WE DON'T WANT IT.
You'd better contribute your share towards food...
HUH ?!
Aniki...
NO, REALLY! IT'S AMAZING! INCREDIBLE, EVEN!
LOOK!!
rummage
rummage

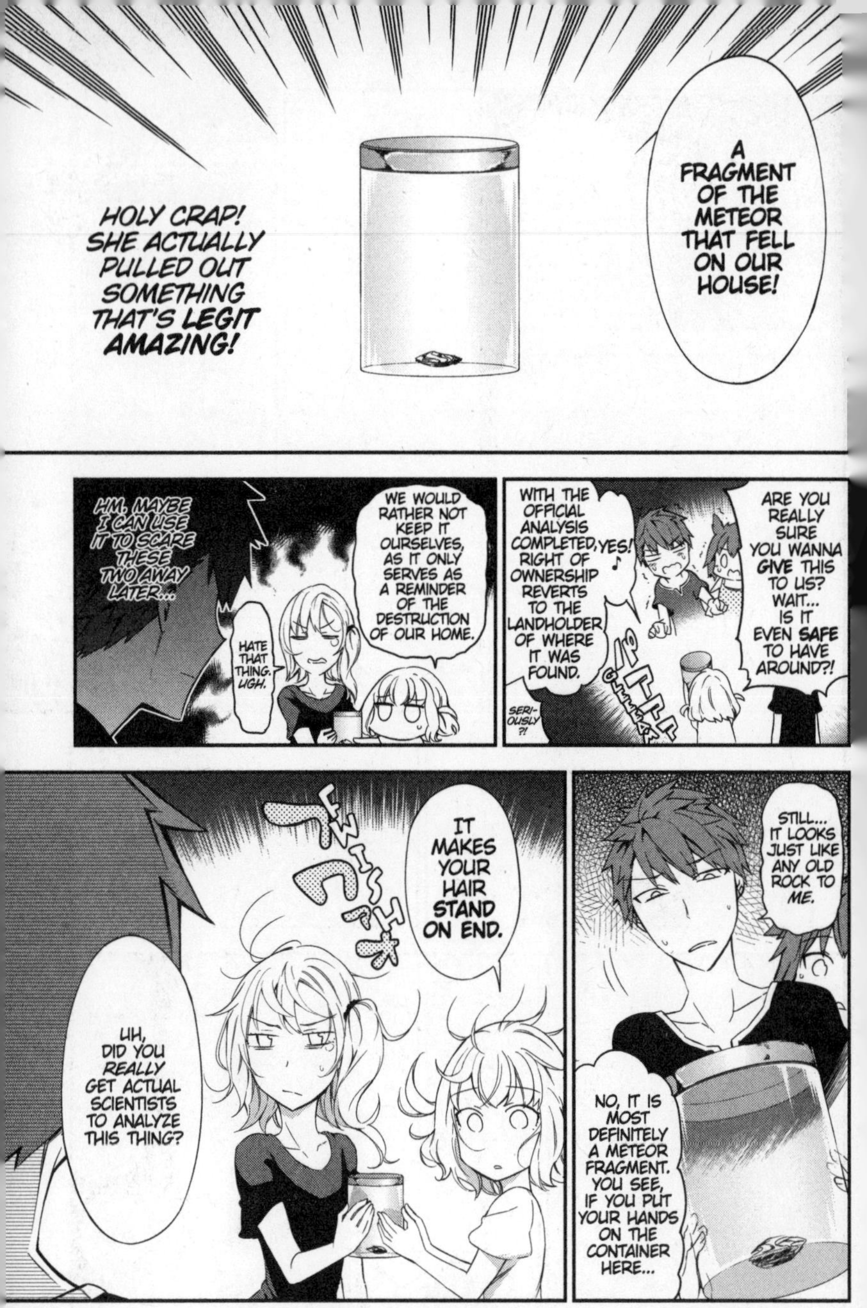
A FRAGMENT OF THE METEOR THAT FELL ON OUR HOUSE!
HOLY CRAP! SHE ACTUALLY PULLED OUT SOMETHING THAT'S LEGIT AMAZING!
ARE YOU REALLY SURE YOU WANNA GIVE THIS TO US? WAIT... IS IT EVEN SAFE TO HAVE AROUND?!
WITH THE OFFICIAL ANALYSIS COMPLETED, RIGHT OF OWNERSHIP REVERTS TO THE LANDHOLDER OF WHERE IT WAS FOUND.
YES! ♪
GLEEEAM
SERI-OUSLY?!
WE WOULD RATHER NOT KEEP IT OURSELVES, AS IT ONLY SERVES AS A REMINDER OF THE DESTRUCTION OF OUR HOME.
HATE THAT THING. UGH.
HM. MAYBE I CAN USE IT TO SCARE THESE TWO AWAY LATER...
STILL... IT LOOKS JUST LIKE ANY OLD ROCK TO ME.
NO, IT IS MOST DEFINITELY A METEOR FRAGMENT. YOU SEE, IF YOU PUT YOUR HANDS ON THE CONTAINER HERE...
IT MAKES YOUR HAIR STAND ON END.
FWISH
UH, DID YOU REALLY GET ACTUAL SCIENTISTS TO ANALYZE THIS THING?

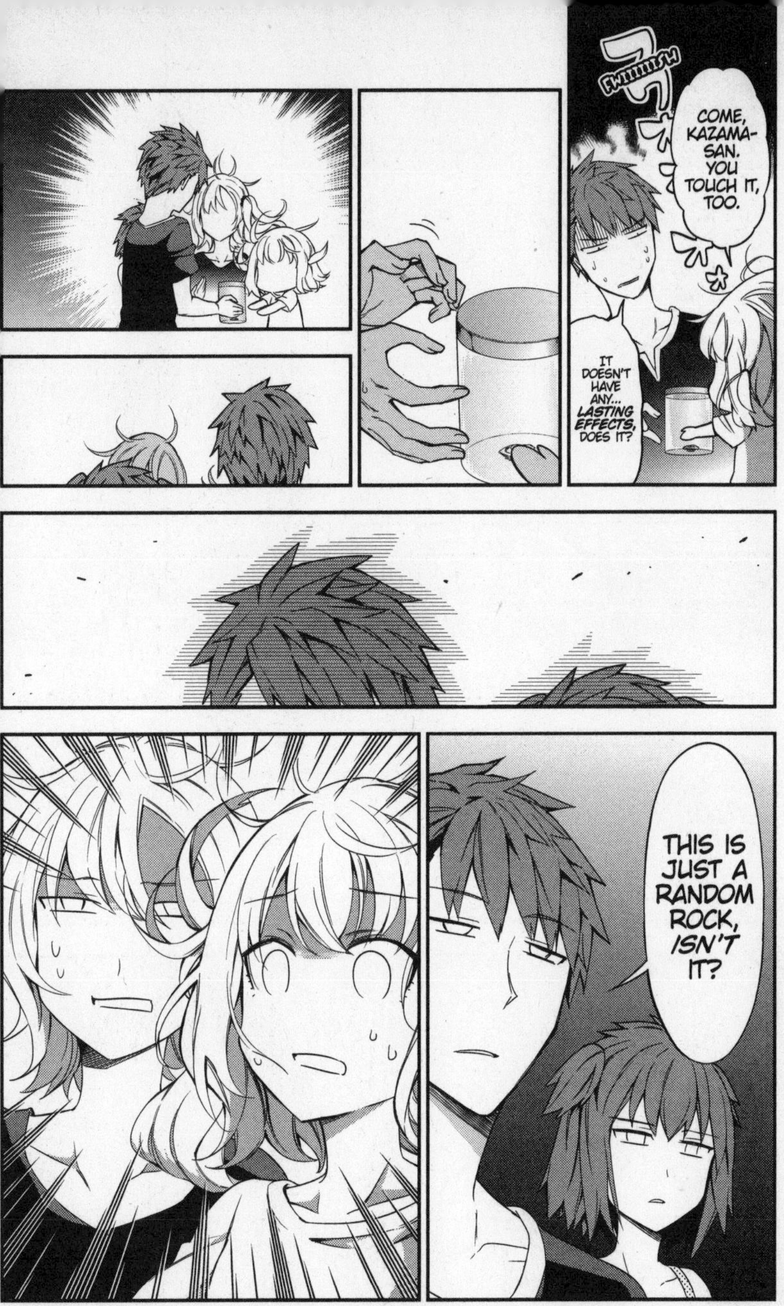
FWIIIIIISH
COME, KAZAMA-SAN. YOU TOUCH IT, TOO.
IT DOESN'T HAVE ANY... LASTING EFFECTS, DOES IT?
THIS IS JUST A RANDOM ROCK, ISN'T IT?

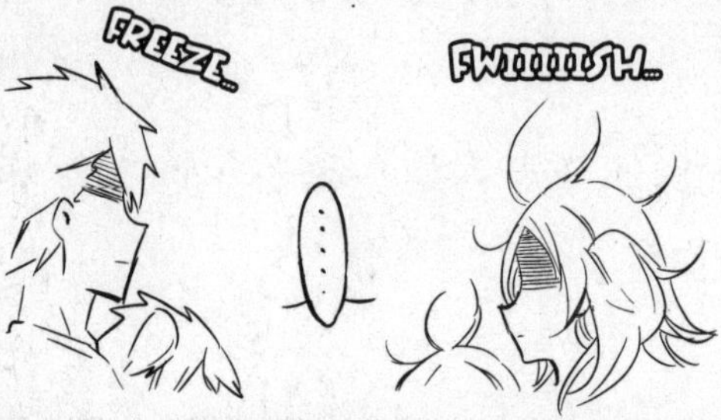
FWIIIIISH...
.....
FREEZE...

D-FRAGMENTS ディーふらぐっ！

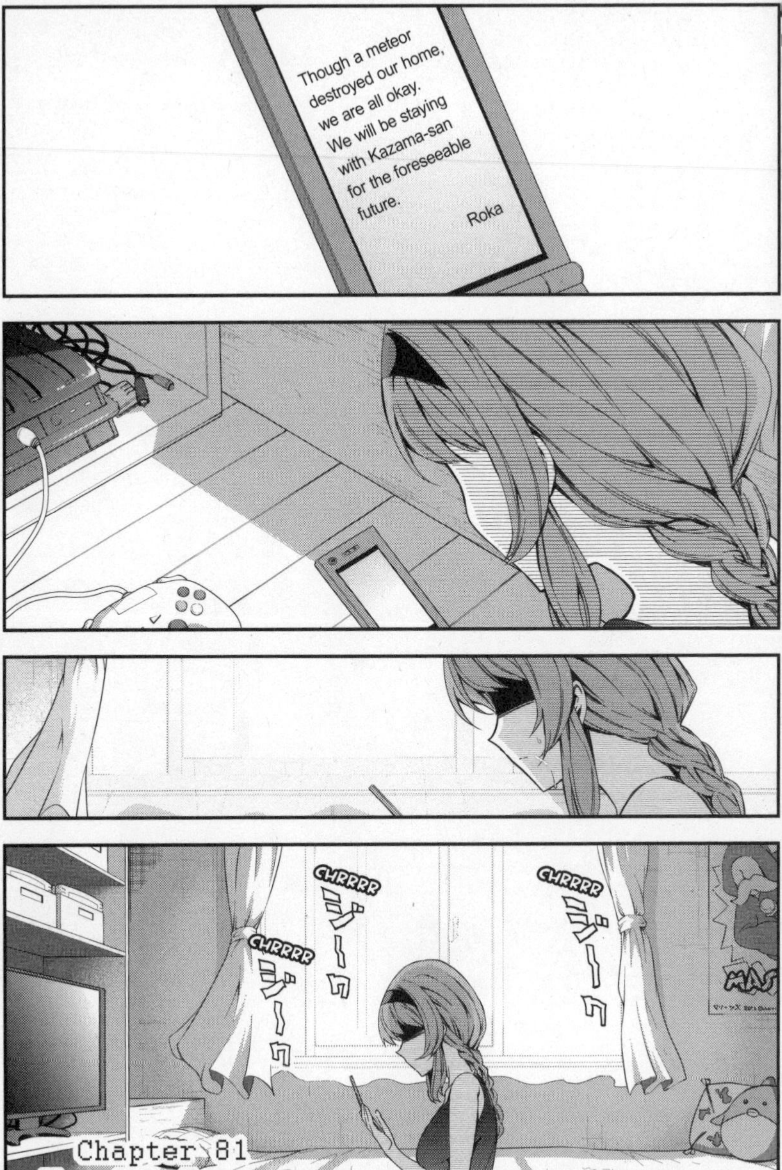
Though a meteor destroyed our home, we are all okay. We will be staying with Kazama-san for the foreseeable future.
Roka
CHRRRR
ジ〜ク
CHRRRR
ジ〜ク
CHRRRR
ジ〜ク
Chapter 81
You Can Say...

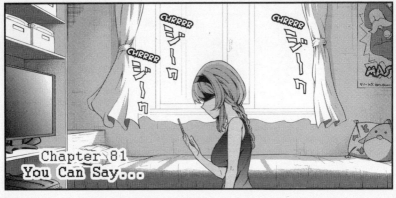

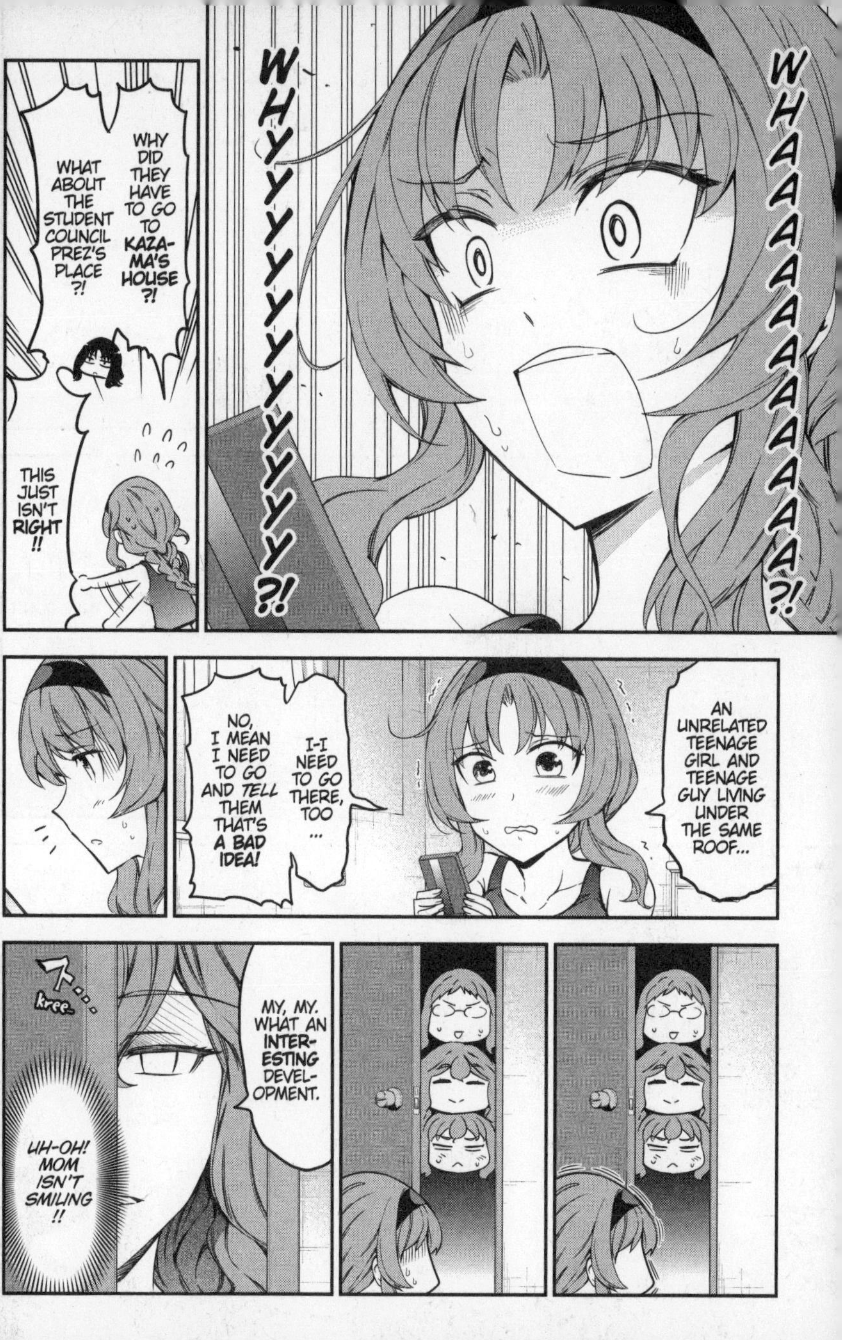
WHAAAAAAAAAAAAAAAA?!
WHYYYYYYYYYYYYYYYY?!
WHY DID THEY HAVE TO GO TO KAZAMA'S HOUSE?!
WHAT ABOUT THE STUDENT COUNCIL PREZ'S PLACE?!
THIS JUST ISN'T RIGHT!!
AN UNRELATED TEENAGE GIRL AND TEENAGE GUY LIVING UNDER THE SAME ROOF...
I-I NEED TO GO THERE, TOO...
NO, I MEAN I NEED TO GO AND TELL THEM THAT'S A BAD IDEA!
MY, MY. WHAT AN INTERESTING DEVELOPMENT.
kree...
UH-OH! MOM ISN'T SMILING!!

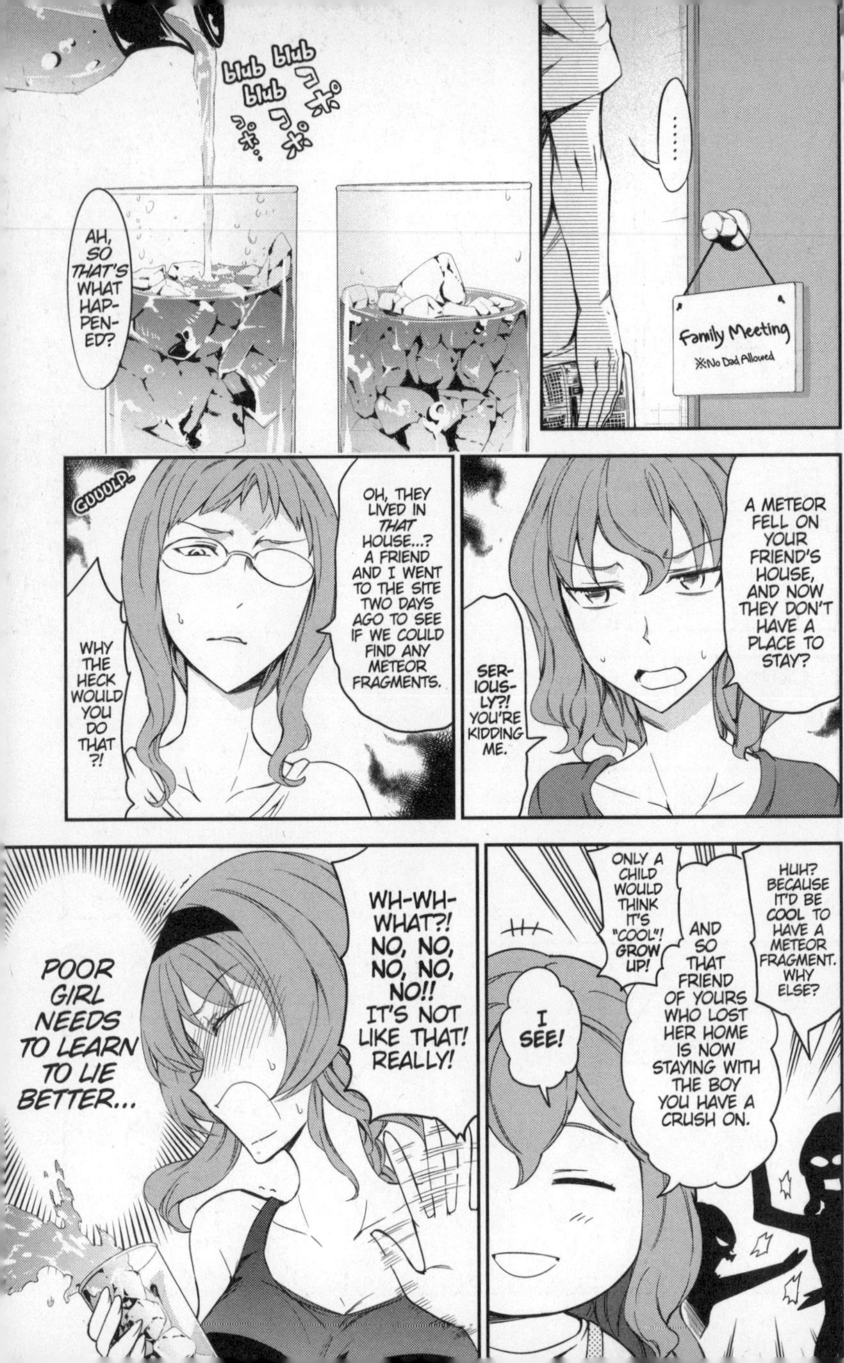
......
Family Meeting
※No Dad Allowed
blub blub blub
AH, SO THAT'S WHAT HAPPENED?
A METEOR FELL ON YOUR FRIEND'S HOUSE, AND NOW THEY DON'T HAVE A PLACE TO STAY?
SERIOUSLY?! YOU'RE KIDDING ME.
OH, THEY LIVED IN *THAT* HOUSE...? A FRIEND AND I WENT TO THE SITE TWO DAYS AGO TO SEE IF WE COULD FIND ANY METEOR FRAGMENTS.
GUUULP.
WHY THE HECK WOULD YOU DO THAT?!
HUH? BECAUSE IT'D BE COOL TO HAVE A METEOR FRAGMENT. WHY ELSE?
ONLY A CHILD WOULD THINK IT'S "COOL"! GROW UP!
AND SO THAT FRIEND OF YOURS WHO LOST HER HOME IS NOW STAYING WITH THE BOY YOU HAVE A CRUSH ON.
I SEE!
WH-WH-WHAT?! NO, NO, NO, NO, NO!! IT'S NOT LIKE THAT! REALLY!
POOR GIRL NEEDS TO LEARN TO LIE BETTER...

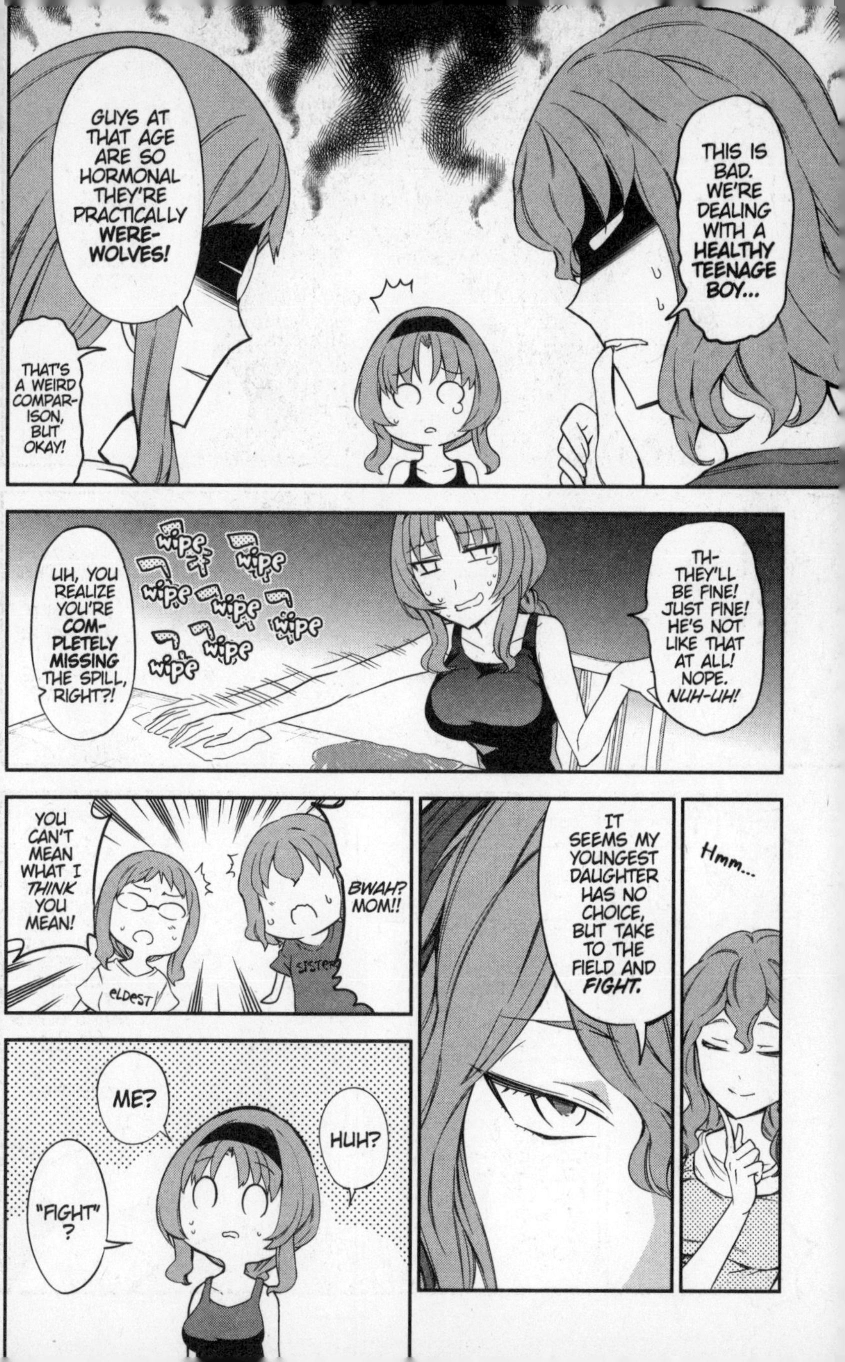
THIS IS BAD. WE'RE DEALING WITH A HEALTHY TEENAGE BOY...
GUYS AT THAT AGE ARE SO HORMONAL THEY'RE PRACTICALLY WERE-WOLVES!
THAT'S A WEIRD COMPAR-ISON, BUT OKAY!
TH-THEY'LL BE FINE! JUST FINE! HE'S NOT LIKE THAT AT ALL! NOPE. NUH-UH!
wipe wipe wipe wipe wipe wipe wipe wipe
UH, YOU REALIZE YOU'RE COM-PLETELY MISSING THE SPILL, RIGHT?!
Hmm...
IT SEEMS MY YOUNGEST DAUGHTER HAS NO CHOICE, BUT TAKE TO THE FIELD AND FIGHT.
BWAH? MOM!!
SISTER
YOU CAN'T MEAN WHAT I THINK YOU MEAN!
eLDEST
HUH?
ME?
"FIGHT"?

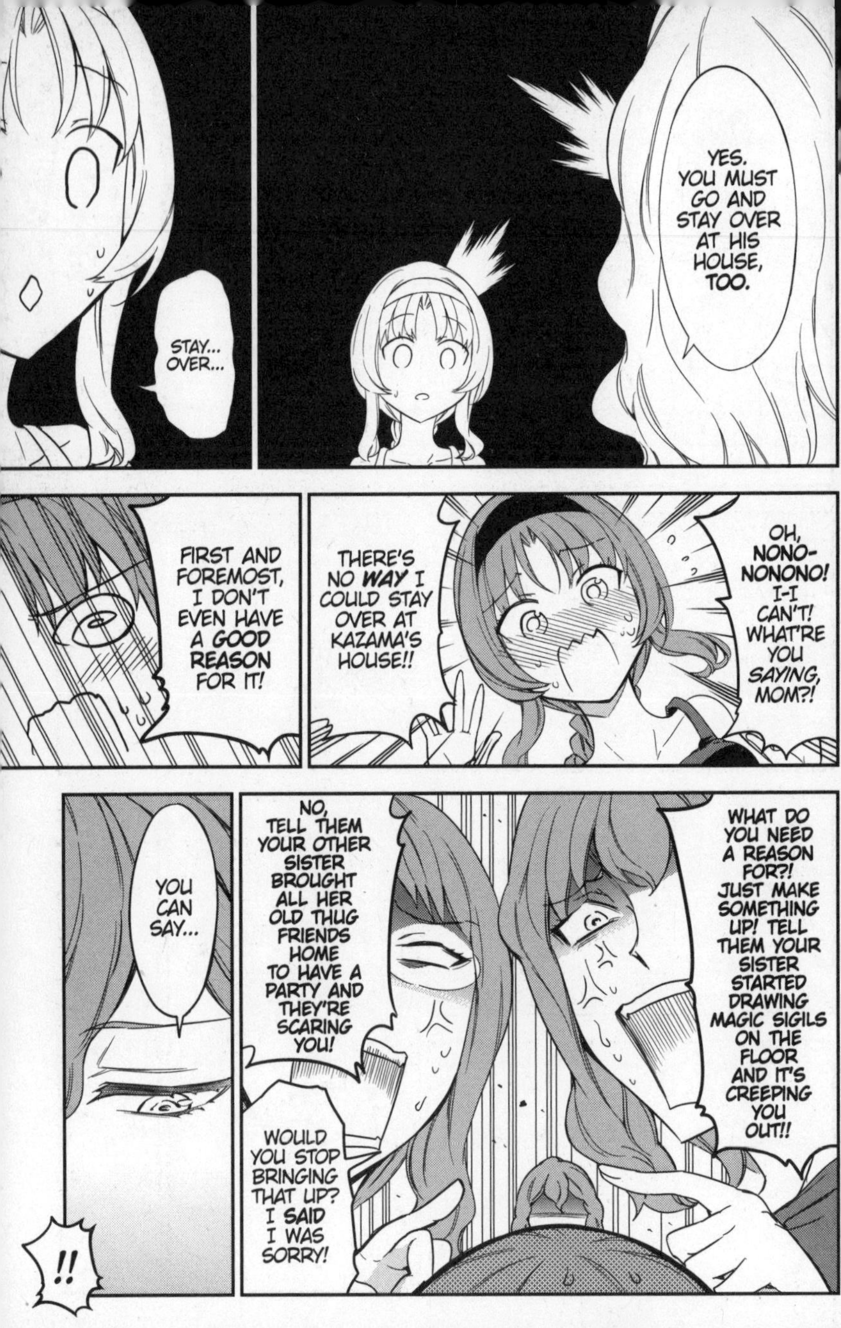
YES. YOU MUST GO AND STAY OVER AT HIS HOUSE, TOO.
STAY... OVER...
OH, NONO-NONONO! I-I CAN'T! WHAT'RE YOU *SAYING*, MOM?!
THERE'S NO ***WAY*** I COULD STAY OVER AT KAZAMA'S HOUSE!!
FIRST AND FOREMOST, I DON'T EVEN HAVE A **GOOD** REASON FOR IT!
WHAT DO YOU NEED A REASON FOR?! JUST MAKE SOMETHING UP! TELL THEM YOUR SISTER STARTED DRAWING MAGIC SIGILS ON THE FLOOR AND IT'S CREEPING YOU OUT!!
NO, TELL THEM YOUR OTHER SISTER BROUGHT ALL HER OLD THUG FRIENDS HOME TO HAVE A PARTY AND THEY'RE SCARING YOU!
WOULD YOU STOP BRINGING THAT UP? I **SAID** I WAS SORRY!
YOU CAN SAY...
!!

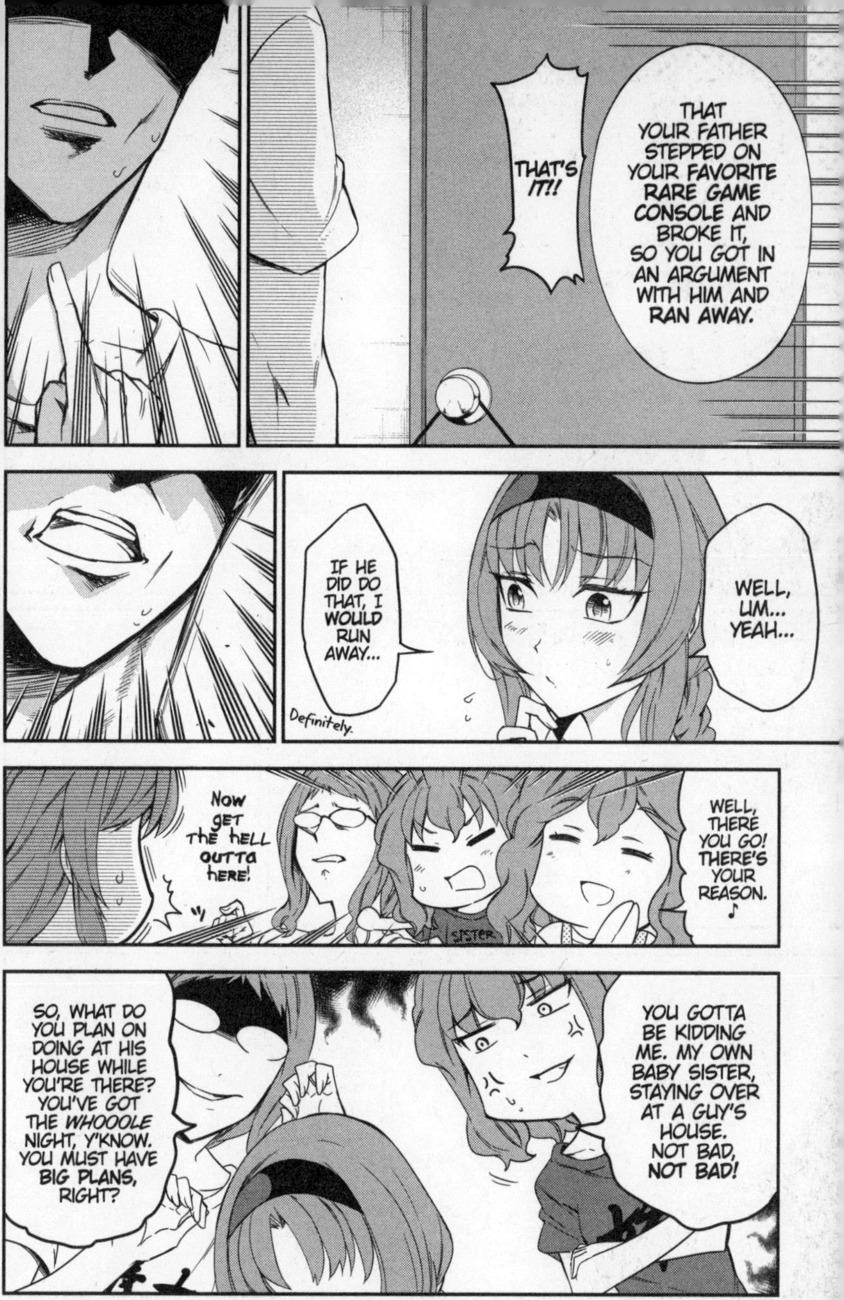
THAT YOUR FATHER STEPPED ON YOUR FAVORITE RARE GAME CONSOLE AND BROKE IT, SO YOU GOT IN AN ARGUMENT WITH HIM AND RAN AWAY.
THAT'S IT!!
WELL, UM... YEAH...
IF HE DID DO THAT, I WOULD RUN AWAY...
Definitely.
WELL, THERE YOU GO! THERE'S YOUR REASON. ♪
Now get the hell outta here!
SISTER
YOU GOTTA BE KIDDING ME. MY OWN BABY SISTER, STAYING OVER AT A GUY'S HOUSE. NOT BAD, NOT BAD!
SO, WHAT DO YOU PLAN ON DOING AT HIS HOUSE WHILE YOU'RE THERE? YOU'VE GOT THE WHOOOLE NIGHT, Y'KNOW. YOU MUST HAVE BIG PLANS, RIGHT?

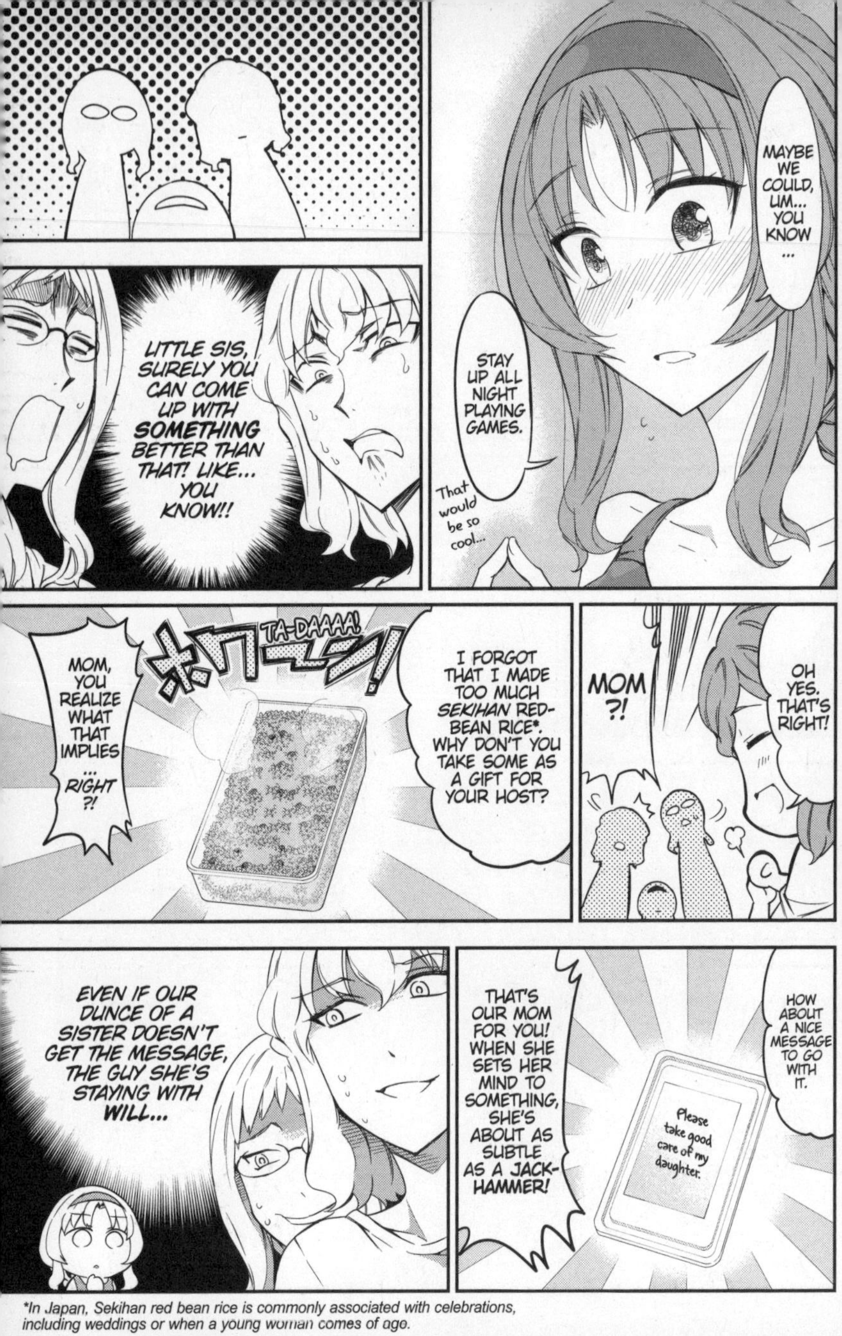
MAYBE WE COULD, UM... YOU KNOW...
STAY UP ALL NIGHT PLAYING GAMES.
That would be so cool...
LITTLE SIS, SURELY YOU CAN COME UP WITH SOMETHING BETTER THAN THAT! LIKE... YOU KNOW!!
OH YES. THAT'S RIGHT!
MOM ?!
I FORGOT THAT I MADE TOO MUCH SEKIHAN RED-BEAN RICE*. WHY DON'T YOU TAKE SOME AS A GIFT FOR YOUR HOST?
TA-DAAAA!
MOM, YOU REALIZE WHAT THAT IMPLIES... RIGHT ?!
HOW ABOUT A NICE MESSAGE TO GO WITH IT.
Please take good care of my daughter.
THAT'S OUR MOM FOR YOU! WHEN SHE SETS HER MIND TO SOMETHING, SHE'S ABOUT AS SUBTLE AS A JACK-HAMMER!
EVEN IF OUR DUNCE OF A SISTER DOESN'T GET THE MESSAGE, THE GUY SHE'S STAYING WITH WILL...

*In Japan, Sekihan red bean rice is commonly associated with celebrations, including weddings or when a young woman comes of age.

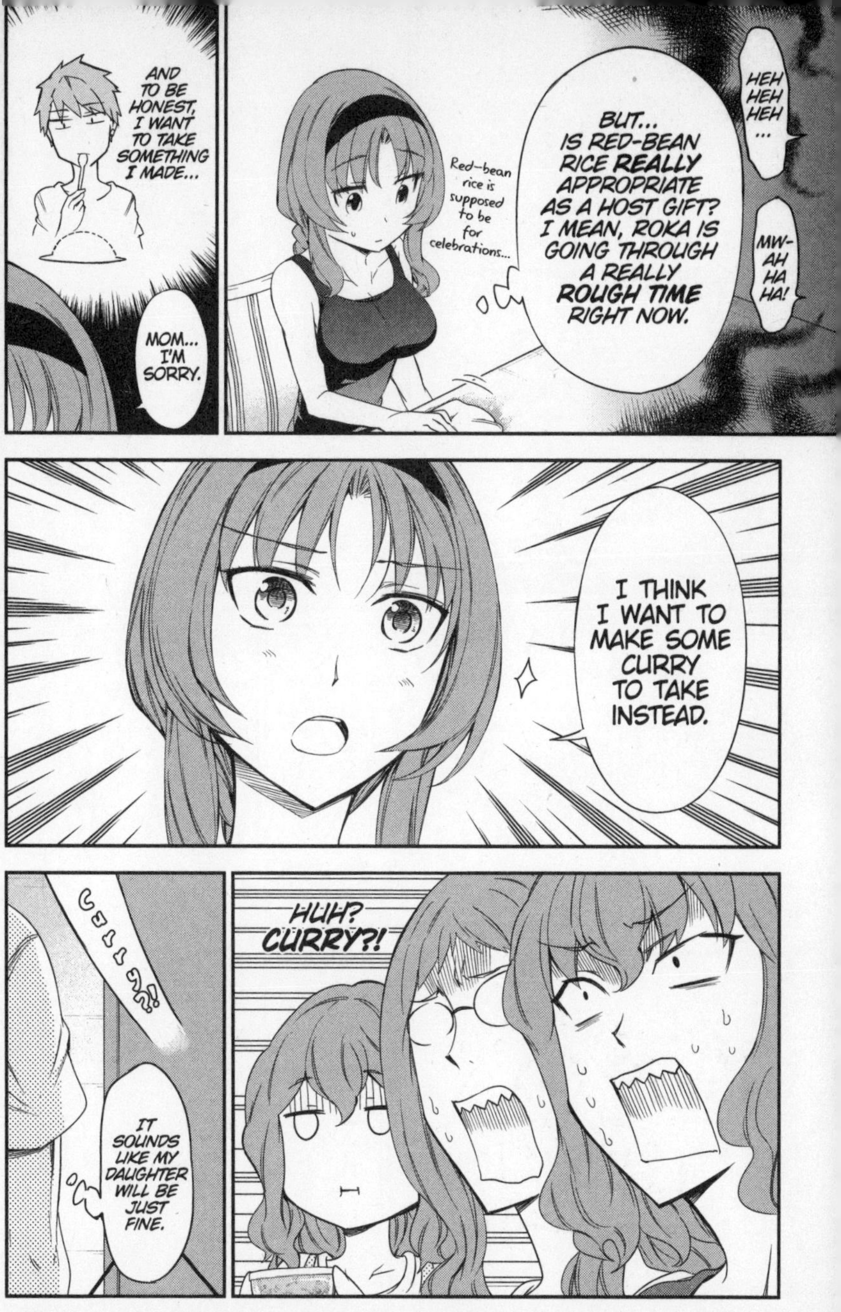
HEH HEH HEH...
MW-AH HA HA!
BUT... IS RED-BEAN RICE REALLY APPROPRIATE AS A HOST GIFT? I MEAN, ROKA IS GOING THROUGH A REALLY ROUGH TIME RIGHT NOW.
Red-bean rice is supposed to be for celebrations...
AND TO BE HONEST, I WANT TO TAKE SOMETHING I MADE...
MOM... I'M SORRY.
I THINK I WANT TO MAKE SOME CURRY TO TAKE INSTEAD.
HUH? CURRY?!
IT SOUNDS LIKE MY DAUGHTER WILL BE JUST FINE.

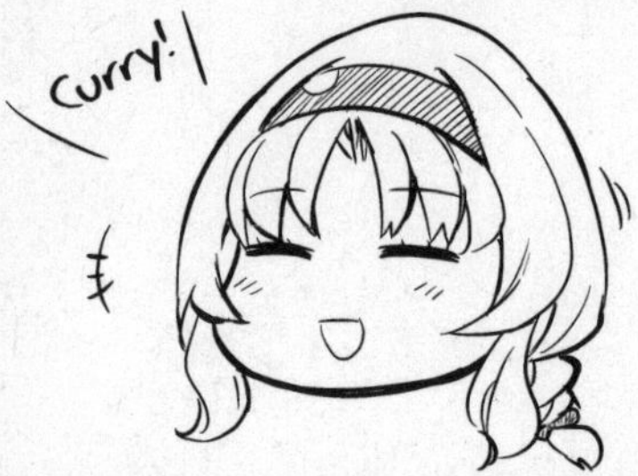
Curry!

D-FRAGMENTS ディー・フラグメンツ!

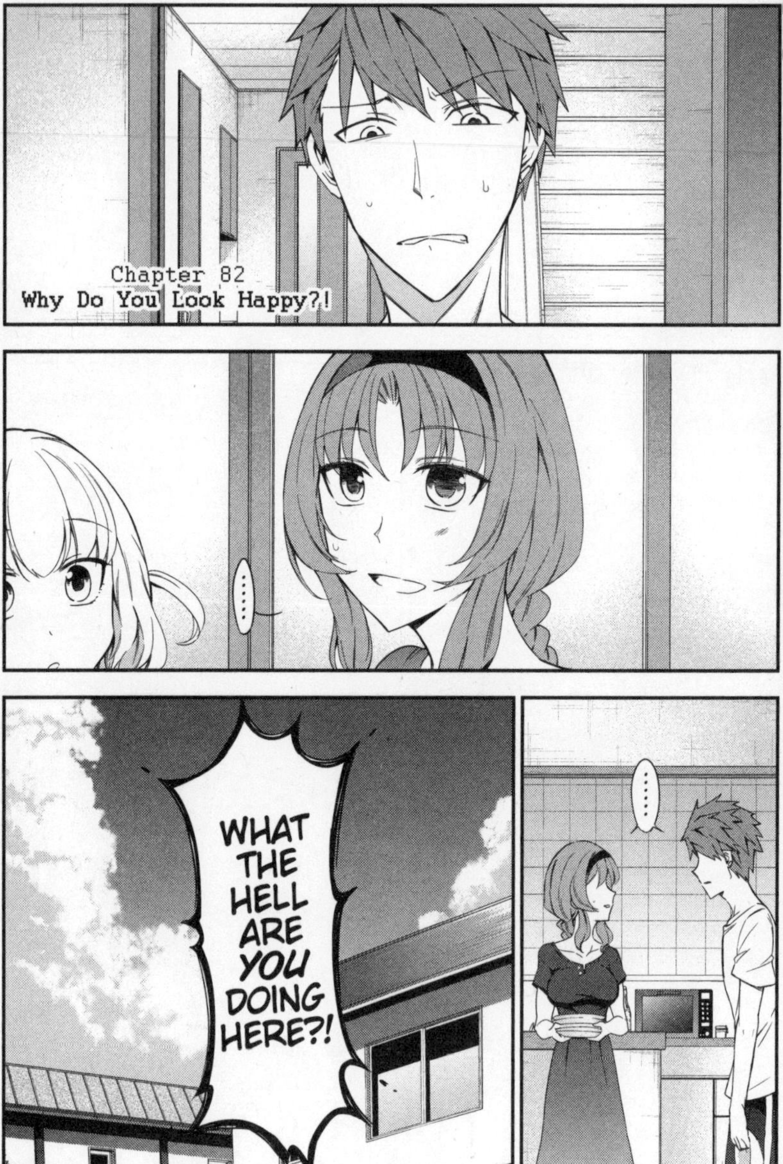
Chapter 82
Why Do You Look Happy?!
......
......
WHAT THE HELL ARE YOU DOING HERE?!

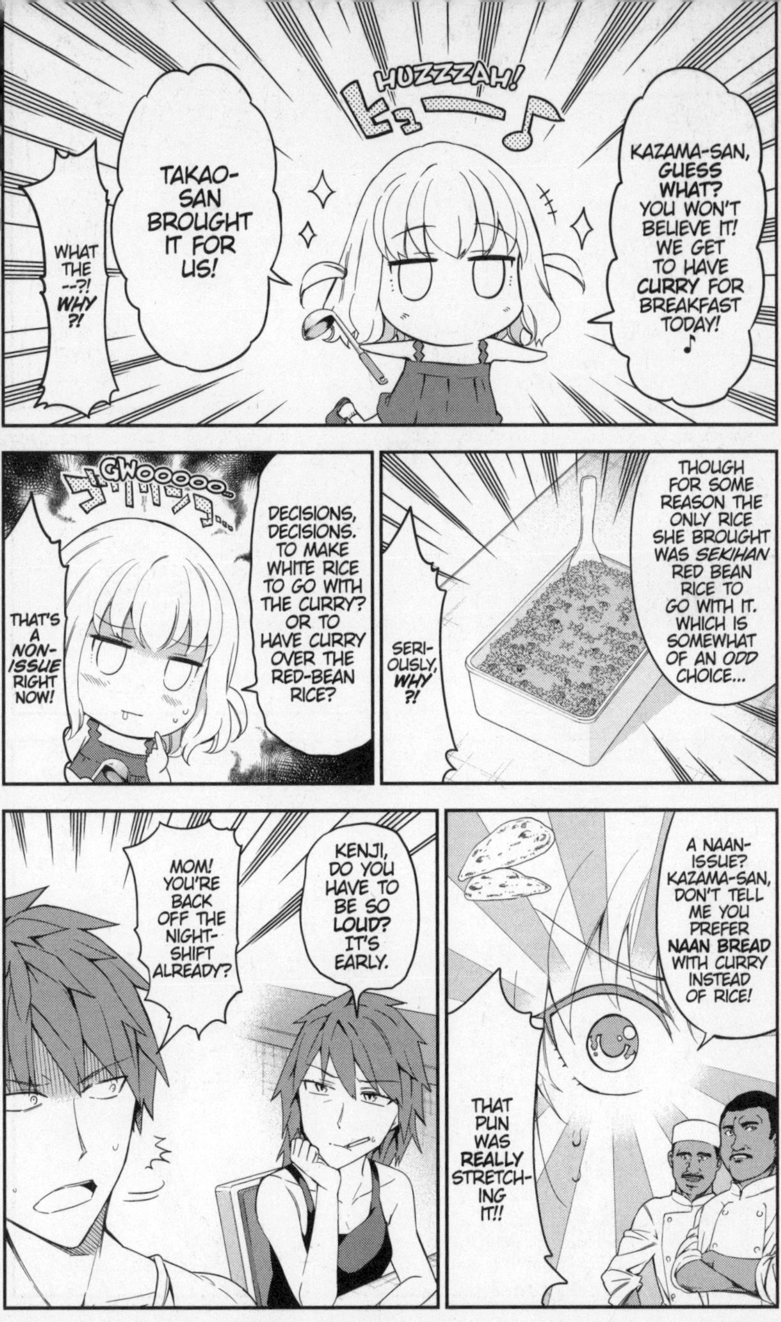
KAZAMA-SAN, GUESS WHAT? YOU WON'T BELIEVE IT! WE GET TO HAVE CURRY FOR BREAKFAST TODAY! ♪
HUZZZZAH!
TAKAO-SAN BROUGHT IT FOR US!
WHAT THE --?! WHY?!
THOUGH FOR SOME REASON THE ONLY RICE SHE BROUGHT WAS SEKIHAN RED BEAN RICE TO GO WITH IT. WHICH IS SOMEWHAT OF AN ODD CHOICE...
SERIOUSLY, WHY?!
GWOOOOO...
DECISIONS, DECISIONS. TO MAKE WHITE RICE TO GO WITH THE CURRY? OR TO HAVE CURRY OVER THE RED-BEAN RICE?
THAT'S A NON-ISSUE RIGHT NOW!
A NAAN-ISSUE? KAZAMA-SAN, DON'T TELL ME YOU PREFER NAAN BREAD WITH CURRY INSTEAD OF RICE!
THAT PUN WAS REALLY STRETCHING IT!!
KENJI, DO YOU HAVE TO BE SO LOUD? IT'S EARLY.
MOM! YOU'RE BACK OFF THE NIGHT-SHIFT ALREADY?

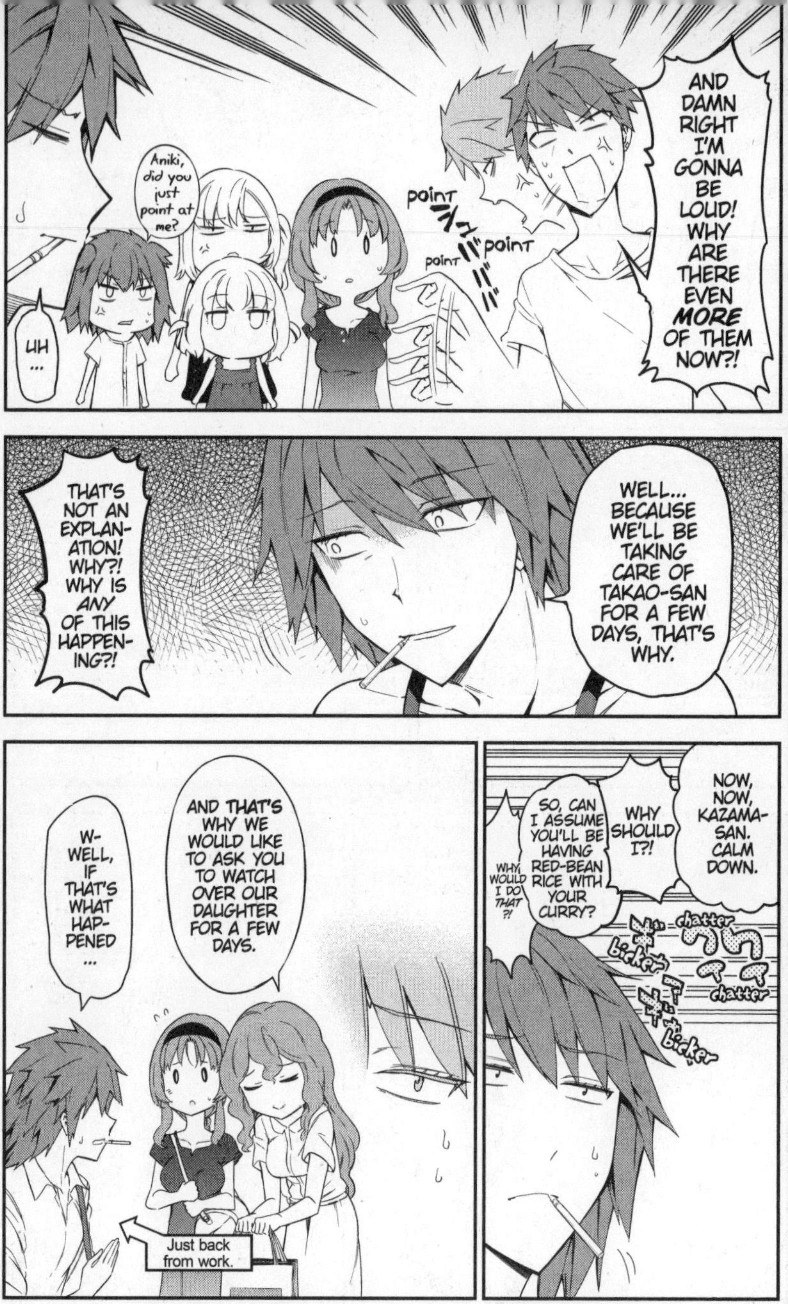

AND DAMN RIGHT I'M GONNA BE LOUD! WHY ARE THERE EVEN MORE OF THEM NOW?!
point point point
Aniki, did you just point at me?
UH ...
WELL... BECAUSE WE'LL BE TAKING CARE OF TAKAO-SAN FOR A FEW DAYS, THAT'S WHY.
THAT'S NOT AN EXPLANATION! WHY?! WHY IS ANY OF THIS HAPPENING?!
NOW, NOW, KAZAMA-SAN. CALM DOWN.
WHY SHOULD I?!
SO, CAN I ASSUME YOU'LL BE HAVING RED-BEAN RICE WITH YOUR CURRY?
WHY WOULD I DO THAT ?!
chatter chatter
bicker bicker
AND THAT'S WHY WE WOULD LIKE TO ASK YOU TO WATCH OVER OUR DAUGHTER FOR A FEW DAYS.
W-WELL, IF THAT'S WHAT HAPPENED ...
Just back from work.

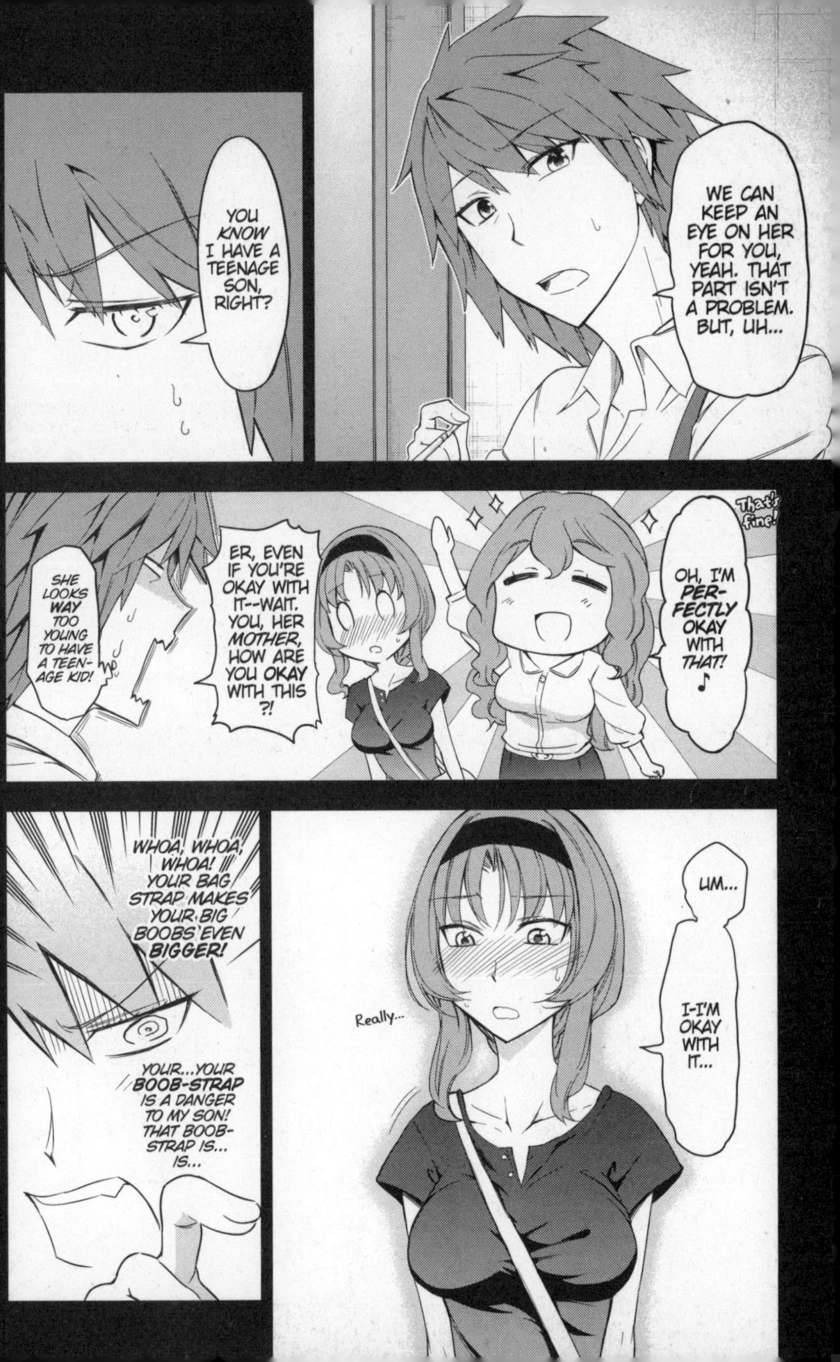
WE CAN KEEP AN EYE ON HER FOR YOU, YEAH. THAT PART ISN'T A PROBLEM. BUT, UH...
YOU KNOW I HAVE A TEENAGE SON, RIGHT?
That's fine!
OH, I'M PERFECTLY OKAY WITH THAT! ♪
ER, EVEN IF YOU'RE OKAY WITH IT--WAIT. YOU, HER MOTHER, HOW ARE YOU OKAY WITH THIS?!
SHE LOOKS WAY TOO YOUNG TO HAVE A TEENAGE KID!
UM...
I-I'M OKAY WITH IT...
Really...
WHOA, WHOA, WHOA! YOUR BAG STRAP MAKES YOUR BIG BOOBS EVEN BIGGER!
YOUR...YOUR BOOB-STRAP IS A DANGER TO MY SON! THAT BOOB-STRAP IS... IS...

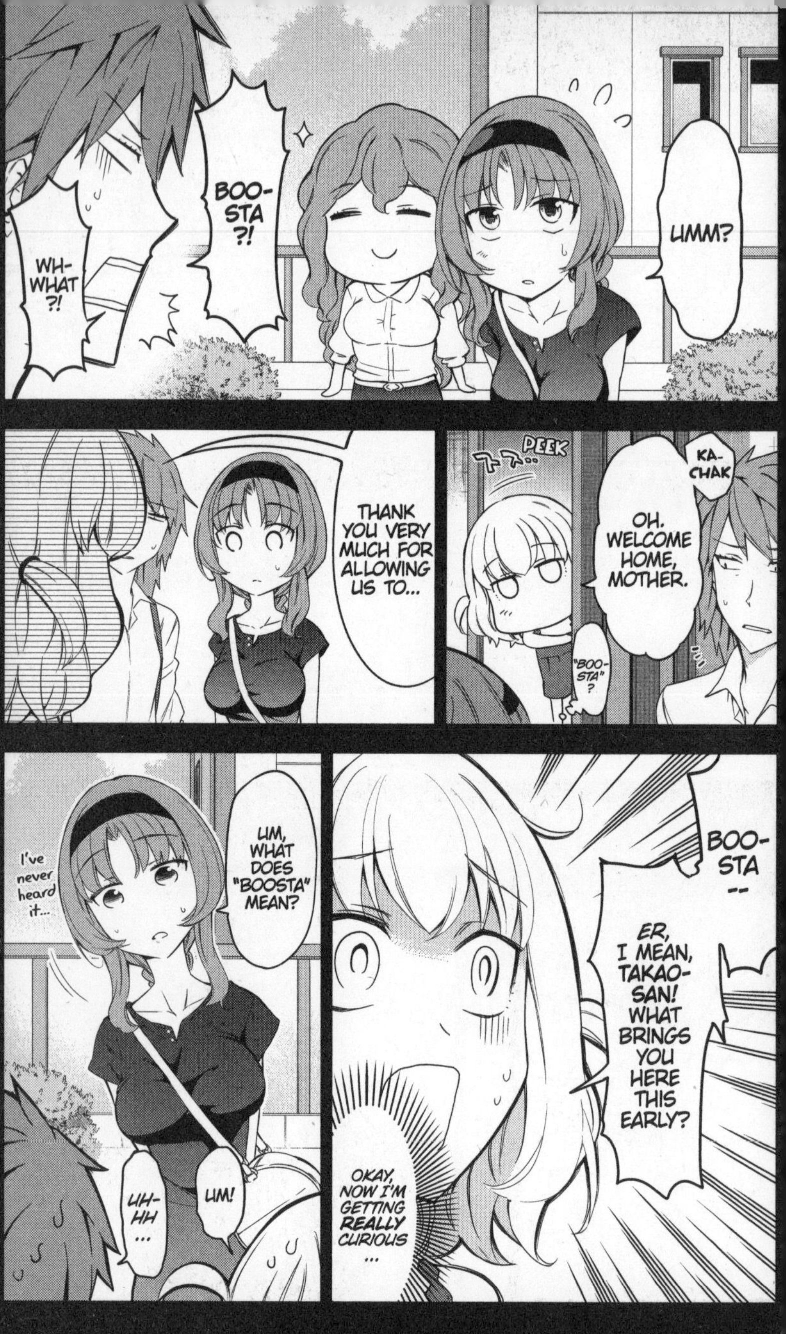
UMM?
BOO-STA?!
WH-WHAT?!
KA-CHAK
OH. WELCOME HOME, MOTHER.
PEEK
"BOO-STA"?
THANK YOU VERY MUCH FOR ALLOWING US TO...
BOO-STA--
ER, I MEAN, TAKAO-SAN! WHAT BRINGS YOU HERE THIS EARLY?
OKAY, NOW I'M GETTING REALLY CURIOUS...
UM, WHAT DOES "BOOSTA" MEAN?
I've never heard it...
UM!
UHHH...

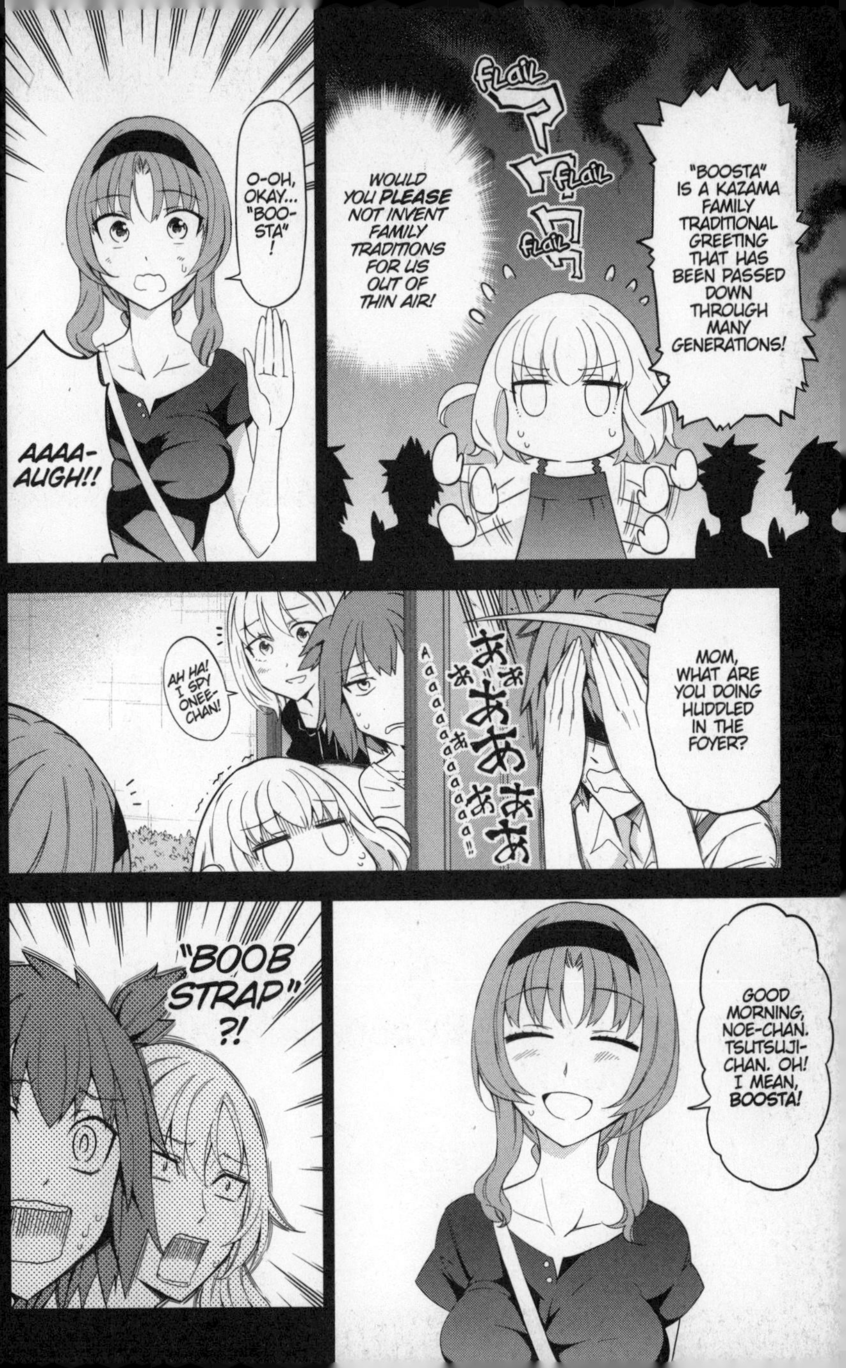
"BOOSTA" IS A KAZAMA FAMILY TRADITIONAL GREETING THAT HAS BEEN PASSED DOWN THROUGH MANY GENERATIONS!
FLAIL
FLAIL
FLAIL
WOULD YOU PLEASE NOT INVENT FAMILY TRADITIONS FOR US OUT OF THIN AIR!
O-OH, OKAY... "BOO-STA" !
AAAA-AUGH!!
MOM, WHAT ARE YOU DOING HUDDLED IN THE FOYER?
AH HA! I SPY ONEE-CHAN!
GOOD MORNING, NOE-CHAN. TSUTSUJI-CHAN. OH! I MEAN, BOOSTA!
"BOOB STRAP" ?!

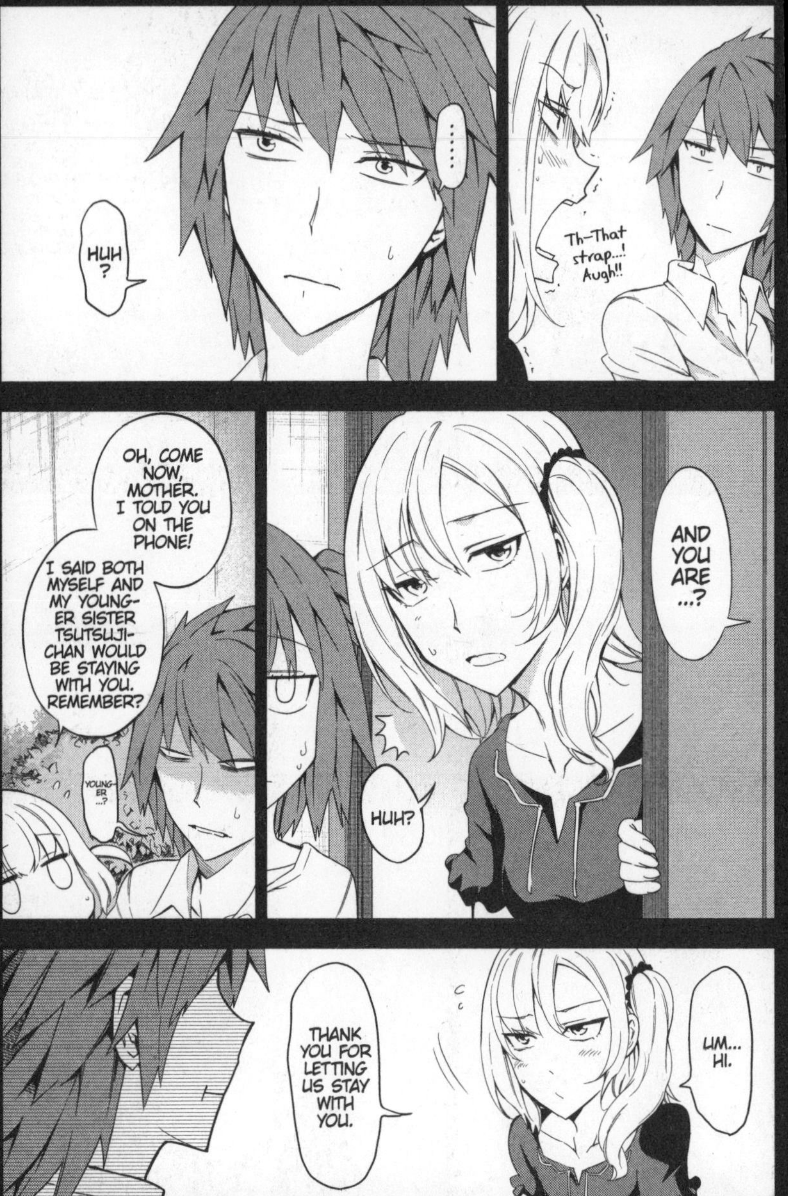
Th-That strap...! Augh!!
......
HUH?
AND YOU ARE ...?
HUH?
OH, COME NOW, MOTHER. I TOLD YOU ON THE PHONE!
I SAID BOTH MYSELF AND MY YOUNGER SISTER TSUTSUJI-CHAN WOULD BE STAYING WITH YOU. REMEMBER?
YOUNGER...?
UM... HI.
THANK YOU FOR LETTING US STAY WITH YOU.

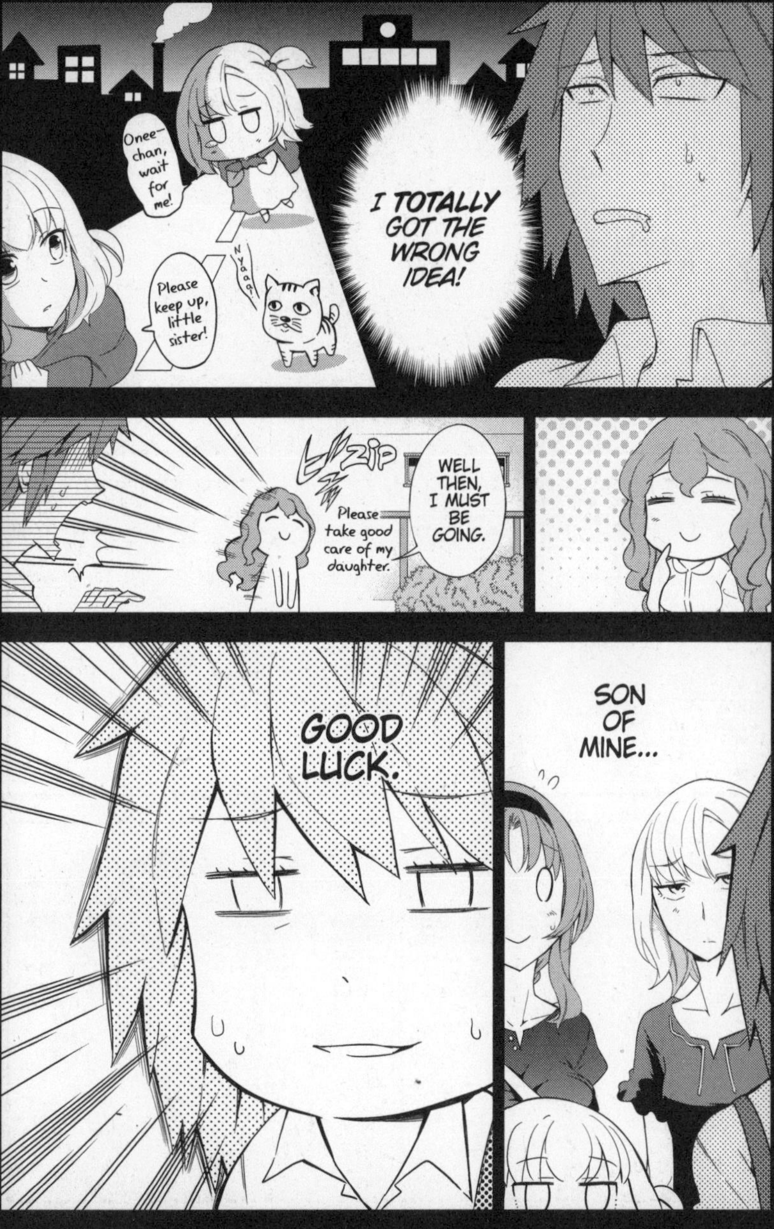
I TOTALLY GOT THE WRONG IDEA!
Onee-chan, wait for me!
Nyaaa!
Please keep up, little sister!
WELL THEN, I MUST BE GOING.
zip
Please take good care of my daughter.
SON OF MINE...
GOOD LUCK.

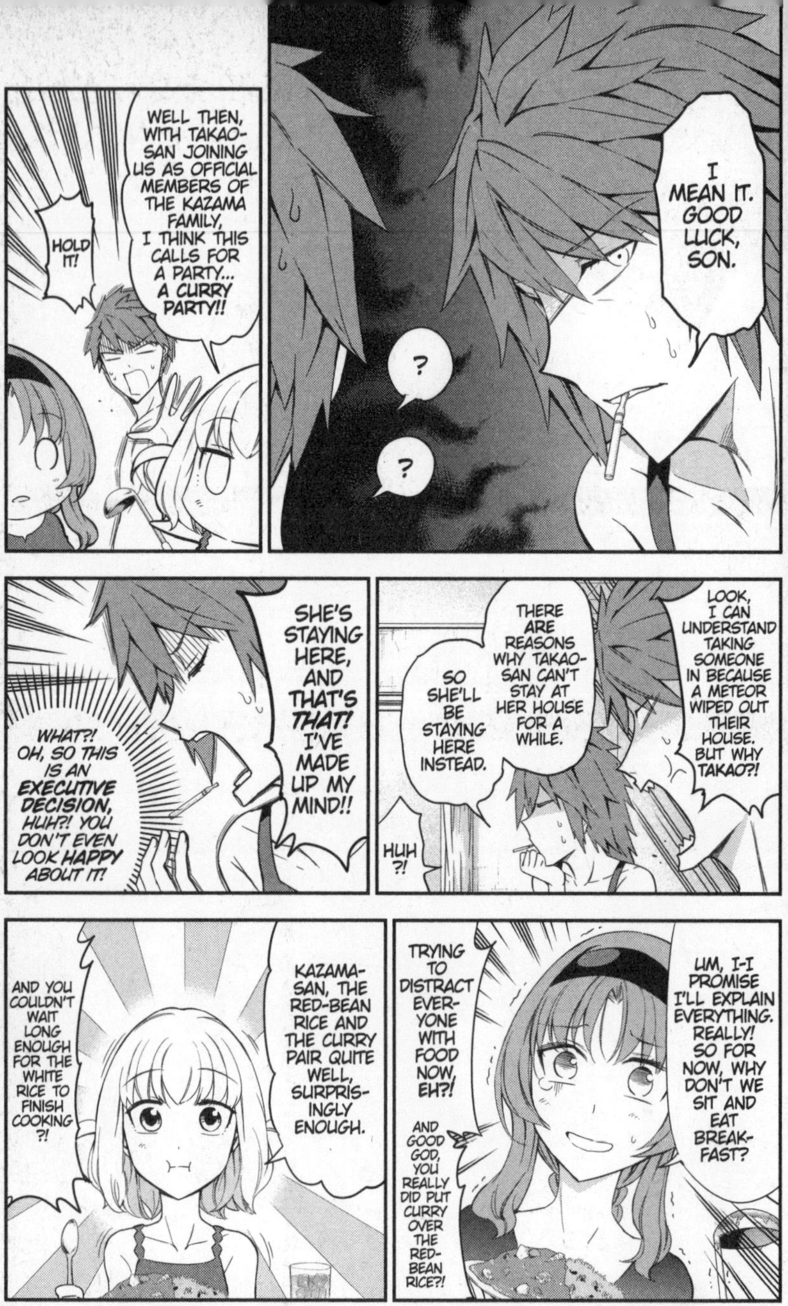
I MEAN IT. GOOD LUCK, SON.
?
?
WELL THEN, WITH TAKAO-SAN JOINING US AS OFFICIAL MEMBERS OF THE KAZAMA FAMILY, I THINK THIS CALLS FOR A PARTY... A CURRY PARTY!!
HOLD IT!
LOOK, I CAN UNDERSTAND TAKING SOMEONE IN BECAUSE A METEOR WIPED OUT THEIR HOUSE. BUT WHY TAKAO?!
THERE ARE REASONS WHY TAKAO-SAN CAN'T STAY AT HER HOUSE FOR A WHILE.
SO SHE'LL BE STAYING HERE INSTEAD.
HUH?!
SHE'S STAYING HERE, AND THAT'S THAT! I'VE MADE UP MY MIND!!
WHAT?! OH, SO THIS IS AN EXECUTIVE DECISION, HUH?! YOU DON'T EVEN LOOK HAPPY ABOUT IT!
UM, I-I PROMISE I'LL EXPLAIN EVERYTHING. REALLY! SO FOR NOW, WHY DON'T WE SIT AND EAT BREAK-FAST?
TRYING TO DISTRACT EVERY-ONE WITH FOOD NOW, EH?!
AND GOOD GOD, YOU REALLY DID PUT CURRY OVER THE RED-BEAN RICE?!
KAZAMA-SAN, THE RED-BEAN RICE AND THE CURRY PAIR QUITE WELL, SURPRIS-INGLY ENOUGH.
AND YOU COULDN'T WAIT LONG ENOUGH FOR THE WHITE RICE TO FINISH COOKING?!

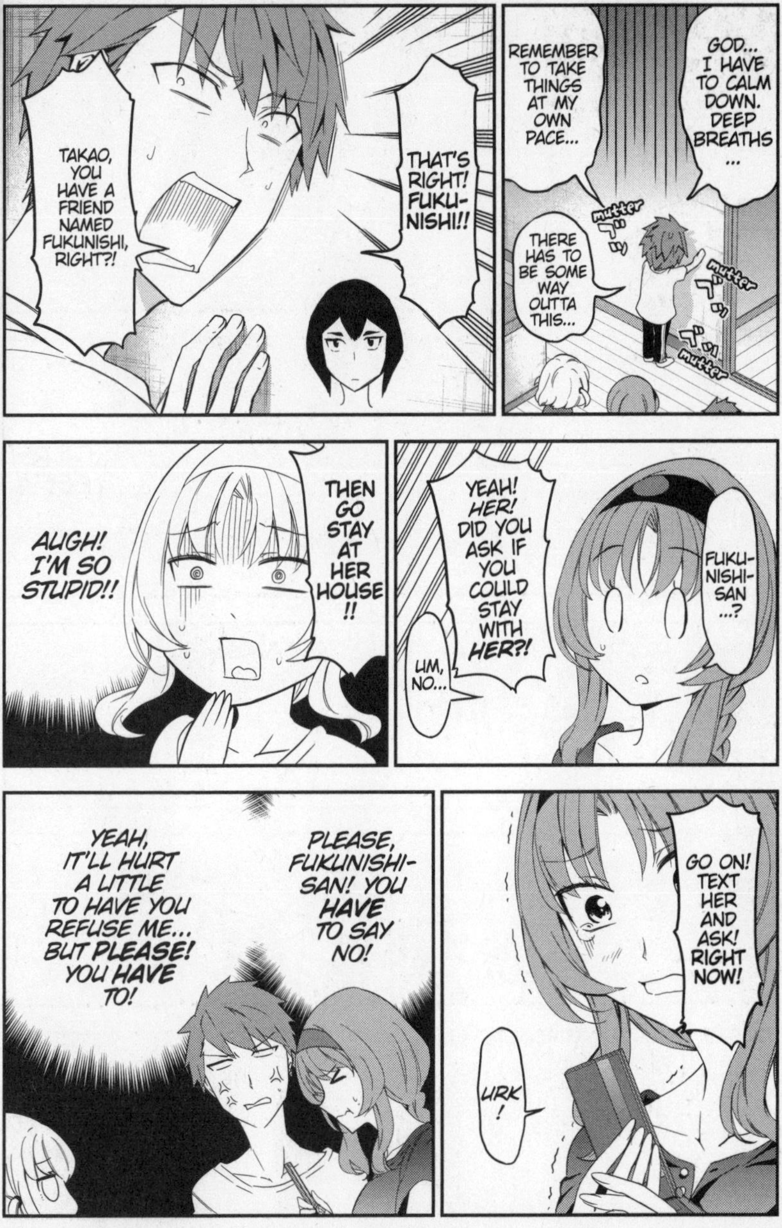
GOD... I HAVE TO CALM DOWN. DEEP BREATHS ...
REMEMBER TO TAKE THINGS AT MY OWN PACE...
mutter
mutter
THERE HAS TO BE SOME WAY OUTTA THIS...
mutter
THAT'S RIGHT! FUKUNISHI!!
TAKAO, YOU HAVE A FRIEND NAMED FUKUNISHI, RIGHT?!
FUKUNISHI-SAN ...?
YEAH! HER! DID YOU ASK IF YOU COULD STAY WITH HER?!
UM, NO...
THEN GO STAY AT HER HOUSE!!
AUGH! I'M SO STUPID!!
GO ON! TEXT HER AND ASK! RIGHT NOW!
URK!
PLEASE, FUKUNISHI-SAN! YOU HAVE TO SAY NO!
YEAH, IT'LL HURT A LITTLE TO HAVE YOU REFUSE ME... BUT PLEASE! YOU HAVE TO!

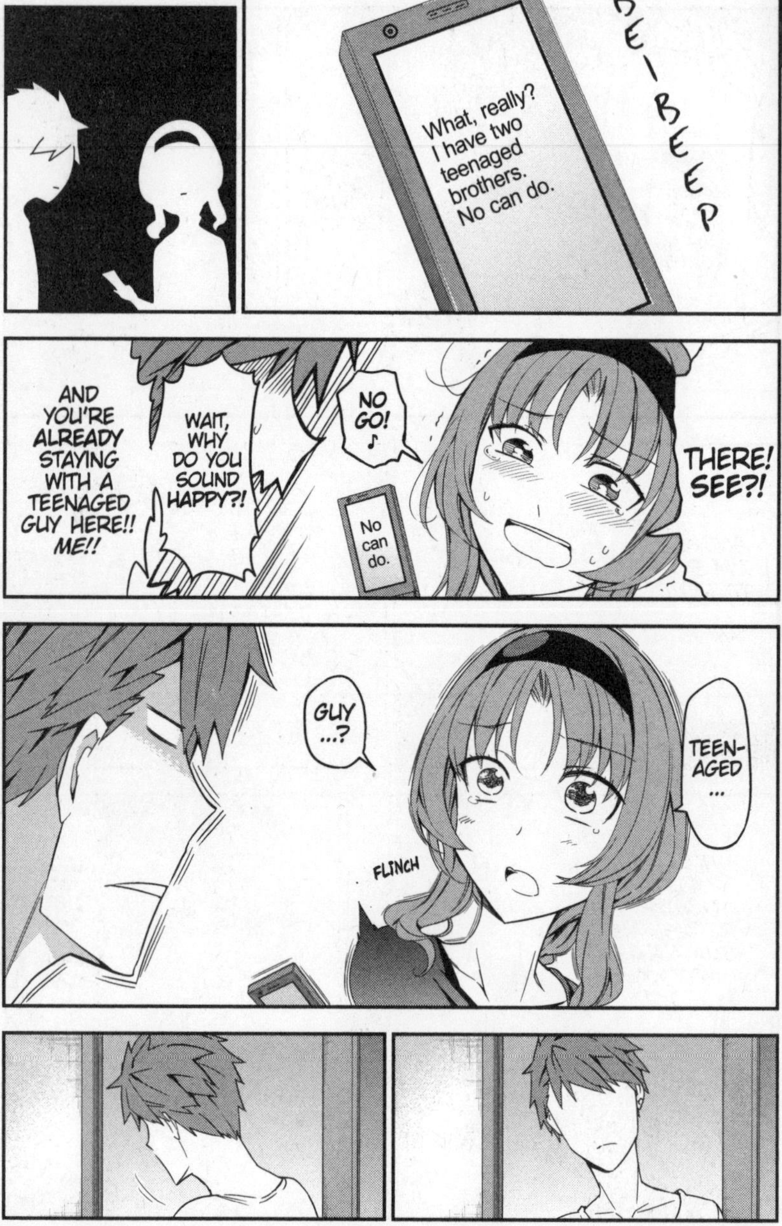
BEIBEEP
What, really? I have two teenaged brothers. No can do.
THERE! SEE?!
NO GO! ♪
No can do.
WAIT, WHY DO YOU SOUND HAPPY?!
AND YOU'RE ALREADY STAYING WITH A TEENAGED GUY HERE!! ME!!
TEEN-AGED ...
GUY ...?
FLINCH

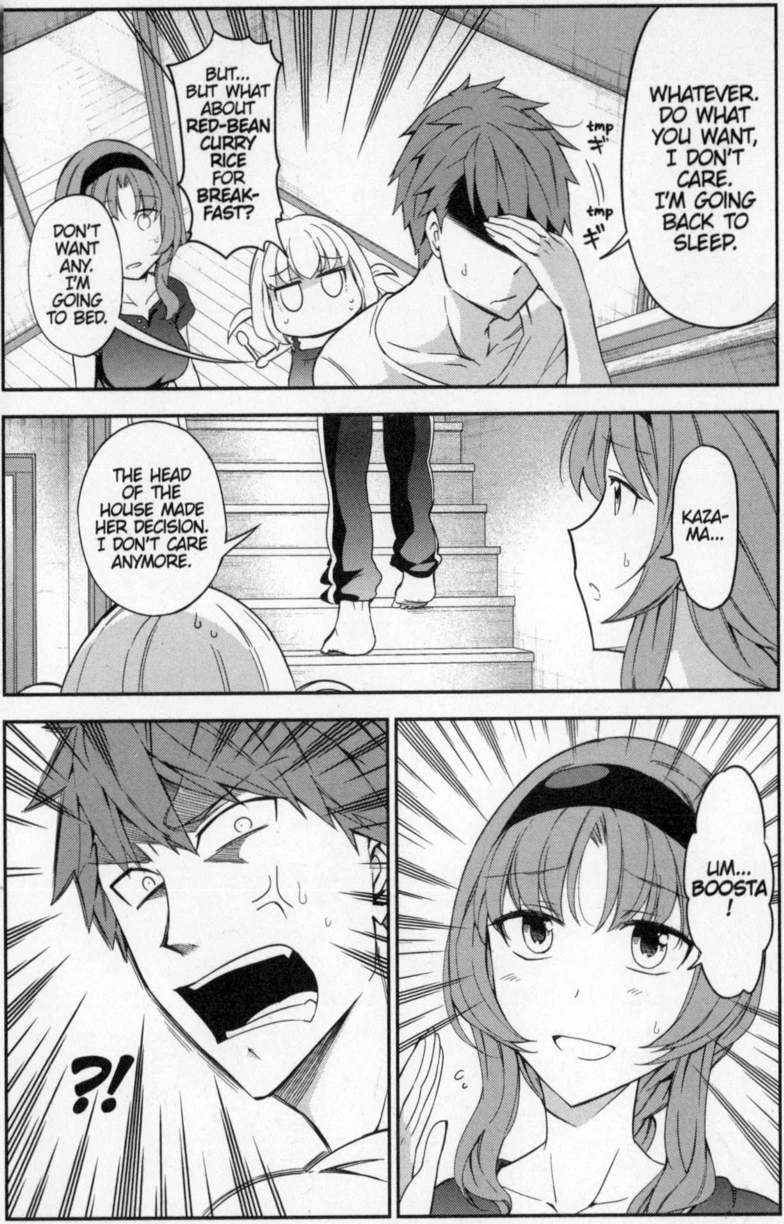
WHATEVER. DO WHAT YOU WANT, I DON'T CARE. I'M GOING BACK TO SLEEP.
tmp ギ
tmp ギ
BUT... BUT WHAT ABOUT RED-BEAN CURRY RICE FOR BREAK-FAST?
DON'T WANT ANY. I'M GOING TO BED.
KAZA-MA...
THE HEAD OF THE HOUSE MADE HER DECISION. I DON'T CARE ANYMORE.
UM... BOOSTA!
?!

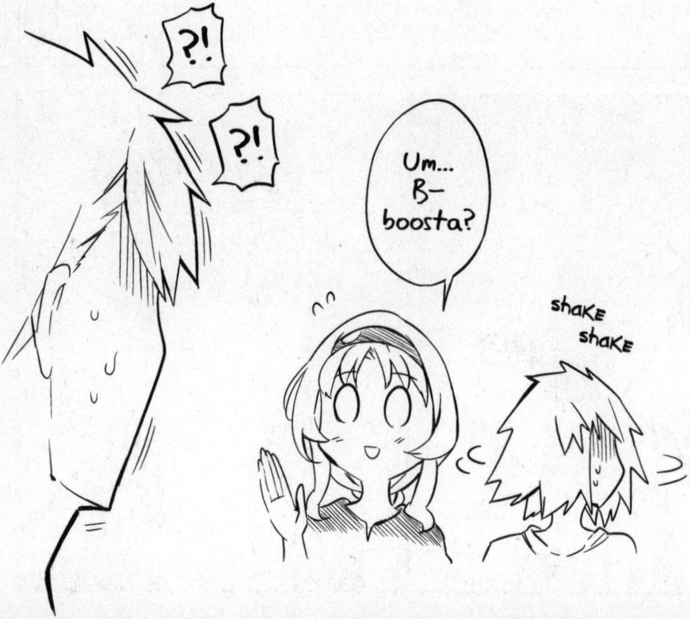
Um... B-boosta?
?!
?!
shake shake

D-FRAGMENTS
ディーフラぐ！

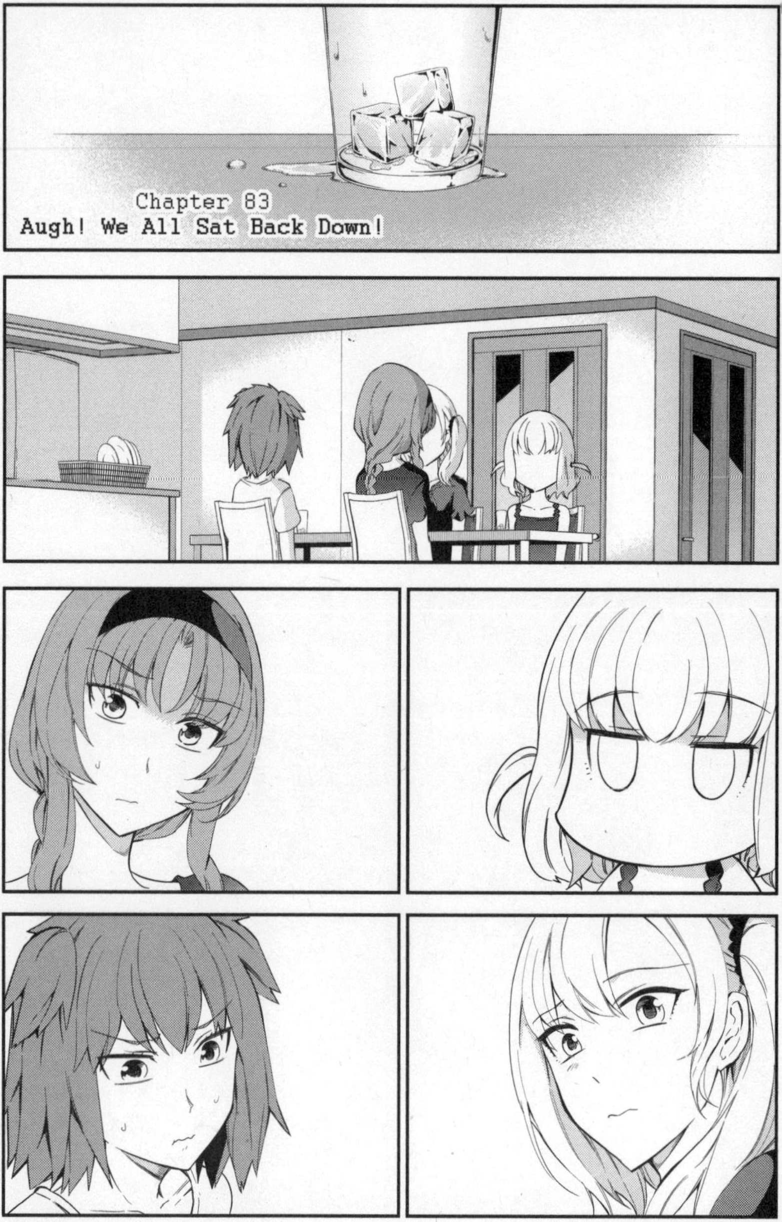
Chapter 83
Augh! We All Sat Back Down!

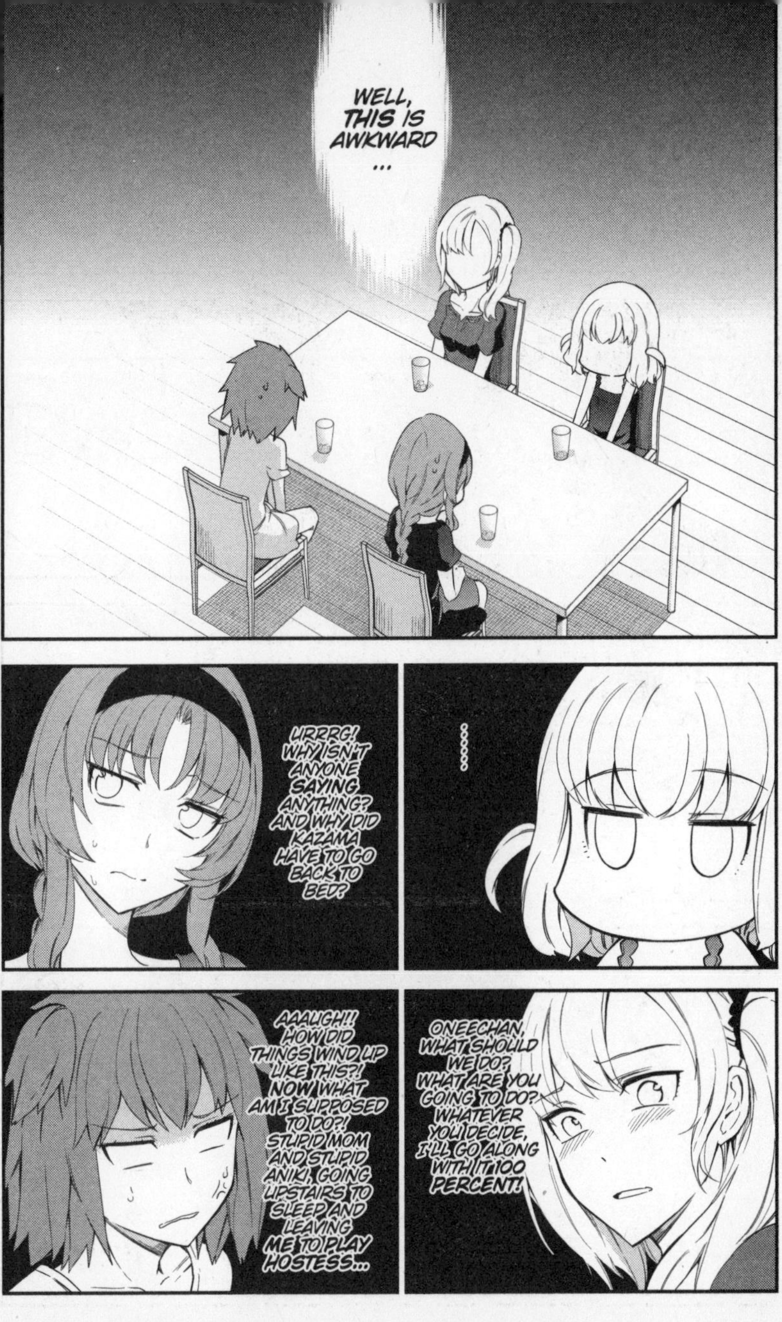
WELL, THIS IS AWKWARD ...
.....
URRRG! WHY ISN'T ANYONE SAYING ANYTHING? AND WHY DID KAZAMA HAVE TO GO BACK TO BED?
ONEECHAN, WHAT SHOULD WE DO? WHAT ARE YOU GOING TO DO? WHATEVER YOU DECIDE, I'LL GO ALONG WITH IT 100 PERCENT!
AAAUGH!! HOW DID THINGS WIND UP LIKE THIS?! NOW WHAT AM I SUPPOSED TO DO?! STUPID MOM AND STUPID ANIKI, GOING UPSTAIRS TO SLEEP AND LEAVING ME TO PLAY HOSTESS...

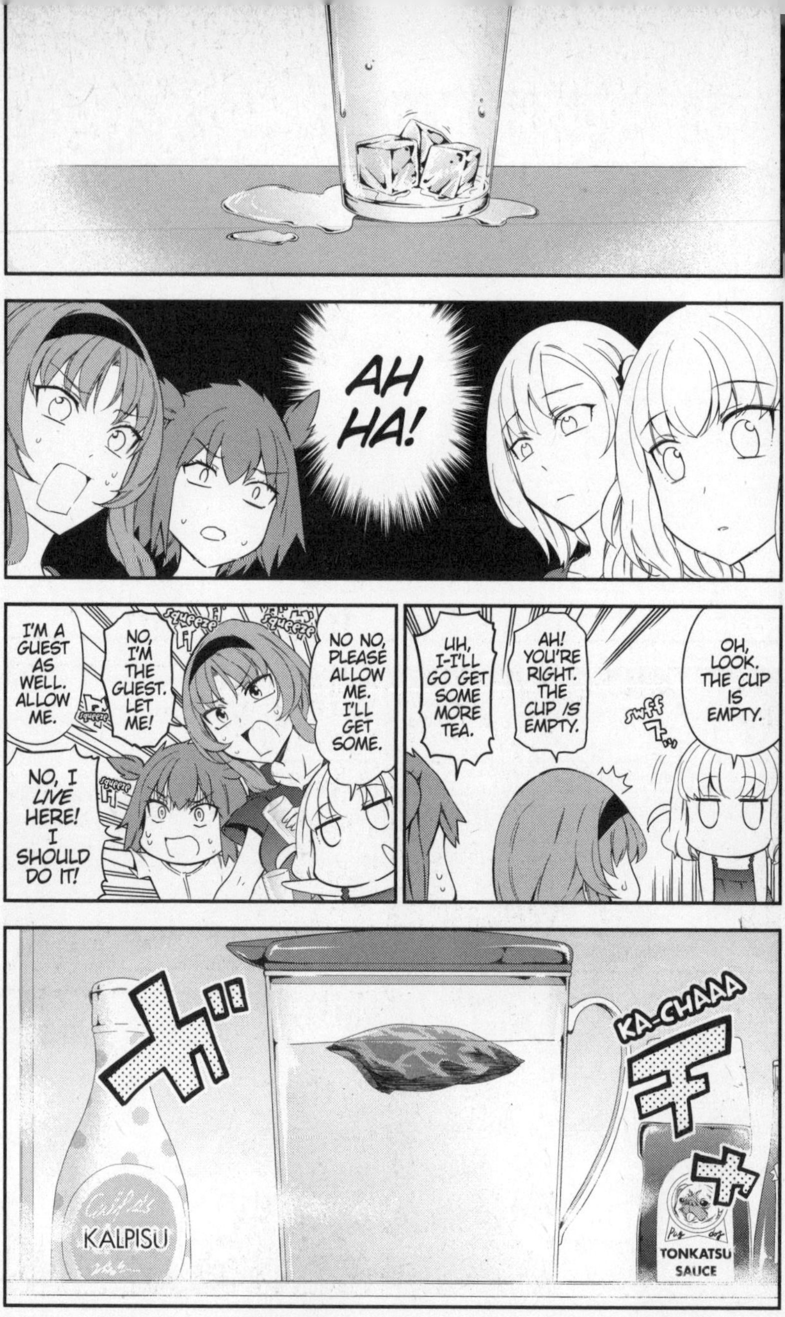
AH HA!
OH, LOOK. THE CUP IS EMPTY.
swff
AH! YOU'RE RIGHT. THE CUP IS EMPTY.
UH, I-I'LL GO GET SOME MORE TEA.
squeeze
squeeze
NO NO, PLEASE ALLOW ME. I'LL GET SOME.
NO, I'M THE GUEST. LET ME!
I'M A GUEST AS WELL. ALLOW ME.
squeeze
squeeze
NO, I *LIVE* HERE! I SHOULD DO IT!
KA-CHAAA
KALPISU
Pug dog
TONKATSU SAUCE

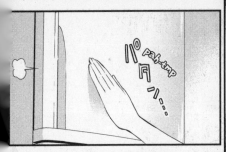

パタンプ pahtmp

AH. THE BAG HASN'T STEEPED LONG ENOUGH.

TRUE...

ストーン... PLUNK.

AUGH! WE ALL SAT BACK DOWN!!

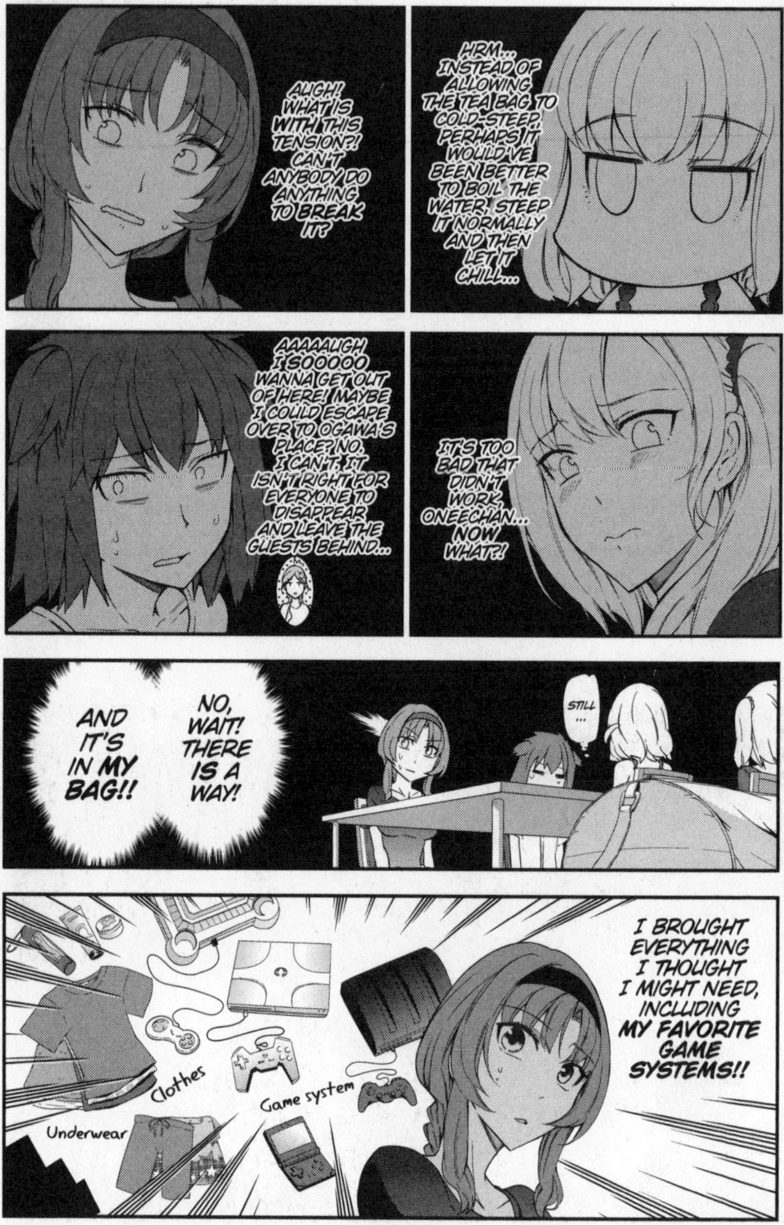
HRM... INSTEAD OF ALLOWING THE TEA BAG TO COLD-STEEP, PERHAPS IT WOULD'VE BEEN BETTER TO BOIL THE WATER, STEEP IT NORMALLY AND THEN LET IT CHILL...
AUGH! WHAT IS WITH THIS TENSION?! CAN'T ANYBODY DO ANYTHING TO BREAK IT?
IT'S TOO BAD THAT DIDN'T WORK, ONEECHAN... NOW WHAT?!
AAAAAUGH I SOOOOO WANNA GET OUT OF HERE! MAYBE I COULD ESCAPE OVER TO OGAWA'S PLACE? NO, I CAN'T. IT ISN'T RIGHT FOR EVERYONE TO DISAPPEAR AND LEAVE THE GUESTS BEHIND...
STILL ...
NO, WAIT! THERE IS A WAY!
AND IT'S IN MY BAG!!
I BROUGHT EVERYTHING I THOUGHT I MIGHT NEED, INCLUDING MY FAVORITE GAME SYSTEMS!!
Game system
Clothes
Underwear

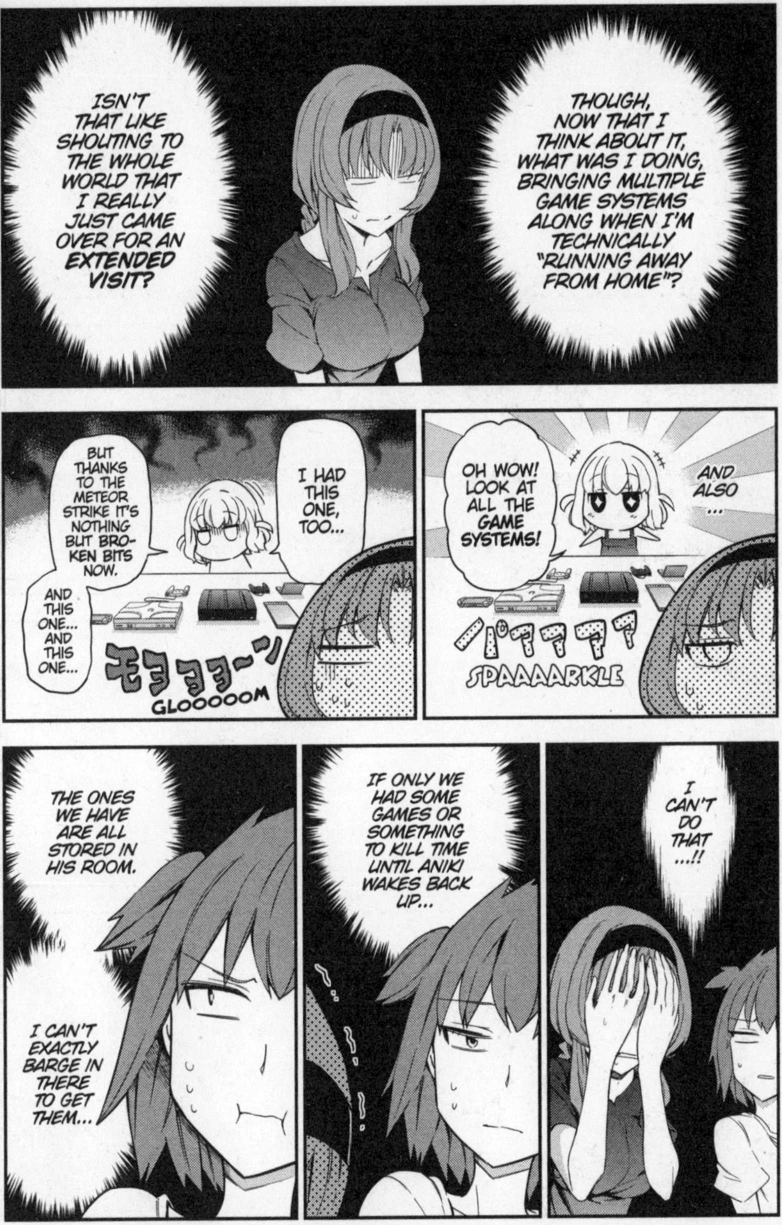
THOUGH, NOW THAT I THINK ABOUT IT, WHAT WAS I DOING, BRINGING MULTIPLE GAME SYSTEMS ALONG WHEN I'M TECHNICALLY "RUNNING AWAY FROM HOME"?
ISN'T THAT LIKE SHOUTING TO THE WHOLE WORLD THAT I REALLY JUST CAME OVER FOR AN EXTENDED VISIT?
AND ALSO ...
OH WOW! LOOK AT ALL THE GAME SYSTEMS!
SPAAAARKLE
I HAD THIS ONE, TOO...
BUT THANKS TO THE METEOR STRIKE IT'S NOTHING BUT BRO-KEN BITS NOW.
AND THIS ONE... AND THIS ONE...
GLOOOOOM
I CAN'T DO THAT ...!!
IF ONLY WE HAD SOME GAMES OR SOMETHING TO KILL TIME UNTIL ANIKI WAKES BACK UP...
THE ONES WE HAVE ARE ALL STORED IN HIS ROOM.
I CAN'T EXACTLY BARGE IN THERE TO GET THEM...

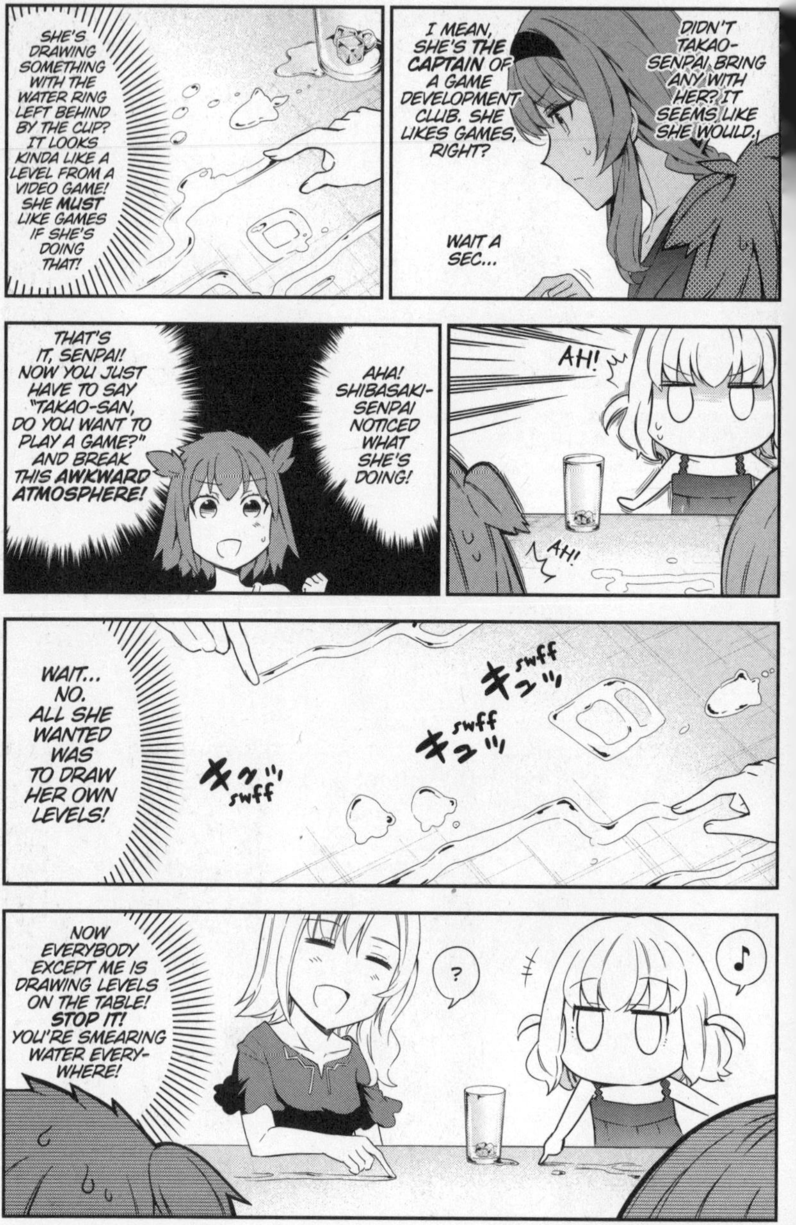
DIDN'T TAKAO-SENPAI BRING ANY WITH HER? IT SEEMS LIKE SHE WOULD.
I MEAN, SHE'S **THE CAPTAIN** OF A GAME DEVELOPMENT CLUB. SHE LIKES GAMES, RIGHT?
WAIT A SEC...
SHE'S DRAWING SOMETHING WITH THE WATER RING LEFT BEHIND BY THE CUP? IT LOOKS KINDA LIKE A LEVEL FROM A VIDEO GAME! SHE **MUST** LIKE GAMES IF SHE'S DOING THAT!
AH!
AH!
AHA! SHIBASAKI-SENPAI NOTICED WHAT SHE'S DOING!
THAT'S IT, SENPAI! NOW YOU JUST HAVE TO SAY "TAKAO-SAN, DO YOU WANT TO PLAY A GAME?" AND BREAK THIS **AWKWARD ATMOSPHERE!**
swff
swff
swff
WAIT... NO. ALL SHE WANTED WAS TO DRAW HER OWN LEVELS!
♪
?
NOW EVERYBODY EXCEPT ME IS DRAWING LEVELS ON THE TABLE! **STOP IT!** YOU'RE SMEARING WATER EVERY-WHERE!

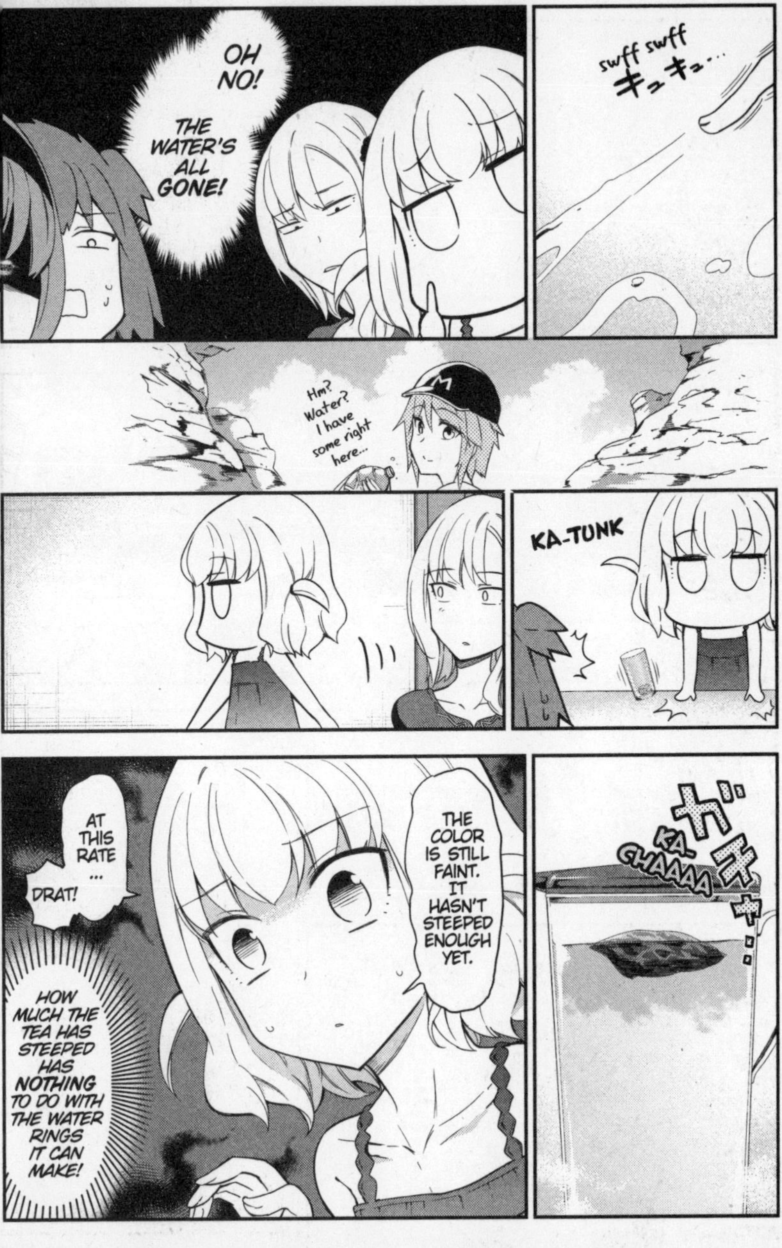

swff swff
キュキュ…
OH NO!
THE WATER'S ALL GONE!
Hm? Water? I have some right here...
KA-TUNK
KA-CHAAAA
ガチャ…
THE COLOR IS STILL FAINT. IT HASN'T STEEPED ENOUGH YET.
AT THIS RATE ...
DRAT!
HOW MUCH THE TEA HAS STEEPED HAS NOTHING TO DO WITH THE WATER RINGS IT CAN MAKE!

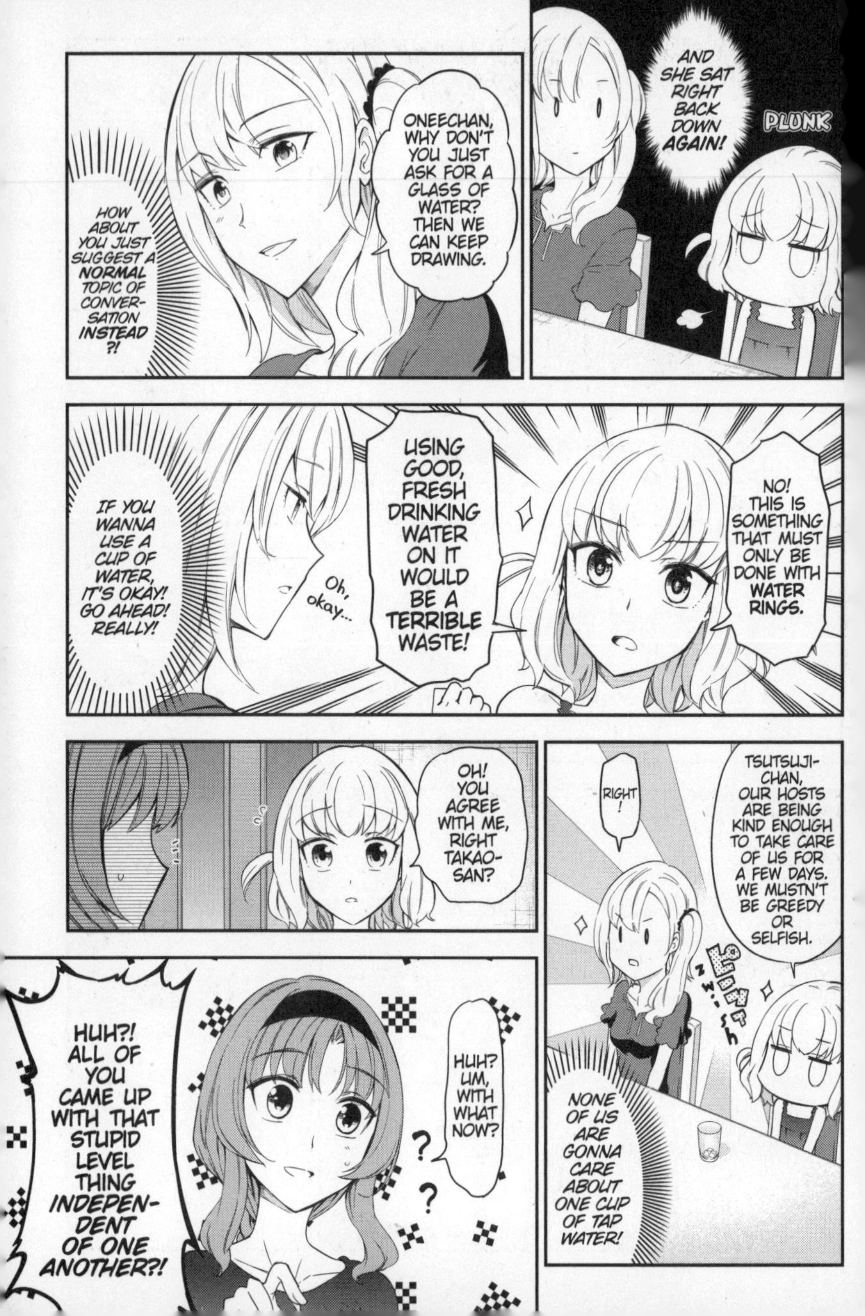
AND SHE SAT RIGHT BACK DOWN AGAIN!
PLUNK
ONEECHAN, WHY DON'T YOU JUST ASK FOR A GLASS OF WATER? THEN WE CAN KEEP DRAWING.
HOW ABOUT YOU JUST SUGGEST A NORMAL TOPIC OF CONVERSATION INSTEAD?!
NO! THIS IS SOMETHING THAT MUST ONLY BE DONE WITH WATER RINGS.
USING GOOD, FRESH DRINKING WATER ON IT WOULD BE A TERRIBLE WASTE!
Oh, okay...
IF YOU WANNA USE A CUP OF WATER, IT'S OKAY! GO AHEAD! REALLY!
TSUTSUJI-CHAN, OUR HOSTS ARE BEING KIND ENOUGH TO TAKE CARE OF US FOR A FEW DAYS. WE MUSTN'T BE GREEDY OR SELFISH.
RIGHT!
NONE OF US ARE GONNA CARE ABOUT ONE CUP OF TAP WATER!
OH! YOU AGREE WITH ME, RIGHT TAKAO-SAN?
HUH? UM, WITH WHAT NOW?
HUH?! ALL OF YOU CAME UP WITH THAT STUPID LEVEL THING INDEPENDENT OF ONE ANOTHER?!

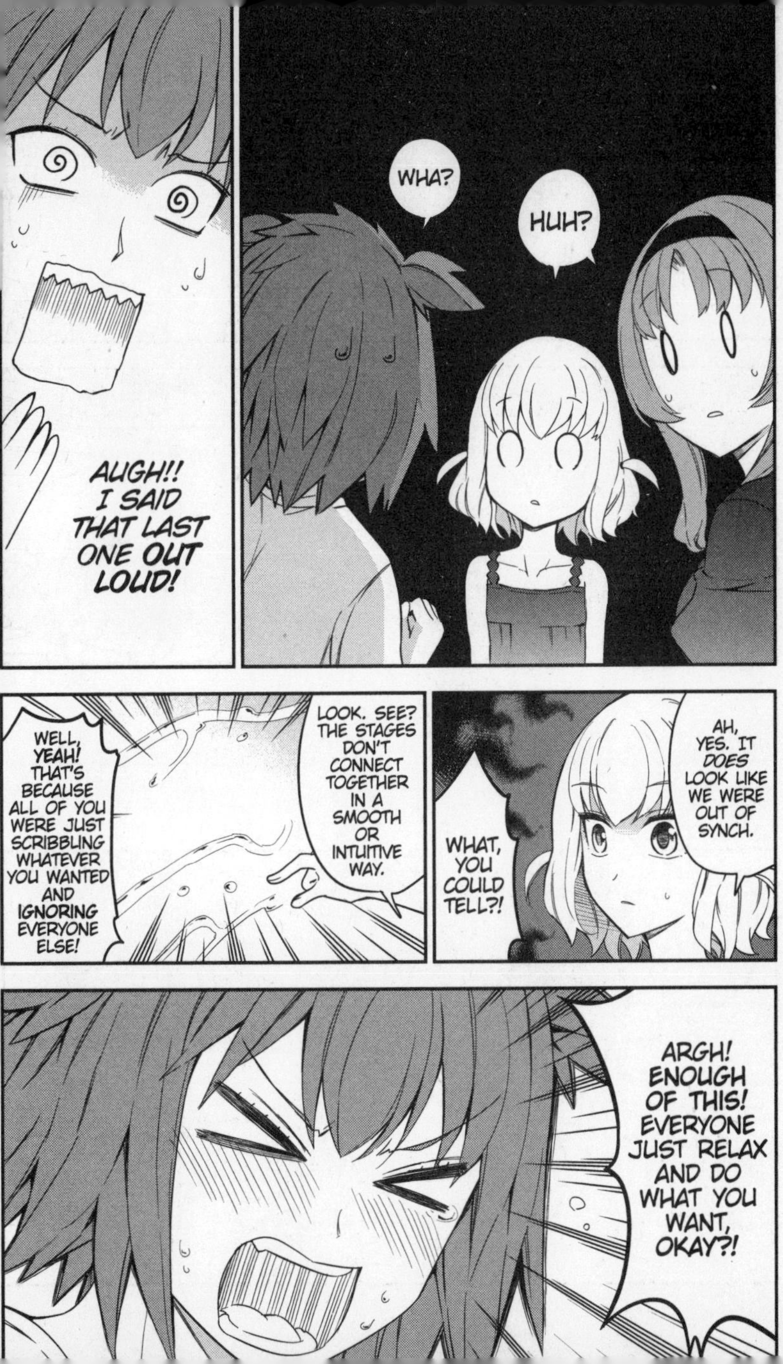
HUH?
WHA?
AUGH!! I SAID THAT LAST ONE OUT LOUD!
AH, YES. IT DOES LOOK LIKE WE WERE OUT OF SYNCH.
WHAT, YOU COULD TELL?!
LOOK. SEE? THE STAGES DON'T CONNECT TOGETHER IN A SMOOTH OR INTUITIVE WAY.
WELL, YEAH! THAT'S BECAUSE ALL OF YOU WERE JUST SCRIBBLING WHATEVER YOU WANTED AND IGNORING EVERYONE ELSE!
ARGH! ENOUGH OF THIS! EVERYONE JUST RELAX AND DO WHAT YOU WANT, OKAY?!

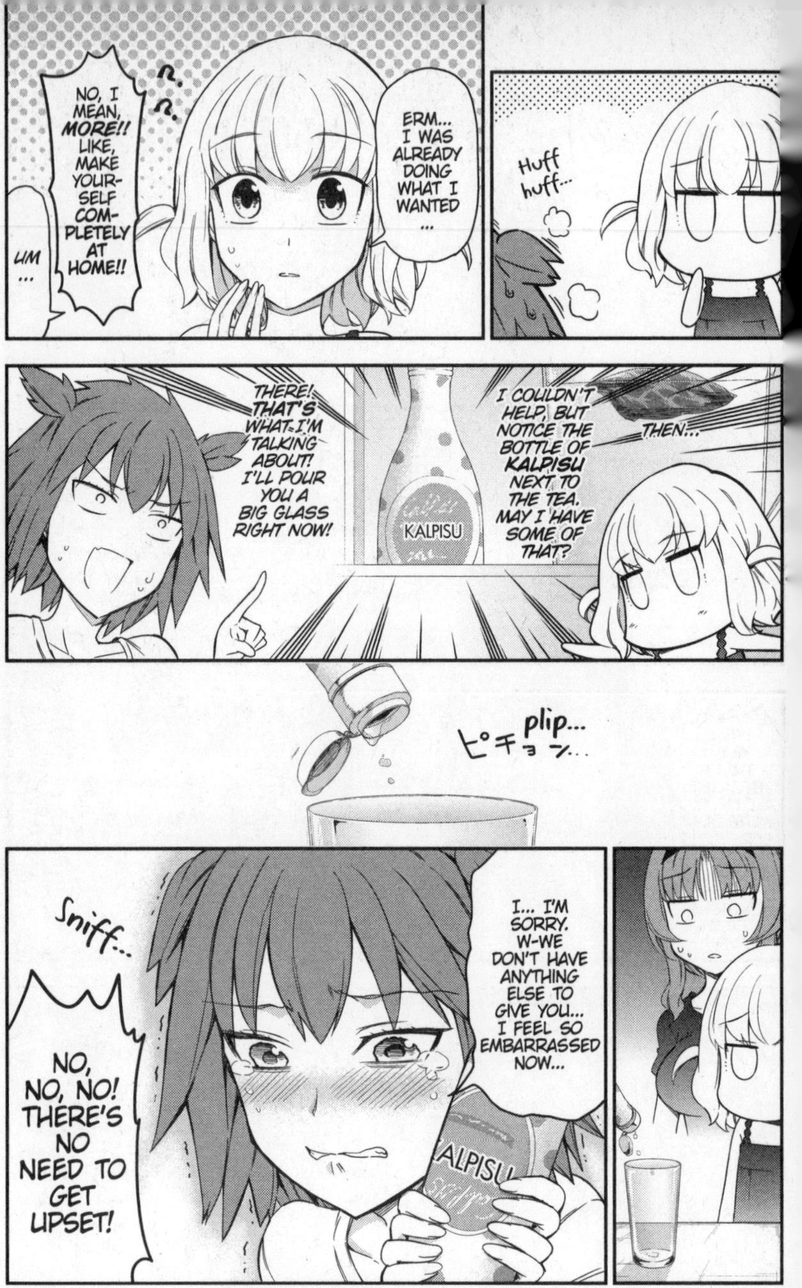
Huff huff...
ERM... I WAS ALREADY DOING WHAT I WANTED...
NO, I MEAN, MORE!! LIKE, MAKE YOURSELF COMPLETELY AT HOME!!
UM...
THEN...
I COULDN'T HELP, BUT NOTICE THE BOTTLE OF KALPISU NEXT TO THE TEA. MAY I HAVE SOME OF THAT?
KALPISU
THERE! THAT'S WHAT I'M TALKING ABOUT! I'LL POUR YOU A BIG GLASS RIGHT NOW!
plip...
ピチョン...
I... I'M SORRY. W-WE DON'T HAVE ANYTHING ELSE TO GIVE YOU... I FEEL SO EMBARRASSED NOW...
KALPISU
Sniff...
NO, NO, NO! THERE'S NO NEED TO GET UPSET!

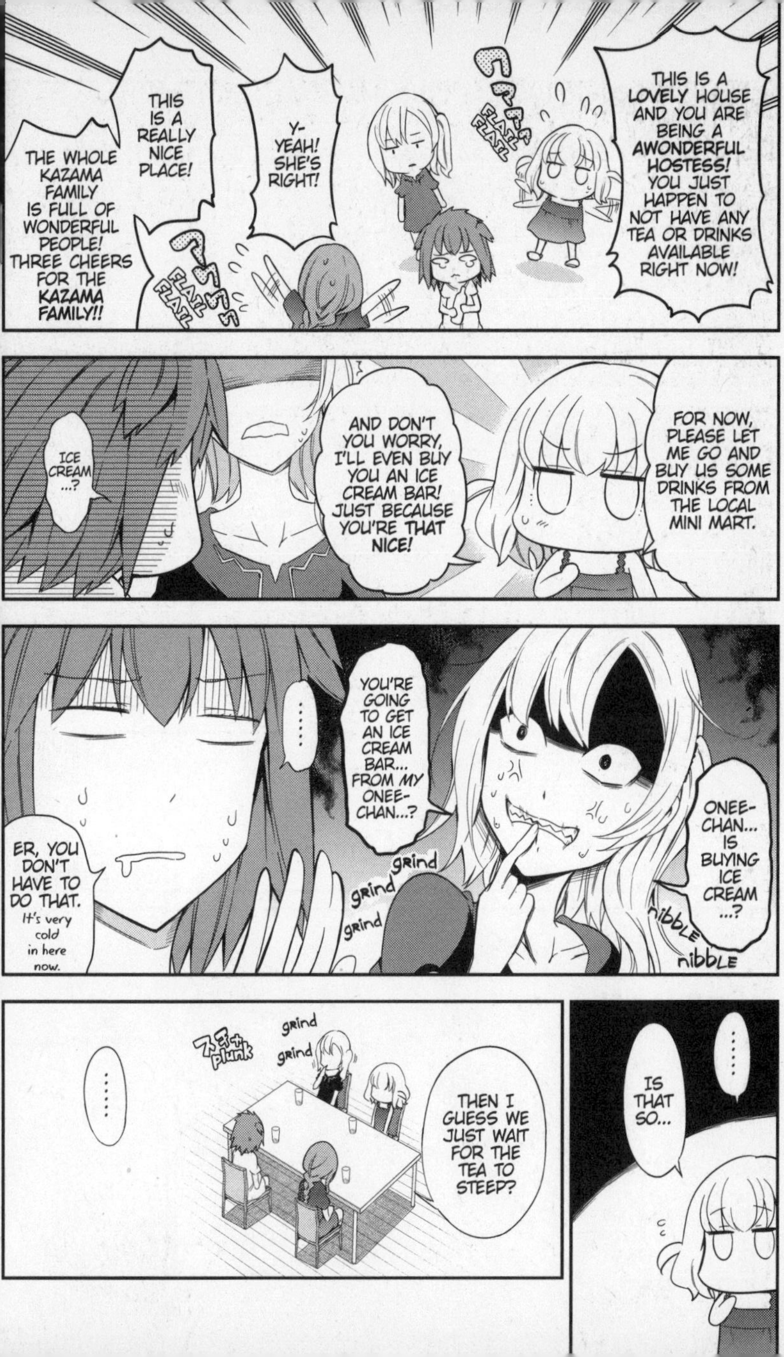
THIS IS A LOVELY HOUSE AND YOU ARE BEING A AWONDERFUL HOSTESS! YOU JUST HAPPEN TO NOT HAVE ANY TEA OR DRINKS AVAILABLE RIGHT NOW!
FLAIL FLAIL
Y-YEAH! SHE'S RIGHT!
THIS IS A REALLY NICE PLACE!
THE WHOLE KAZAMA FAMILY IS FULL OF WONDERFUL PEOPLE! THREE CHEERS FOR THE KAZAMA FAMILY!!
FLAIL FLAIL
FOR NOW, PLEASE LET ME GO AND BUY US SOME DRINKS FROM THE LOCAL MINI MART.
AND DON'T YOU WORRY, I'LL EVEN BUY YOU AN ICE CREAM BAR! JUST BECAUSE YOU'RE THAT NICE!
ICE CREAM ...?
ONEE-CHAN... IS BUYING ICE CREAM ...?
nibble
nibble
YOU'RE GOING TO GET AN ICE CREAM BAR... FROM MY ONEE-CHAN...?
grind
grind
grind
......
ER, YOU DON'T HAVE TO DO THAT.
It's very cold in here now.
......
IS THAT SO...
THEN I GUESS WE JUST WAIT FOR THE TEA TO STEEP?
grind
grind
plunk
......

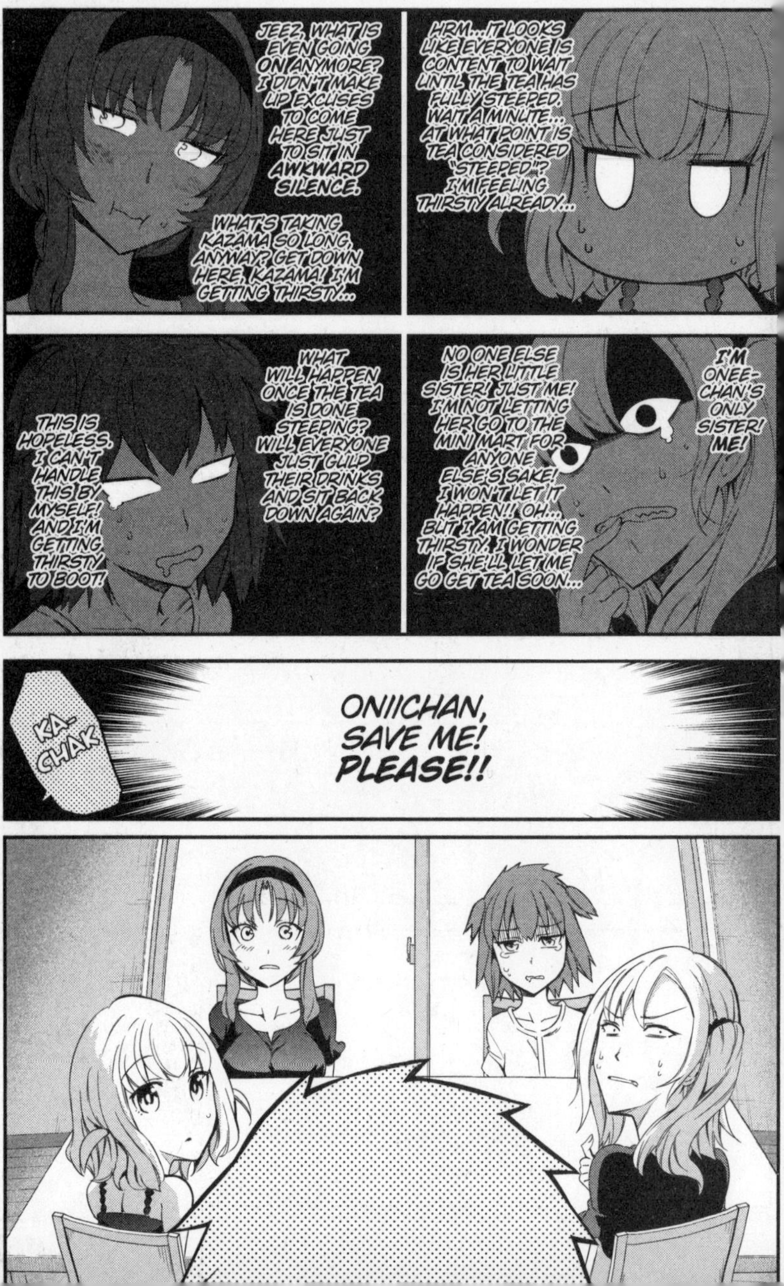
HRM...IT LOOKS LIKE EVERYONE IS CONTENT TO WAIT UNTIL THE TEA HAS FULLY STEEPED. WAIT A MINUTE... AT WHAT POINT IS TEA CONSIDERED "STEEPED"? I'M FEELING THIRSTY ALREADY...
JEEZ, WHAT IS EVEN GOING ON ANYMORE? I DIDN'T MAKE UP EXCUSES TO COME HERE JUST TO SIT IN AWKWARD SILENCE.
WHAT'S TAKING KAZAMA SO LONG, ANYWAY? GET DOWN HERE, KAZAMA! I'M GETTING THIRSTY...
I'M ONEE-CHAN'S ONLY SISTER! ME!
NO ONE ELSE IS HER LITTLE SISTER! JUST ME! I'M NOT LETTING HER GO TO THE MINI MART FOR ANYONE ELSE'S SAKE! I WON'T LET IT HAPPEN!! OH... BUT I AM GETTING THIRSTY. I WONDER IF SHE'LL LET ME GO GET TEA SOON...
WHAT WILL HAPPEN ONCE THE TEA IS DONE STEEPING? WILL EVERYONE JUST GULP THEIR DRINKS AND SIT BACK DOWN AGAIN?
THIS IS HOPELESS. I CAN'T HANDLE THIS BY MYSELF! AND I'M GETTING THIRSTY TO BOOT!
ONIICHAN, SAVE ME! PLEASE!!
KA-CHAK

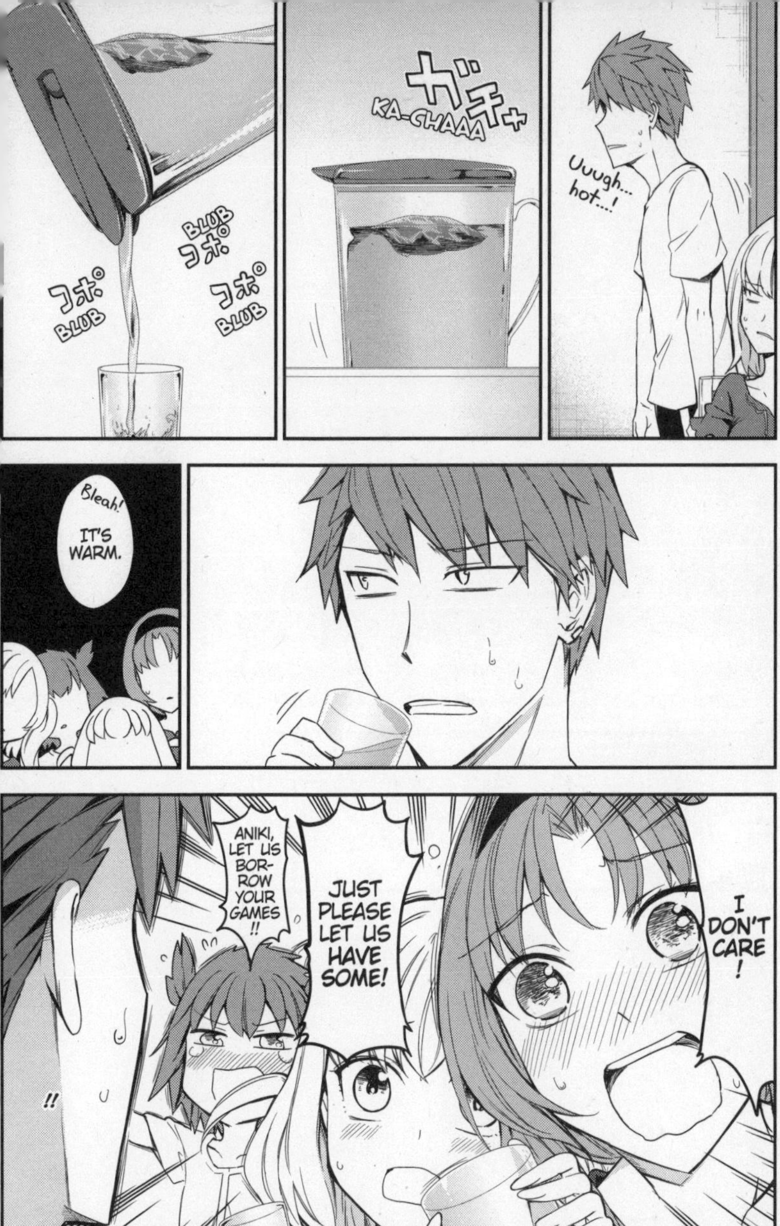
Uuugh... hot...!
ガチャ
KA-CHAAA
フポ
BLUB
フポ
BLUB
フポ
BLUB
Bleah!
IT'S WARM.
I DON'T CARE!
JUST PLEASE LET US HAVE SOME!
ANIKI, LET US BOR-ROW YOUR GAMES!!
!!

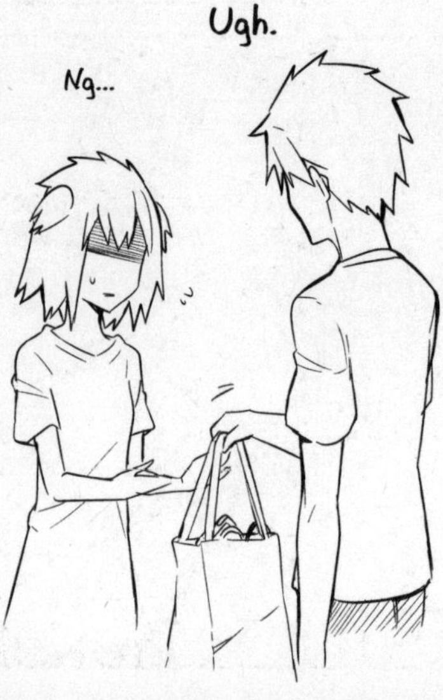
Ugh.
Ng...

D-FRAGMENTS ディーふらぐめんつ!

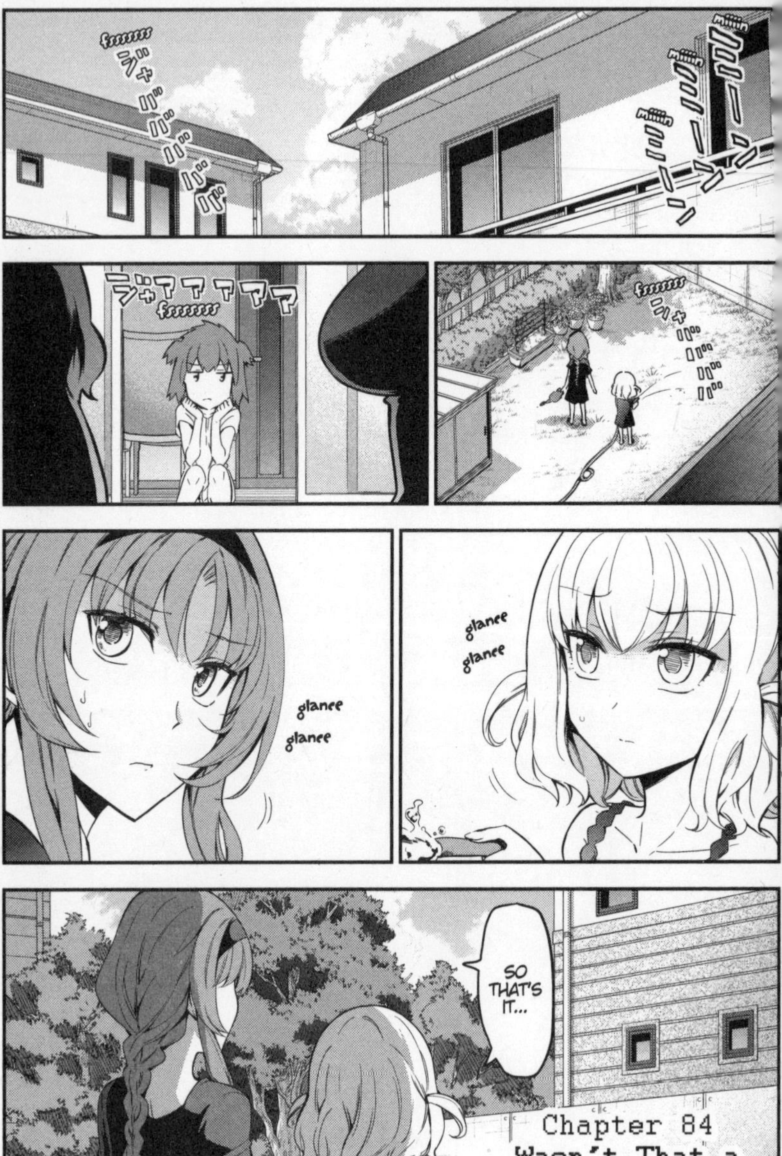
miiin
ミーン
miiin
ミーン
miiin
ミーン
fssssssss
ジャバババババ
fssssssss
シャババババ
ジャアアアアア
fssssssss
glance
glance
glance
glance
SO THAT'S IT...
Chapter 84
Wasn't That a Great Vacation?

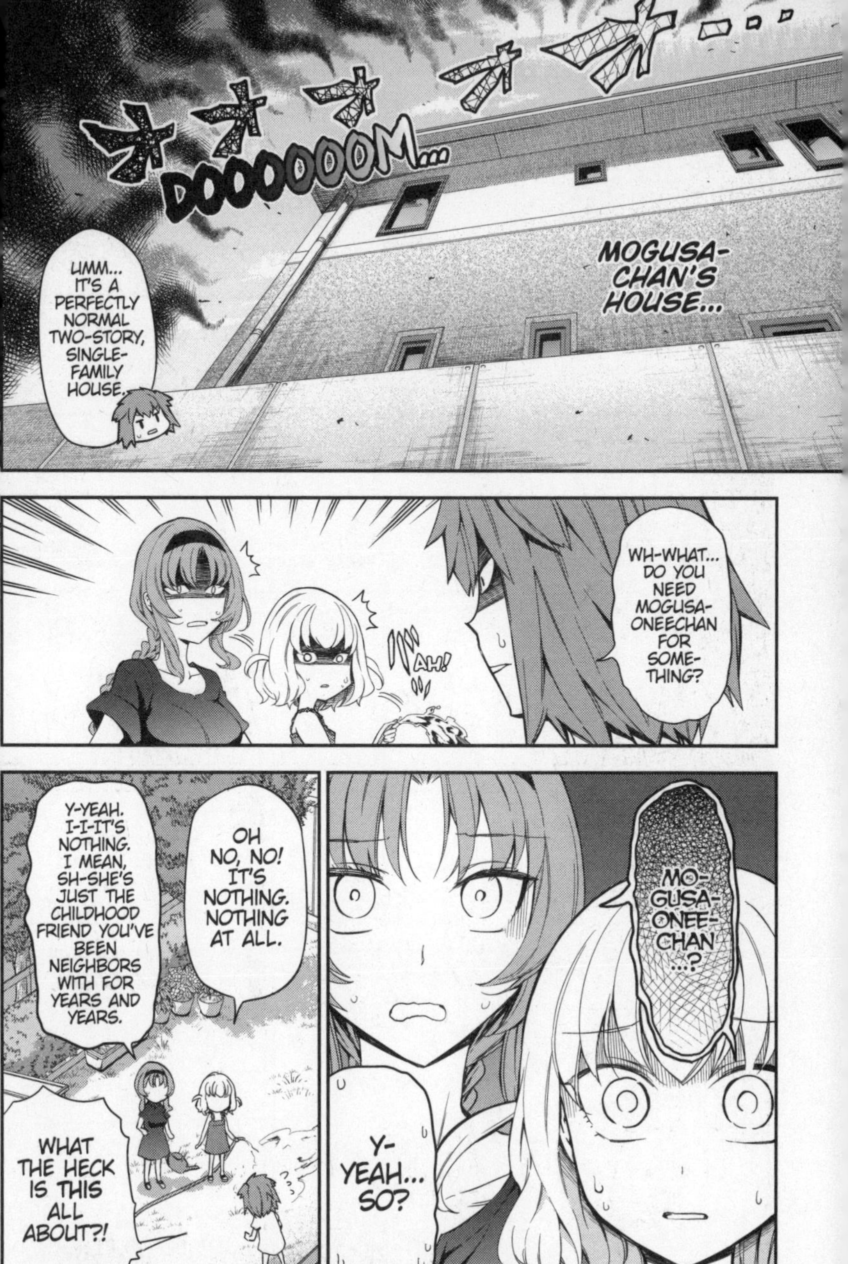
DOOOOOOM...
MOGUSA-CHAN'S HOUSE...
UMM... IT'S A PERFECTLY NORMAL TWO-STORY, SINGLE-FAMILY HOUSE.
WH-WHAT... DO YOU NEED MOGUSA-ONEECHAN FOR SOMETHING?
AH!
MO-GUSA-ONEE-CHAN...?
Y-YEAH... SO?
OH NO, NO! IT'S NOTHING. NOTHING AT ALL.
Y-YEAH. I-I-IT'S NOTHING. I MEAN, SH-SHE'S JUST THE CHILDHOOD FRIEND YOU'VE BEEN NEIGHBORS WITH FOR YEARS AND YEARS.
WHAT THE HECK IS THIS ALL ABOUT?!

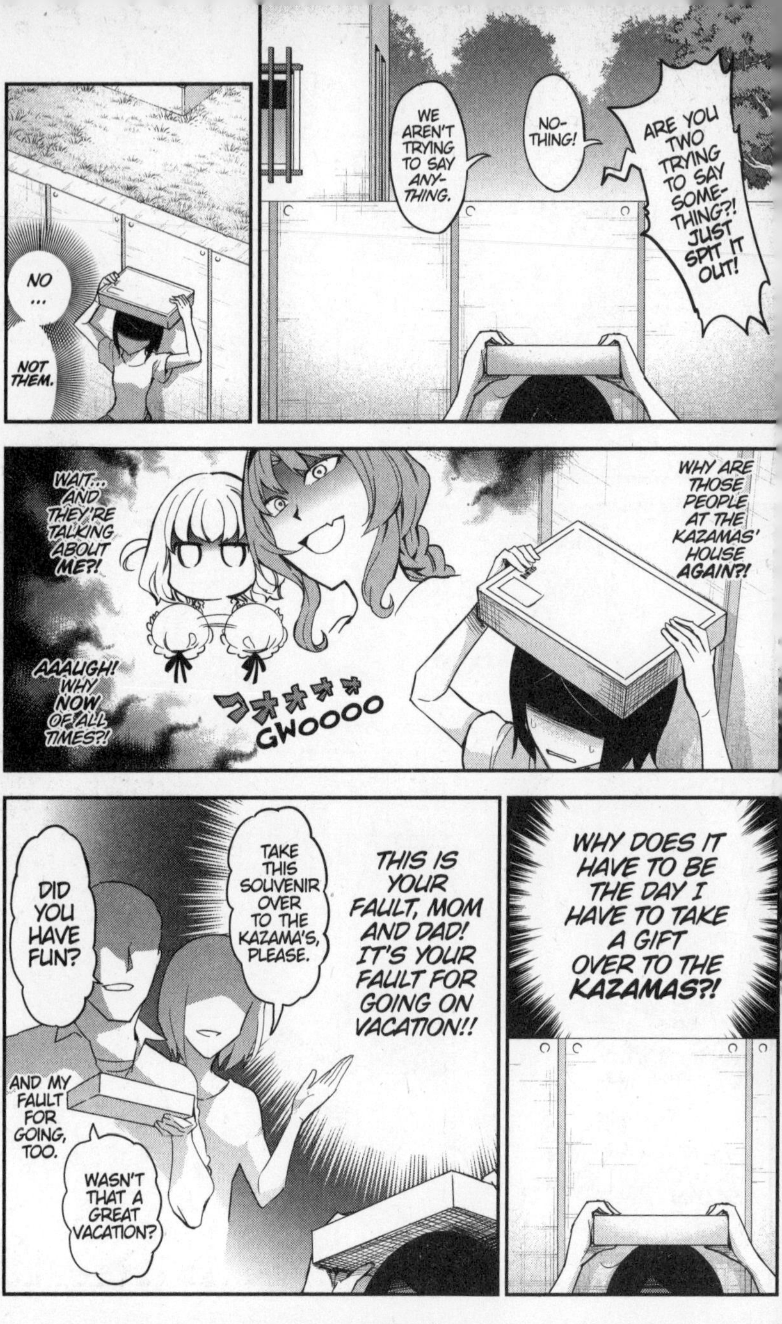
ARE YOU TWO TRYING TO SAY SOMETHING?! JUST SPIT IT OUT!
NO-THING!
WE AREN'T TRYING TO SAY ANYTHING.
NO ...
NOT THEM.
WHY ARE THOSE PEOPLE AT THE KAZAMAS' HOUSE AGAIN?!
WAIT... AND THEY'RE TALKING ABOUT ME?!
AAAUGH! WHY NOW OF ALL TIMES?!
GWOOOO
WHY DOES IT HAVE TO BE THE DAY I HAVE TO TAKE A GIFT OVER TO THE KAZAMAS?!
THIS IS YOUR FAULT, MOM AND DAD! IT'S YOUR FAULT FOR GOING ON VACATION!!
TAKE THIS SOUVENIR OVER TO THE KAZAMA'S, PLEASE.
DID YOU HAVE FUN?
AND MY FAULT FOR GOING, TOO.
WASN'T THAT A GREAT VACATION?

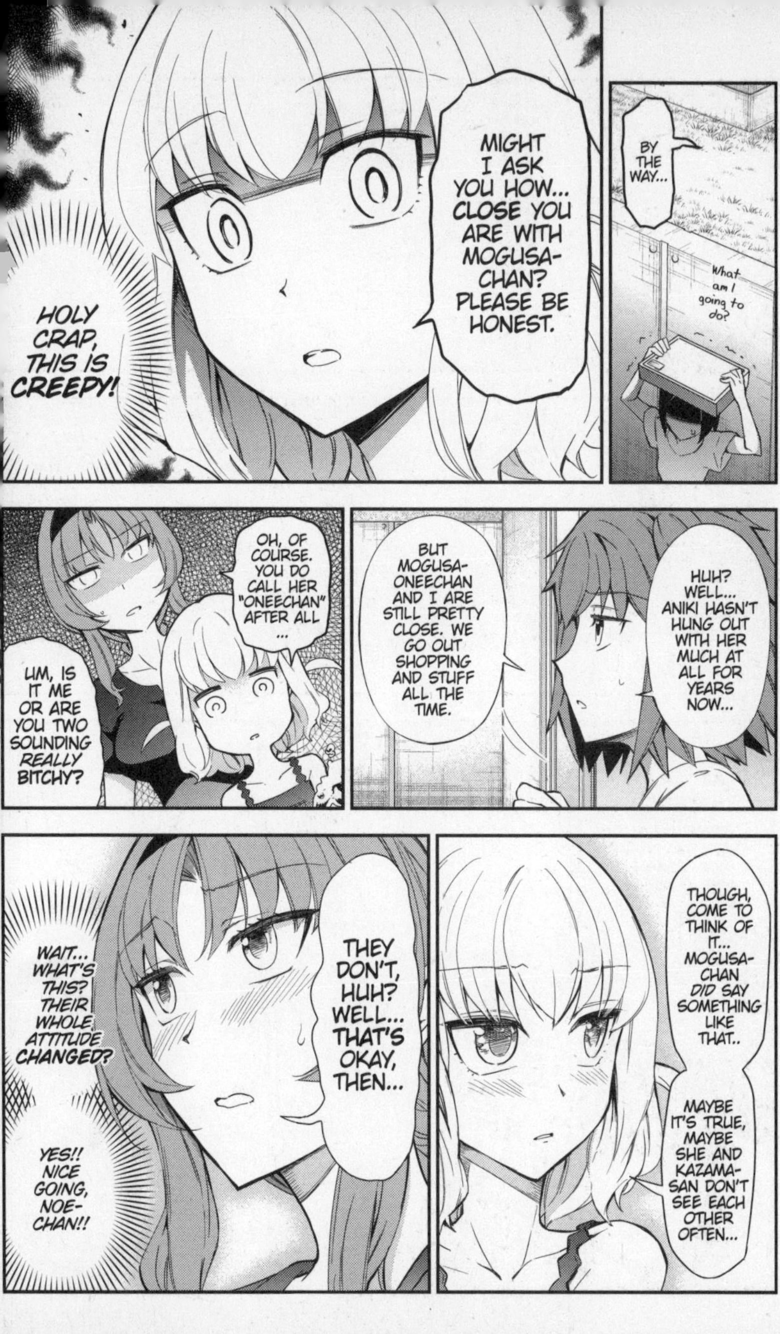
BY THE WAY...
What am I going to do?
MIGHT I ASK YOU HOW... CLOSE YOU ARE WITH MOGUSA-CHAN? PLEASE BE HONEST.
HOLY CRAP, THIS IS CREEPY!
HUH? WELL... ANIKI HASN'T HUNG OUT WITH HER MUCH AT ALL FOR YEARS NOW...
BUT MOGUSA-ONEECHAN AND I ARE STILL PRETTY CLOSE. WE GO OUT SHOPPING AND STUFF ALL THE TIME.
OH, OF COURSE. YOU DO CALL HER "ONEECHAN" AFTER ALL ...
UM, IS IT ME OR ARE YOU TWO SOUNDING *REALLY* BITCHY?
THOUGH, COME TO THINK OF IT... MOGUSA-CHAN *DID* SAY SOMETHING LIKE THAT..
MAYBE IT'S TRUE, MAYBE SHE AND KAZAMA-SAN DON'T SEE EACH OTHER OFTEN...
THEY DON'T, HUH? WELL... THAT'S OKAY, THEN...
WAIT... WHAT'S THIS? THEIR WHOLE ATTITUDE CHANGED?
YES!! NICE GOING, NOE-CHAN!!

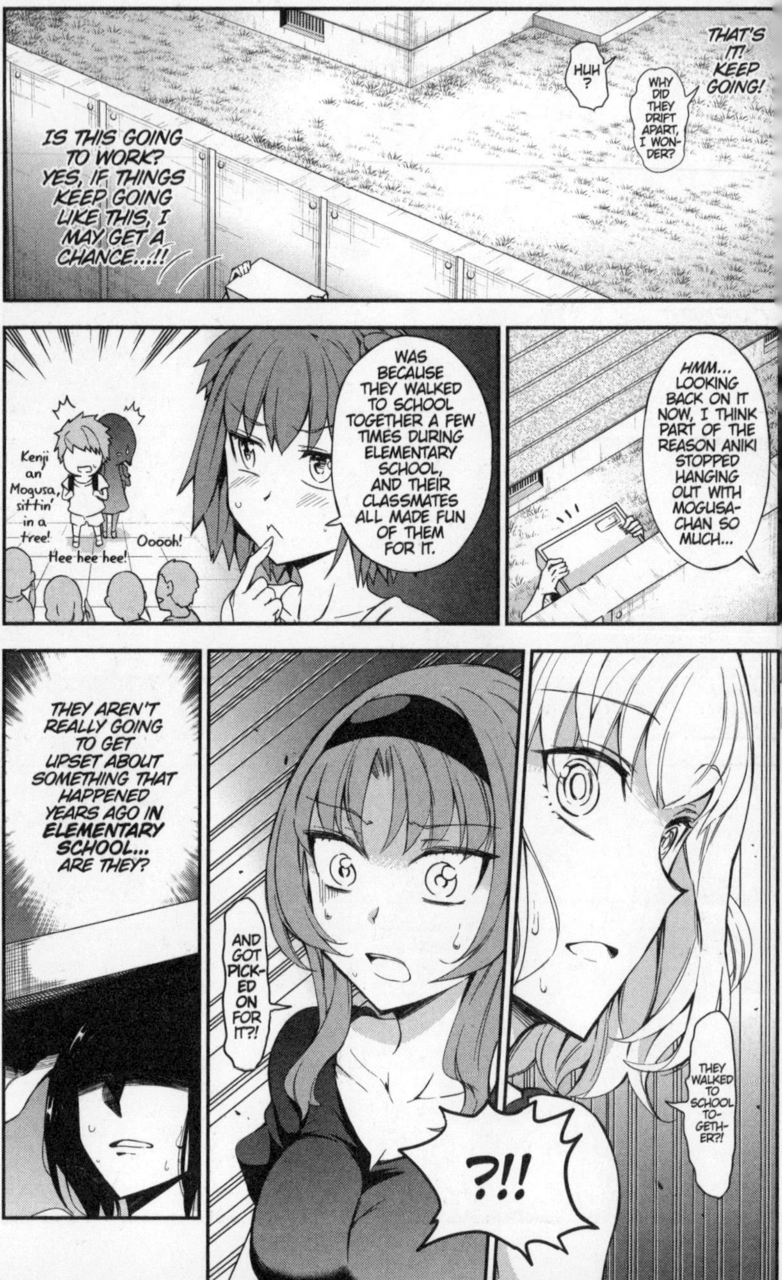
THAT'S IT! KEEP GOING!
WHY DID THEY DRIFT APART, I WONDER?
HUH?
IS THIS GOING TO WORK? YES, IF THINGS KEEP GOING LIKE THIS, I MAY GET A CHANCE...!!
HMM... LOOKING BACK ON IT NOW, I THINK PART OF THE REASON ANIKI STOPPED HANGING OUT WITH MOGUSA-CHAN SO MUCH...
WAS BECAUSE THEY WALKED TO SCHOOL TOGETHER A FEW TIMES DURING ELEMENTARY SCHOOL, AND THEIR CLASSMATES ALL MADE FUN OF THEM FOR IT.
Kenji an Mogusa, sittin' in a tree!
Ooooh!
Hee hee hee!
THEY WALKED TO SCHOOL TOGETHER?!
?!!
AND GOT PICKED ON FOR IT?!
THEY AREN'T REALLY GOING TO GET UPSET ABOUT SOMETHING THAT HAPPENED YEARS AGO IN ELEMENTARY SCHOOL... ARE THEY?

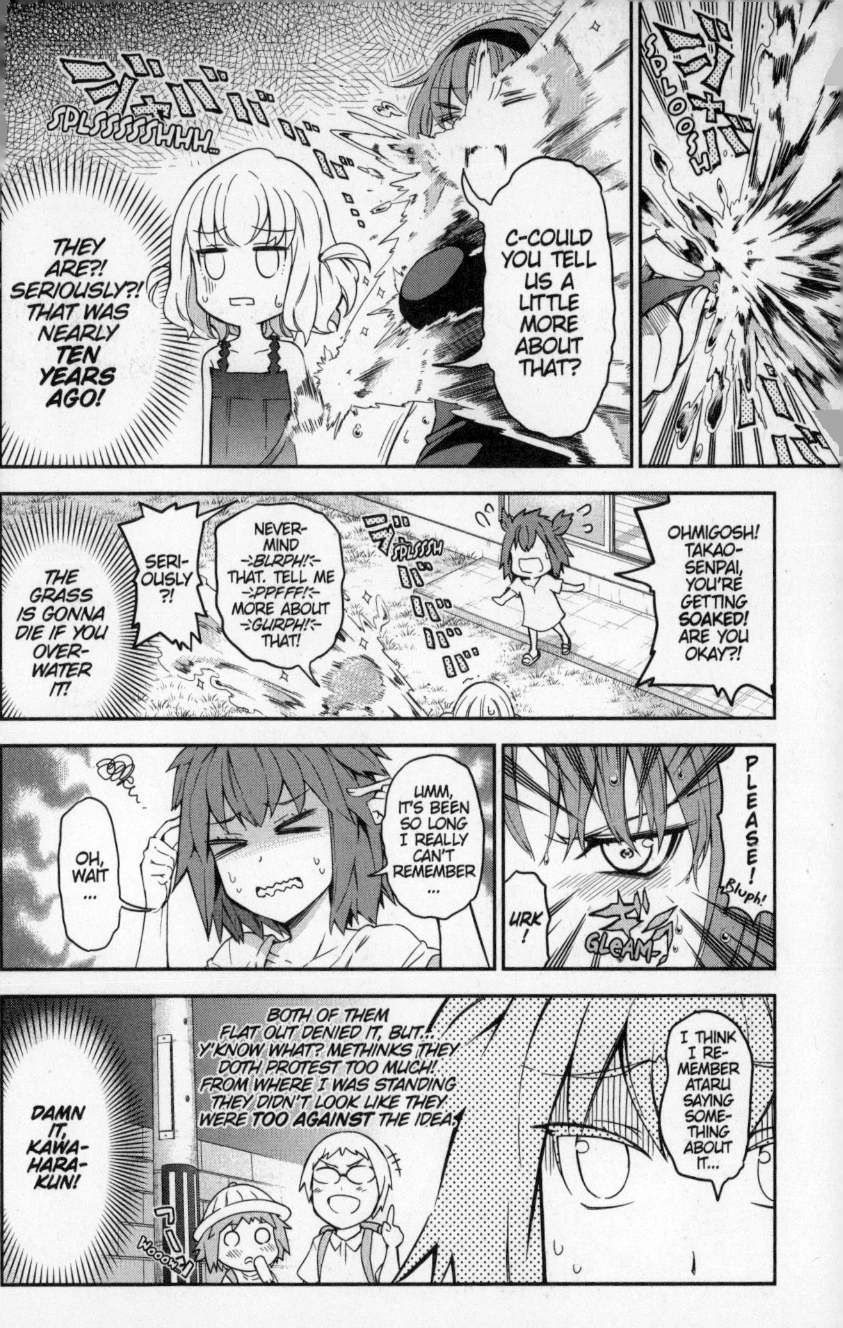
SPLOOOSH
SPLSSSSSHHH...
C-COULD YOU TELL US A LITTLE MORE ABOUT THAT?
THEY ARE?! SERIOUSLY?! THAT WAS NEARLY TEN YEARS AGO!
OHMIGOSH! TAKAO-SENPAI, YOU'RE GETTING SOAKED! ARE YOU OKAY?!
SPLSSSH
NEVER-MIND -BLRPH!- THAT. TELL ME -PPFFF!- MORE ABOUT -GURPH!- THAT!
SERI-OUSLY?!
THE GRASS IS GONNA DIE IF YOU OVER-WATER IT!
PLEASE!
Bluph!
GLEAM
URK!
UMM, IT'S BEEN SO LONG I REALLY CAN'T REMEMBER...
OH, WAIT...
I THINK I RE-MEMBER ATARU SAYING SOME-THING ABOUT IT...
BOTH OF THEM FLAT OUT DENIED IT, BUT... Y'KNOW WHAT? METHINKS THEY DOTH PROTEST TOO MUCH! FROM WHERE I WAS STANDING THEY DIDN'T LOOK LIKE THEY WERE TOO AGAINST THE IDEA!
DAMN IT, KAWA-HARA-KUN!
Wooow!

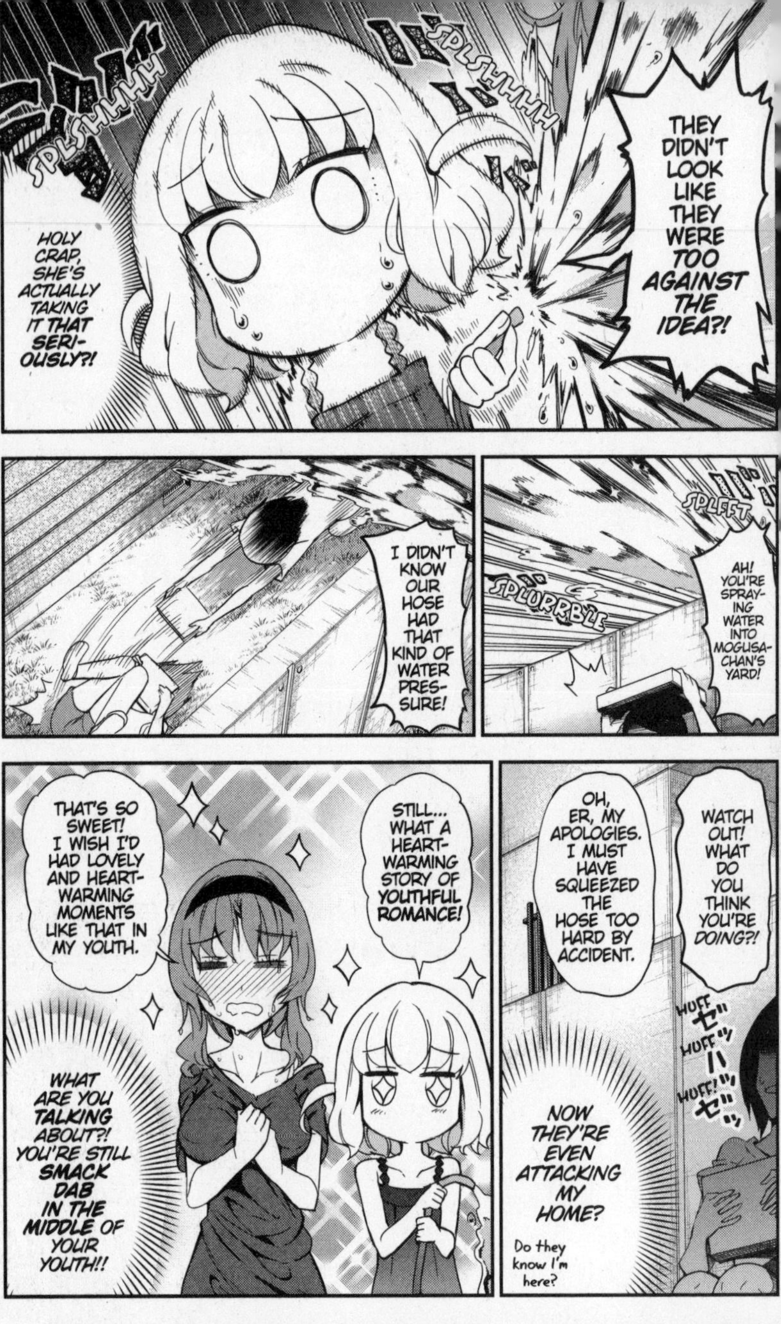
THEY DIDN'T LOOK LIKE THEY WERE TOO AGAINST THE IDEA?!
SPLSHHHHH
SPLSHHHHH
HOLY CRAP, SHE'S ACTUALLY TAKING IT THAT SERI-OUSLY?!
SPLFFT
SPLURRBLE
AH! YOU'RE SPRAY-ING WATER INTO MOGUSA-CHAN'S YARD!
I DIDN'T KNOW OUR HOSE HAD THAT KIND OF WATER PRES-SURE!
WATCH OUT! WHAT DO YOU THINK YOU'RE DOING?!
OH, ER, MY APOLOGIES. I MUST HAVE SQUEEZED THE HOSE TOO HARD BY ACCIDENT.
HUFF HUFF HUFF!
NOW THEY'RE EVEN ATTACKING MY HOME?
Do they know I'm here?
STILL... WHAT A HEART-WARMING STORY OF YOUTHFUL ROMANCE!
THAT'S SO SWEET! I WISH I'D HAD LOVELY AND HEART-WARMING MOMENTS LIKE THAT IN MY YOUTH.
WHAT ARE YOU TALKING ABOUT?! YOU'RE STILL SMACK DAB IN THE MIDDLE OF YOUR YOUTH!!

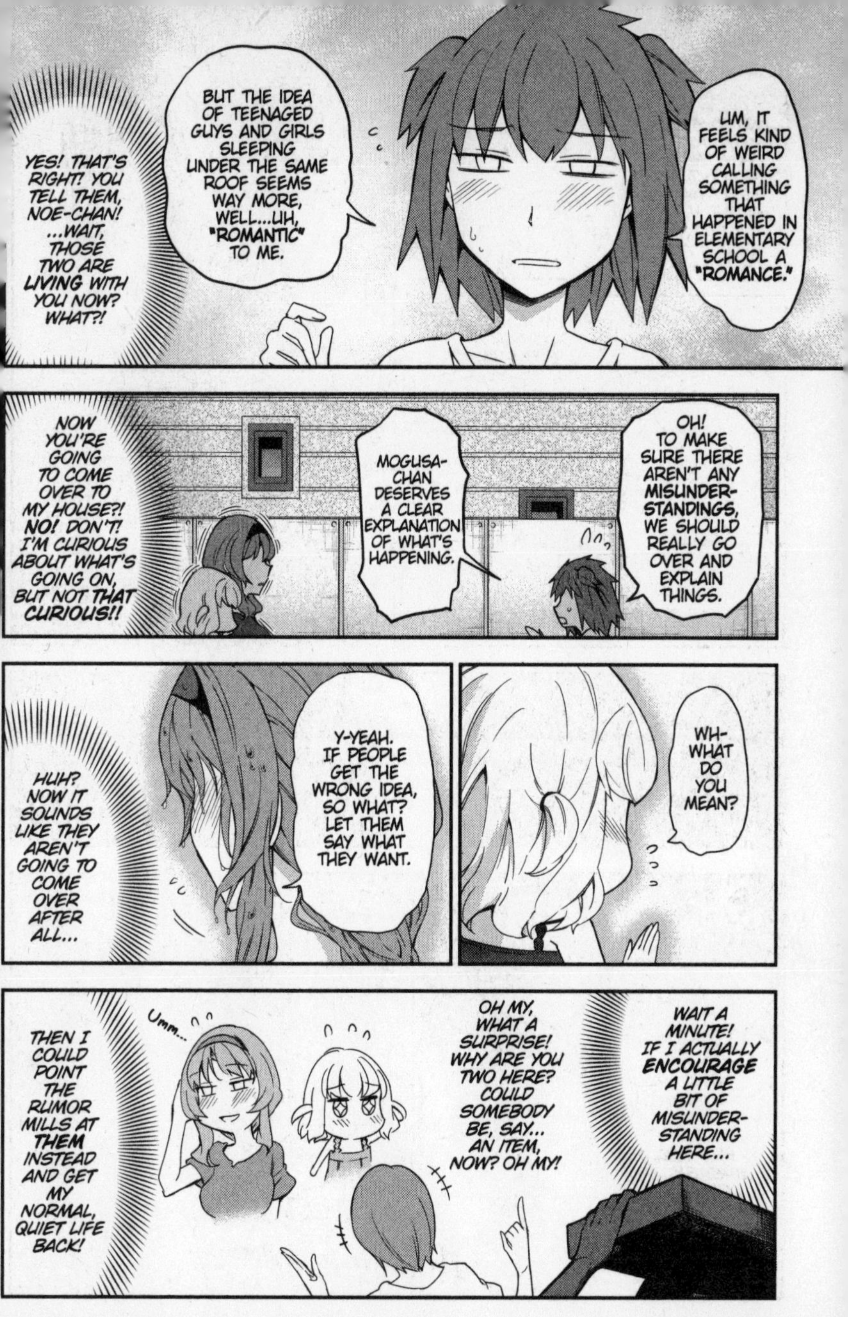
UM, IT FEELS KIND OF WEIRD CALLING SOMETHING THAT HAPPENED IN ELEMENTARY SCHOOL A "ROMANCE."
BUT THE IDEA OF TEENAGED GUYS AND GIRLS SLEEPING UNDER THE SAME ROOF SEEMS WAY MORE, WELL...UH, "ROMANTIC" TO ME.
YES! THAT'S RIGHT! YOU TELL THEM, NOE-CHAN! ...WAIT, THOSE TWO ARE LIVING WITH YOU NOW? WHAT?!
OH! TO MAKE SURE THERE AREN'T ANY MISUNDER-STANDINGS, WE SHOULD REALLY GO OVER AND EXPLAIN THINGS.
MOGUSA-CHAN DESERVES A CLEAR EXPLANATION OF WHAT'S HAPPENING.
NOW YOU'RE GOING TO COME OVER TO MY HOUSE?! NO! DON'T! I'M CURIOUS ABOUT WHAT'S GOING ON, BUT NOT THAT CURIOUS!!
WH-WHAT DO YOU MEAN?
Y-YEAH. IF PEOPLE GET THE WRONG IDEA, SO WHAT? LET THEM SAY WHAT THEY WANT.
HUH? NOW IT SOUNDS LIKE THEY AREN'T GOING TO COME OVER AFTER ALL...
WAIT A MINUTE! IF I ACTUALLY ENCOURAGE A LITTLE BIT OF MISUNDER-STANDING HERE...
OH MY, WHAT A SURPRISE! WHY ARE YOU TWO HERE? COULD SOMEBODY BE, SAY... AN ITEM, NOW? OH MY!
Umm...
THEN I COULD POINT THE RUMOR MILLS AT THEM INSTEAD AND GET MY NORMAL, QUIET LIFE BACK!

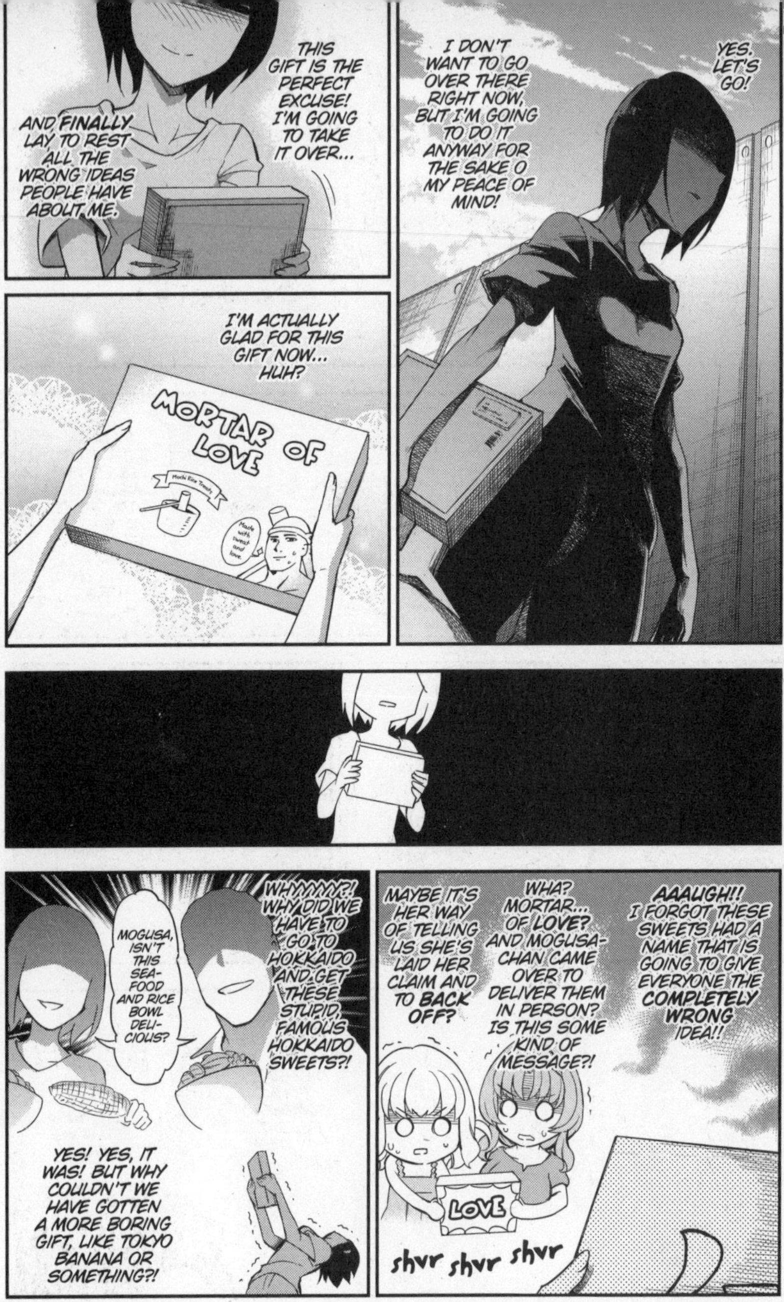
YES. LET'S GO!
I DON'T WANT TO GO OVER THERE RIGHT NOW, BUT I'M GOING TO DO IT ANYWAY FOR THE SAKE O MY PEACE OF MIND!
THIS GIFT IS THE PERFECT EXCUSE! I'M GOING TO TAKE IT OVER...
AND FINALLY LAY TO REST ALL THE WRONG IDEAS PEOPLE HAVE ABOUT ME.
I'M ACTUALLY GLAD FOR THIS GIFT NOW... HUH?
MORTAR OF LOVE
Mochi Rice Treats
Made with sweat and love.
AAAUGH!! I FORGOT THESE SWEETS HAD A NAME THAT IS GOING TO GIVE EVERYONE THE COMPLETELY WRONG IDEA!!
WHA? MORTAR... OF LOVE? AND MOGUSA-CHAN CAME OVER TO DELIVER THEM IN PERSON? IS THIS SOME KIND OF MESSAGE?!
MAYBE IT'S HER WAY OF TELLING US SHE'S LAID HER CLAIM AND TO BACK OFF?
LOVE
shvr shvr shvr
WHYYYYY?! WHY DID WE HAVE TO GO TO HOKKAIDO AND GET THESE STUPID, FAMOUS HOKKAIDO SWEETS?!
MOGUSA, ISN'T THIS SEA-FOOD AND RICE BOWL DELI-CIOUS?
YES! YES, IT WAS! BUT WHY COULDN'T WE HAVE GOTTEN A MORE BORING GIFT, LIKE TOKYO BANANA OR SOMETHING?!

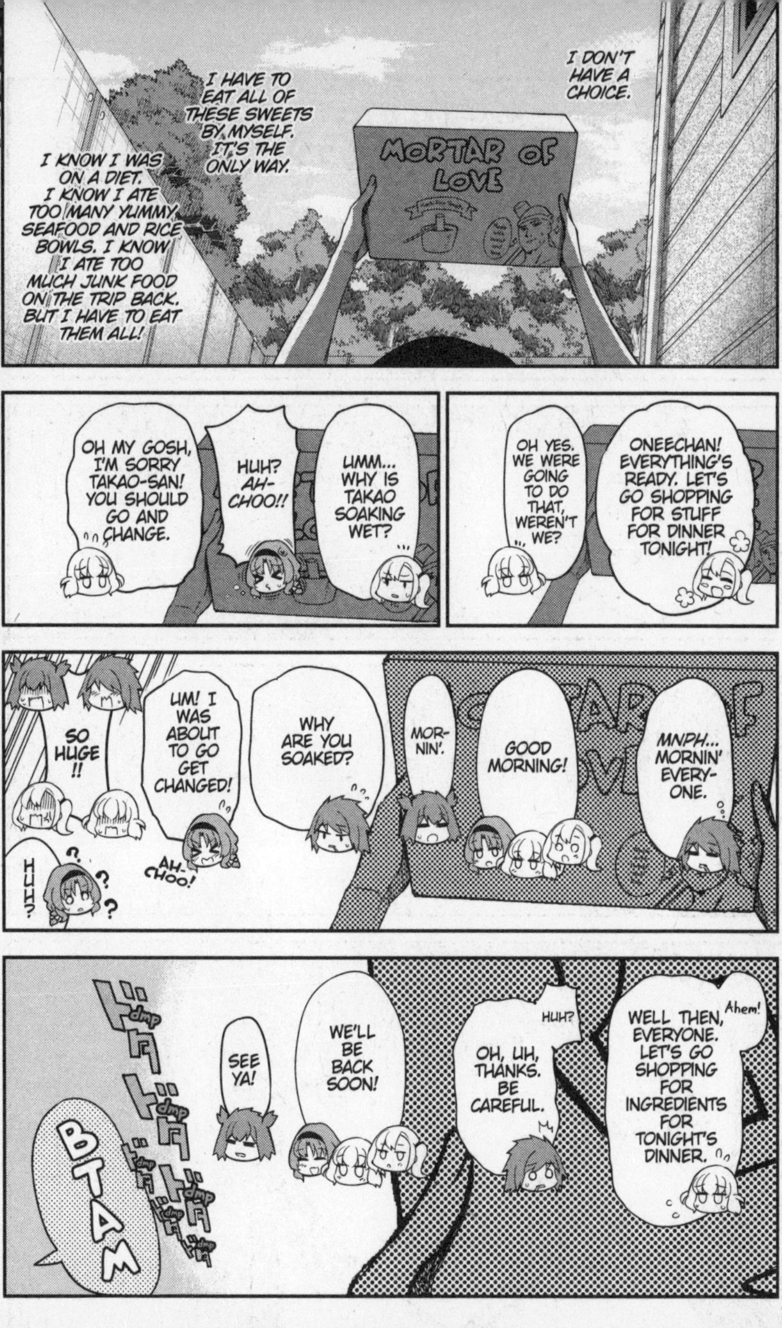
I DON'T HAVE A CHOICE.
MORTAR OF LOVE
I HAVE TO EAT ALL OF THESE SWEETS BY MYSELF. IT'S THE ONLY WAY.
I KNOW I WAS ON A DIET. I KNOW I ATE TOO MANY YUMMY SEAFOOD AND RICE BOWLS. I KNOW I ATE TOO MUCH JUNK FOOD ON THE TRIP BACK. BUT I HAVE TO EAT THEM ALL!
ONEECHAN! EVERYTHING'S READY. LET'S GO SHOPPING FOR STUFF FOR DINNER TONIGHT!
OH YES. WE WERE GOING TO DO THAT, WEREN'T WE?
UMM... WHY IS TAKAO SOAKING WET?
HUH? AH-CHOO!!
OH MY GOSH, I'M SORRY TAKAO-SAN! YOU SHOULD GO AND CHANGE.
MNPH... MORNIN' EVERY-ONE.
GOOD MORNING!
MOR-NIN'.
WHY ARE YOU SOAKED?
UM! I WAS ABOUT TO GO GET CHANGED!
AH-CHOO!
SO HUGE!!
HUH?
Ahem!
WELL THEN, EVERYONE. LET'S GO SHOPPING FOR INGREDIENTS FOR TONIGHT'S DINNER.
HUH?
OH, UH, THANKS. BE CAREFUL.
WE'LL BE BACK SOON!
SEE YA!
BTAM

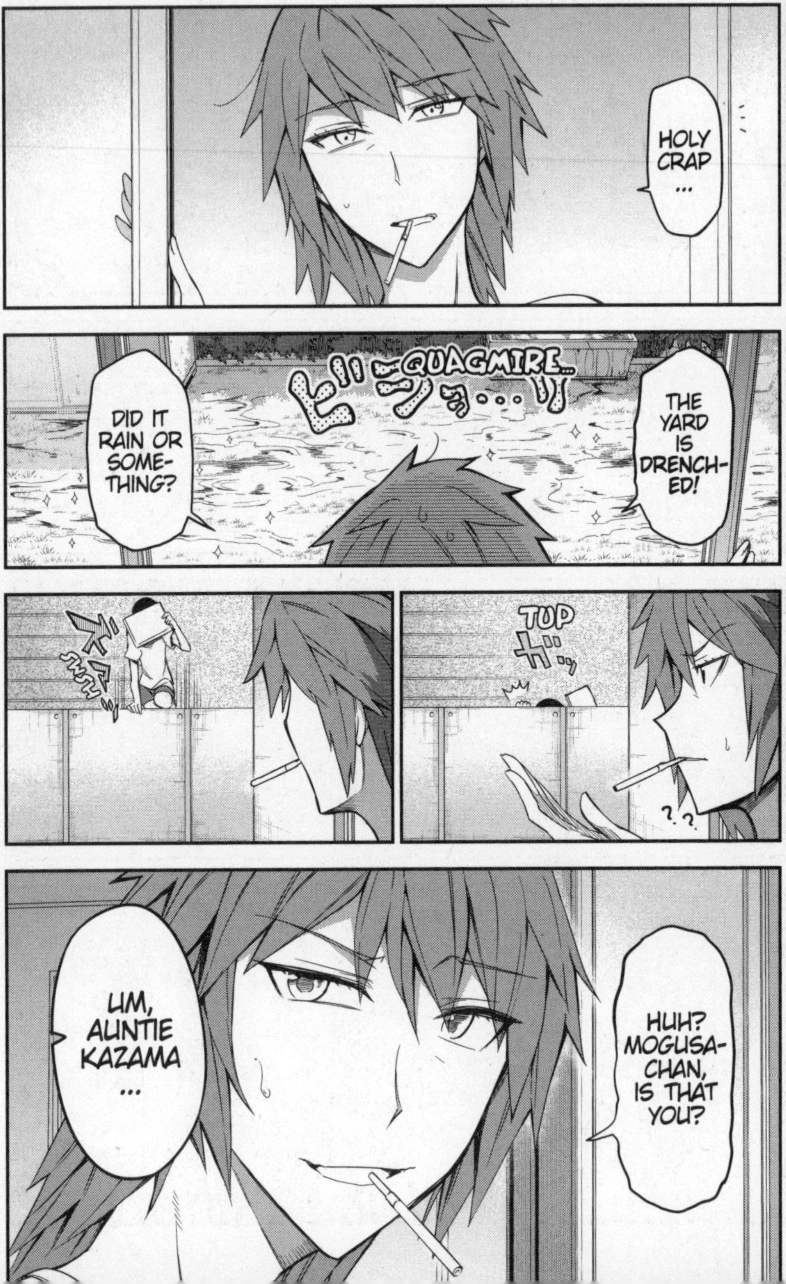
HOLY CRAP ...
THE YARD IS DRENCH-ED!
QUAGMIRE...
DID IT RAIN OR SOME-THING?
TUP
?.?
SWISH
HUH? MOGUSA-CHAN, IS THAT YOU?
UM, AUNTIE KAZAMA ...

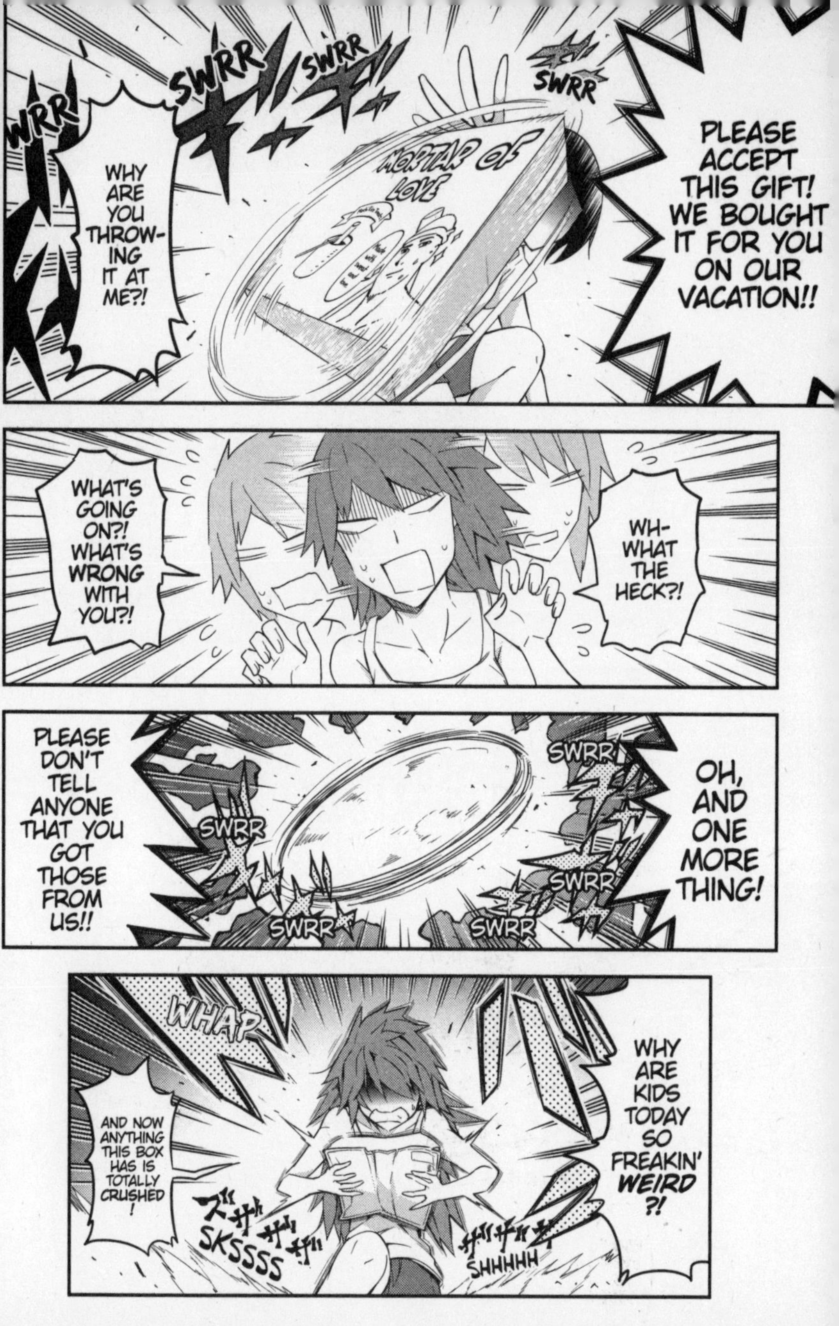
SWRR
PLEASE ACCEPT THIS GIFT! WE BOUGHT IT FOR YOU ON OUR VACATION!!
MORTAR OF LOVE
SWRR
SWRR
WRR
WHY ARE YOU THROWING IT AT ME?!
WH-WHAT THE HECK?!
WHAT'S GOING ON?! WHAT'S WRONG WITH YOU?!
OH, AND ONE MORE THING!
SWRR
SWRR
SWRR
SWRR
SWRR
PLEASE DON'T TELL ANYONE THAT YOU GOT THOSE FROM US!!
WHY ARE KIDS TODAY SO FREAKIN' *WEIRD* ?!
WHAP
SHHHHH
AND NOW ANYTHING THIS BOX HAS IS TOTALLY CRUSHED!
SKSSSS

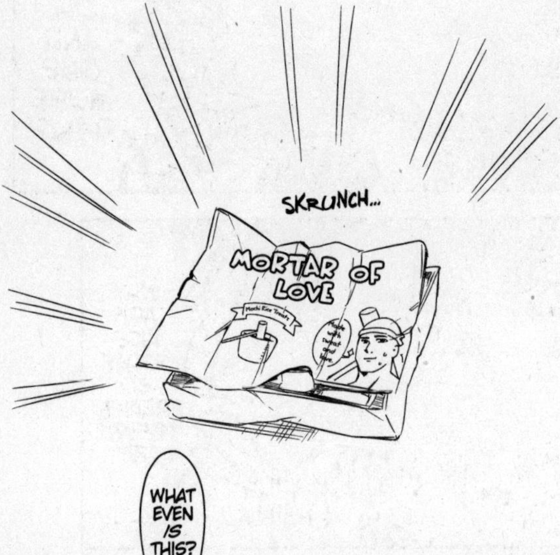
SKRUNCH...
MORTAR OF LOVE
Mochi Rice Treats
Made with sweat and love.
WHAT EVEN IS THIS?

D-FRAGMENTS ディーふらぐ！

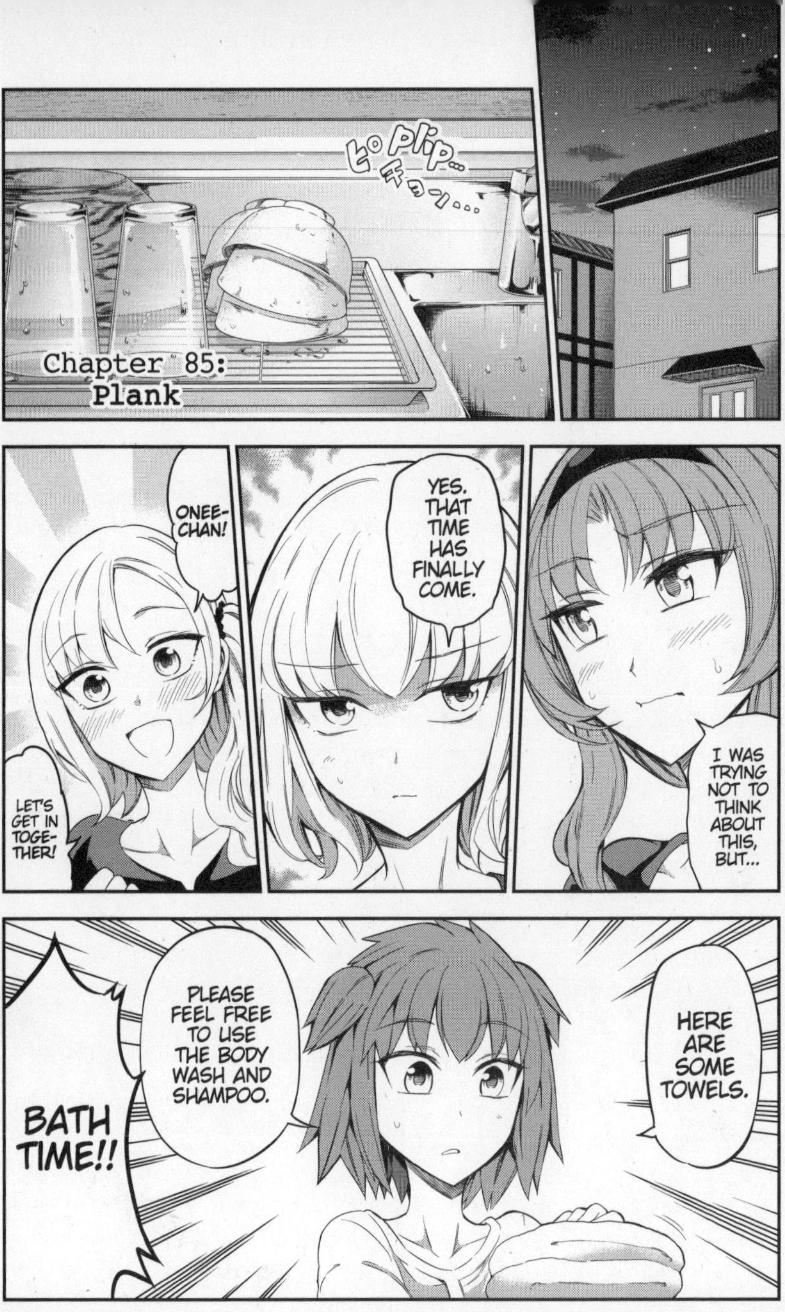
plip...
Chapter 85: Plank
I WAS TRYING NOT TO THINK ABOUT THIS, BUT...
YES. THAT TIME HAS FINALLY COME.
ONEE-CHAN!
LET'S GET IN TOGE-THER!
HERE ARE SOME TOWELS.
PLEASE FEEL FREE TO USE THE BODY WASH AND SHAMPOO.
BATH TIME!!

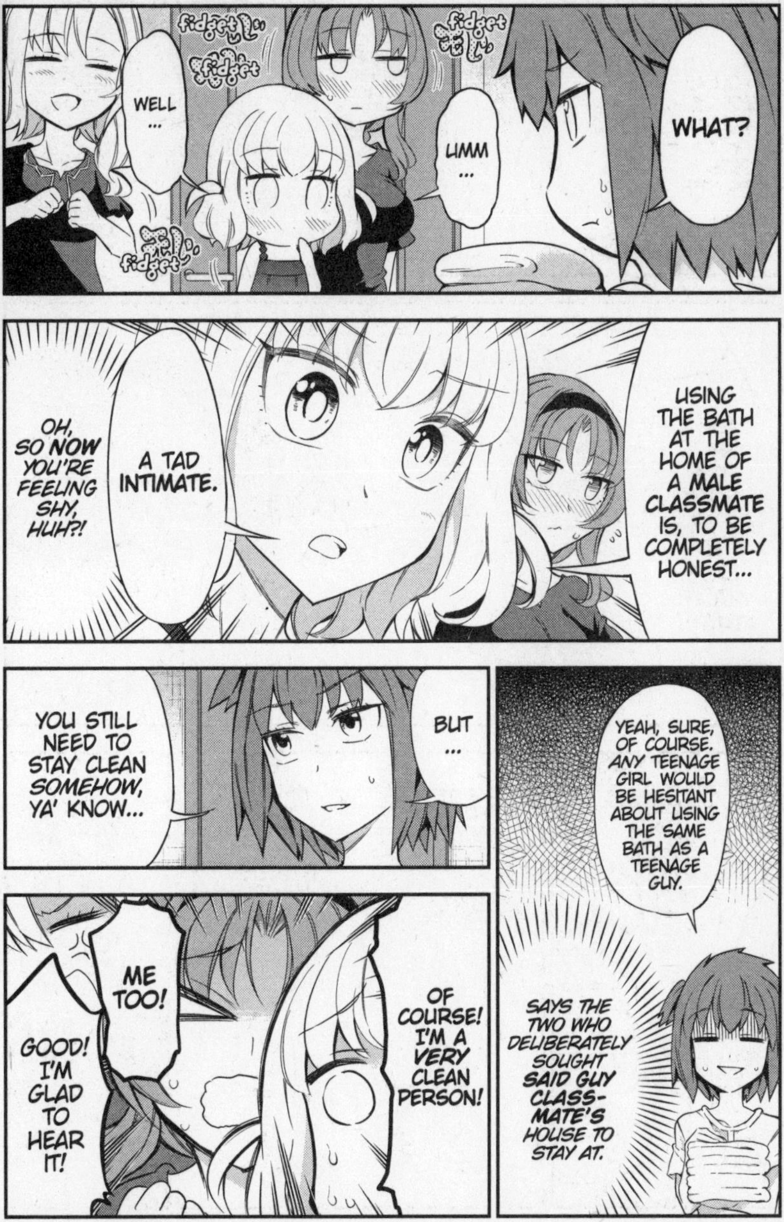
WHAT?
fidget
UMM ...
fidget
fidget
WELL ...
fidget
USING THE BATH AT THE HOME OF A MALE CLASSMATE IS, TO BE COMPLETELY HONEST...
A TAD INTIMATE.
OH, SO NOW YOU'RE FEELING SHY, HUH?!
YEAH, SURE, OF COURSE. ANY TEENAGE GIRL WOULD BE HESITANT ABOUT USING THE SAME BATH AS A TEENAGE GUY.
SAYS THE TWO WHO DELIBERATELY SOUGHT SAID GUY CLASS-MATE'S HOUSE TO STAY AT.
BUT ...
YOU STILL NEED TO STAY CLEAN SOMEHOW, YA' KNOW...
OF COURSE! I'M A VERY CLEAN PERSON!
ME TOO!
GOOD! I'M GLAD TO HEAR IT!

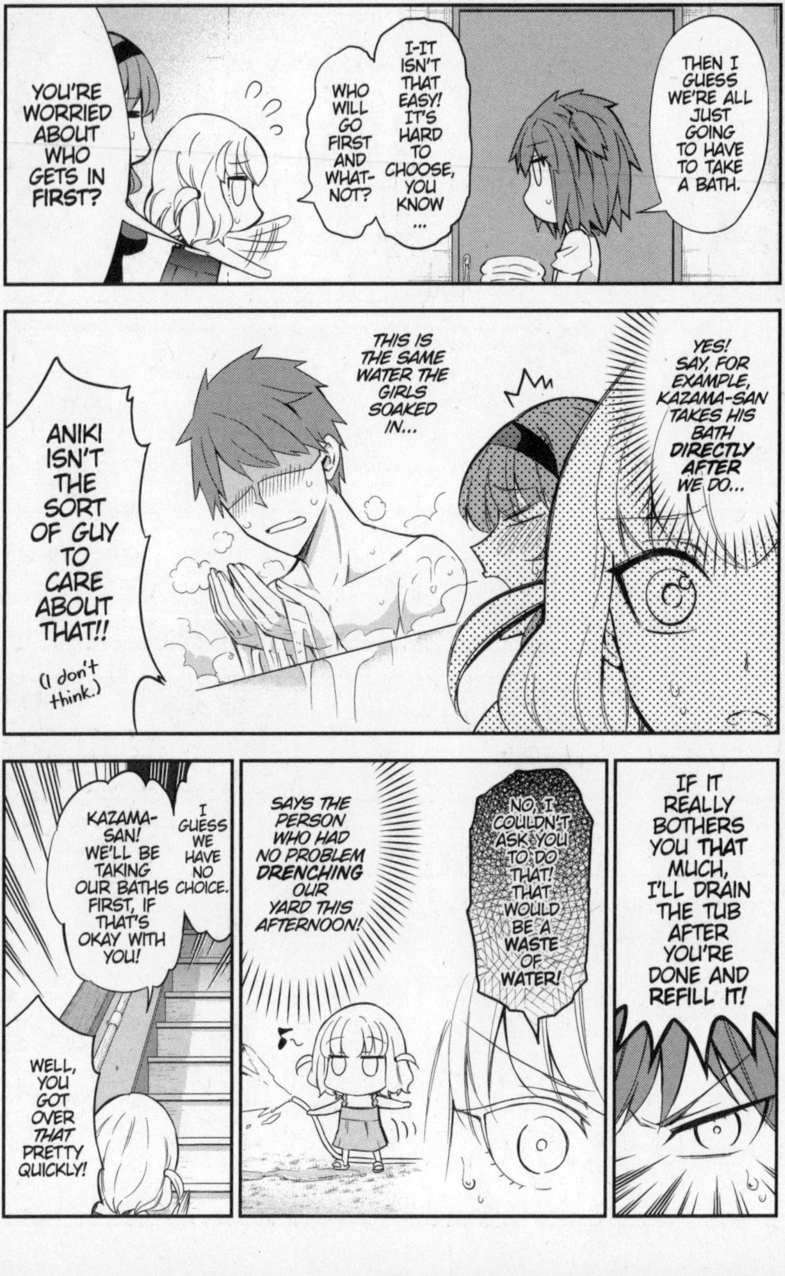
THEN I GUESS WE'RE ALL JUST GOING TO HAVE TO TAKE A BATH.
I-IT ISN'T THAT EASY! IT'S HARD TO CHOOSE, YOU KNOW...
WHO WILL GO FIRST AND WHAT-NOT?
YOU'RE WORRIED ABOUT WHO GETS IN FIRST?
YES! SAY, FOR EXAMPLE, KAZAMA-SAN TAKES HIS BATH **DIRECTLY AFTER** WE DO...
THIS IS THE SAME WATER THE GIRLS SOAKED IN...
ANIKI ISN'T THE SORT OF GUY TO CARE ABOUT THAT!!
(I don't think.)
IF IT REALLY BOTHERS YOU THAT MUCH, I'LL DRAIN THE TUB AFTER YOU'RE DONE AND REFILL IT!
NO, I COULDN'T ASK YOU TO DO THAT! THAT WOULD BE A WASTE OF WATER!
SAYS THE PERSON WHO HAD NO PROBLEM **DRENCHING** OUR YARD THIS AFTERNOON!
I GUESS WE HAVE NO CHOICE.
KAZAMA-SAN! WE'LL BE TAKING OUR BATHS FIRST, IF THAT'S OKAY WITH YOU!
WELL, YOU GOT OVER *THAT* PRETTY QUICKLY!

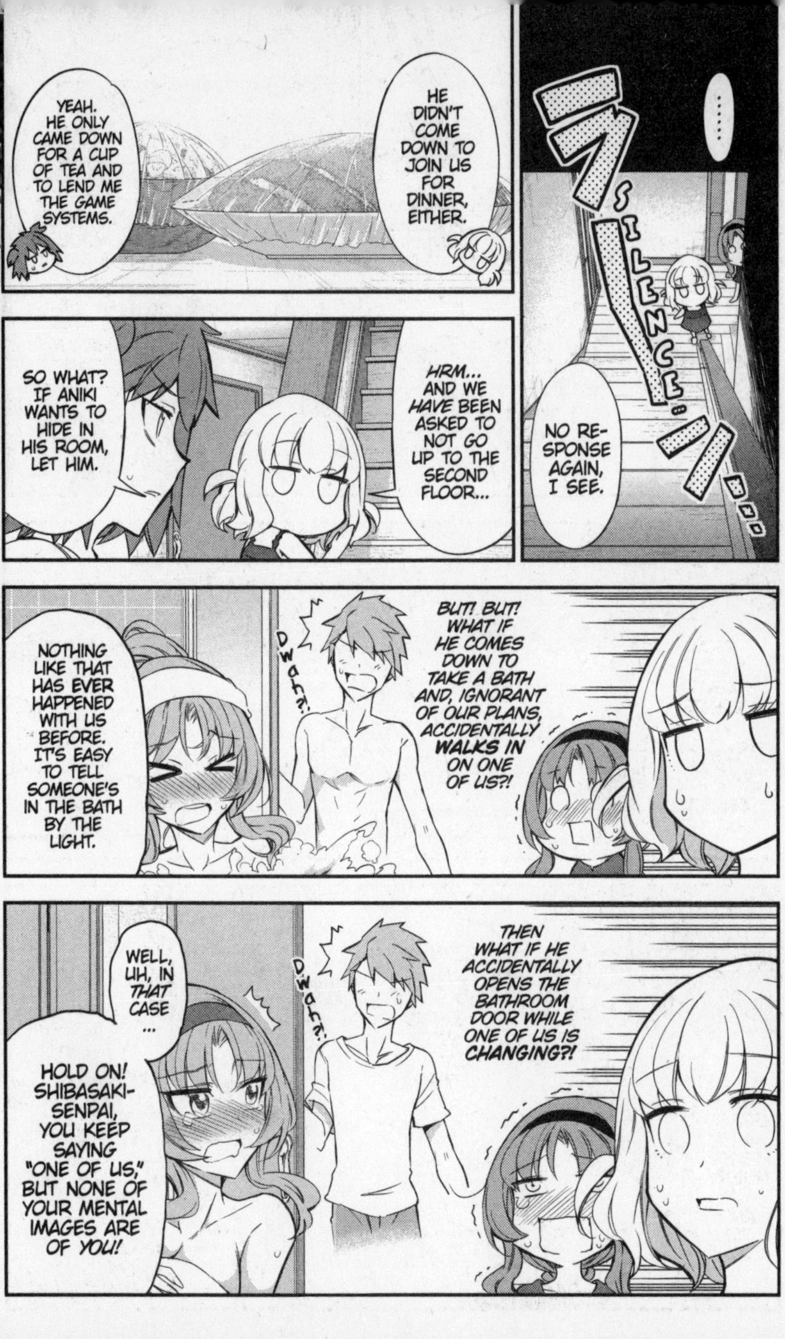
......
SILENCE...
NO RESPONSE AGAIN, I SEE.
HE DIDN'T COME DOWN TO JOIN US FOR DINNER, EITHER.
YEAH. HE ONLY CAME DOWN FOR A CUP OF TEA AND TO LEND ME THE GAME SYSTEMS.
HRM... AND WE *HAVE* BEEN ASKED TO NOT GO UP TO THE SECOND FLOOR...
SO WHAT? IF ANIKI WANTS TO HIDE IN HIS ROOM, LET HIM.
BUT! BUT! WHAT IF HE COMES DOWN TO TAKE A BATH AND, IGNORANT OF OUR PLANS, ACCIDENTALLY **WALKS IN** ON ONE OF US?!
Dwah?!
NOTHING LIKE THAT HAS EVER HAPPENED WITH US BEFORE. IT'S EASY TO TELL SOMEONE'S IN THE BATH BY THE LIGHT.
THEN WHAT IF HE ACCIDENTALLY OPENS THE BATHROOM DOOR WHILE ONE OF US IS **CHANGING?!**
Dwah?!
WELL, UH, IN *THAT* CASE ...
HOLD ON! SHIBASAKI-SENPAI, YOU KEEP SAYING "ONE OF US," BUT NONE OF YOUR MENTAL IMAGES ARE OF *YOU!*

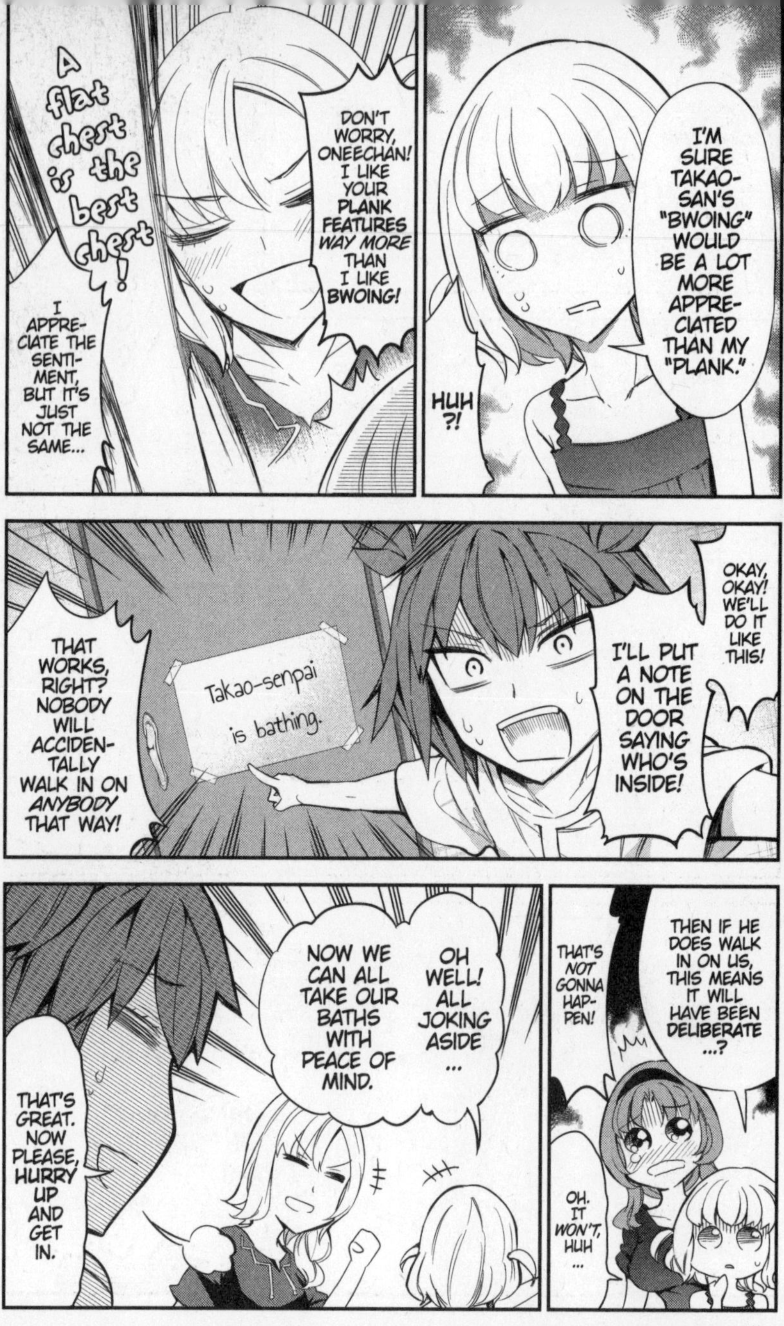
I'M SURE TAKAO-SAN'S "BWOING" WOULD BE A LOT MORE APPRECIATED THAN MY "PLANK."
HUH ?!
DON'T WORRY, ONEECHAN! I LIKE YOUR PLANK FEATURES WAY MORE THAN I LIKE BWOING!
A flat chest is the best chest!
I APPRECIATE THE SENTIMENT, BUT IT'S JUST NOT THE SAME...
OKAY, OKAY! WE'LL DO IT LIKE THIS!
I'LL PUT A NOTE ON THE DOOR SAYING WHO'S INSIDE!
Takao-senpai is bathing.
THAT WORKS, RIGHT? NOBODY WILL ACCIDENTALLY WALK IN ON ANYBODY THAT WAY!
THEN IF HE DOES WALK IN ON US, THIS MEANS IT WILL HAVE BEEN DELIBERATE ...?
THAT'S NOT GONNA HAPPEN!
OH. IT WON'T, HUH ...
OH WELL! ALL JOKING ASIDE ...
NOW WE CAN ALL TAKE OUR BATHS WITH PEACE OF MIND.
THAT'S GREAT. NOW PLEASE, HURRY UP AND GET IN.

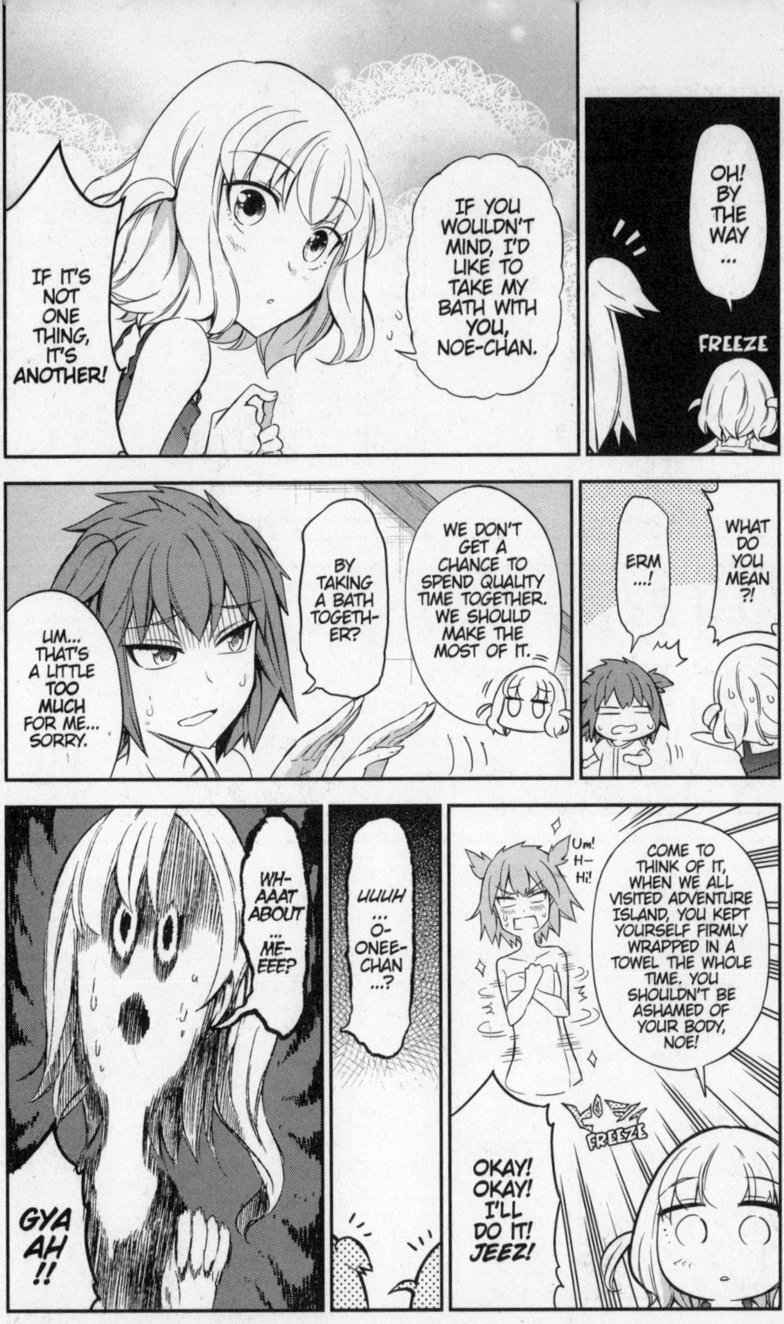
OH! BY THE WAY ...
FREEZE
IF YOU WOULDN'T MIND, I'D LIKE TO TAKE MY BATH WITH YOU, NOE-CHAN.
IF IT'S NOT ONE THING, IT'S ANOTHER!
WHAT DO YOU MEAN?!
ERM ...!
WE DON'T GET A CHANCE TO SPEND QUALITY TIME TOGETHER. WE SHOULD MAKE THE MOST OF IT.
BY TAKING A BATH TOGETH-ER?
UM... THAT'S A LITTLE TOO MUCH FOR ME... SORRY.
COME TO THINK OF IT, WHEN WE ALL VISITED ADVENTURE ISLAND, YOU KEPT YOURSELF FIRMLY WRAPPED IN A TOWEL THE WHOLE TIME. YOU SHOULDN'T BE ASHAMED OF YOUR BODY, NOE!
Um! H-Hi!
FREEZE
OKAY! OKAY! I'LL DO IT! JEEZ!
UUUH ... O-ONEE-CHAN ...?
WH-AAAT ABOUT ... ME-EEE?
GYAAH!!

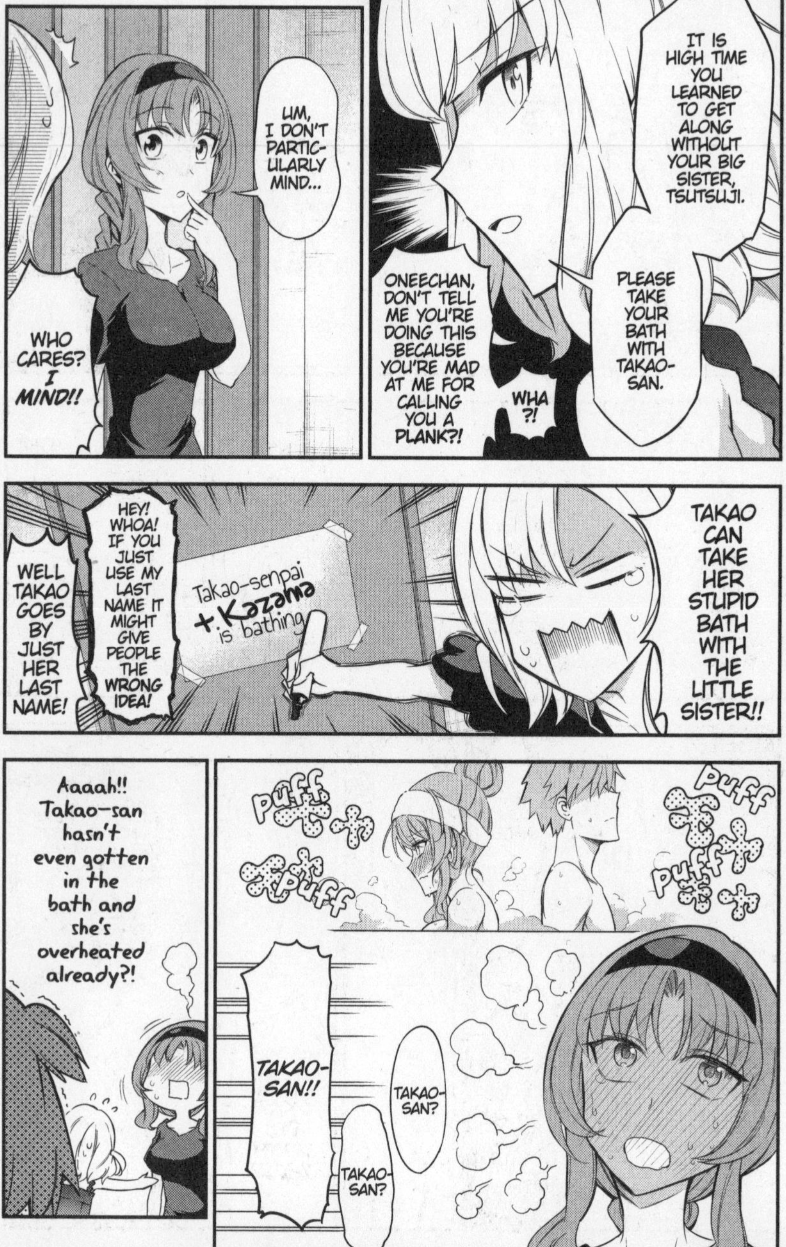

IT IS HIGH TIME YOU LEARNED TO GET ALONG WITHOUT YOUR BIG SISTER, TSUTSUJI.
PLEASE TAKE YOUR BATH WITH TAKAO-SAN.
WHA?!
ONEECHAN, DON'T TELL ME YOU'RE DOING THIS BECAUSE YOU'RE MAD AT ME FOR CALLING YOU A PLANK?!
UM, I DON'T PARTICULARLY MIND...
WHO CARES? I MIND!!
TAKAO CAN TAKE HER STUPID BATH WITH THE LITTLE SISTER!!
Takao-senpai + Kazama is bathing
HEY! WHOA! IF YOU JUST USE MY LAST NAME IT MIGHT GIVE PEOPLE THE WRONG IDEA!
WELL TAKAO GOES BY JUST HER LAST NAME!
puff
puff
puff
puff
TAKAO-SAN?
TAKAO-SAN?
TAKAO-SAN!!
Aaaah!! Takao-san hasn't even gotten in the bath and she's overheated already?!

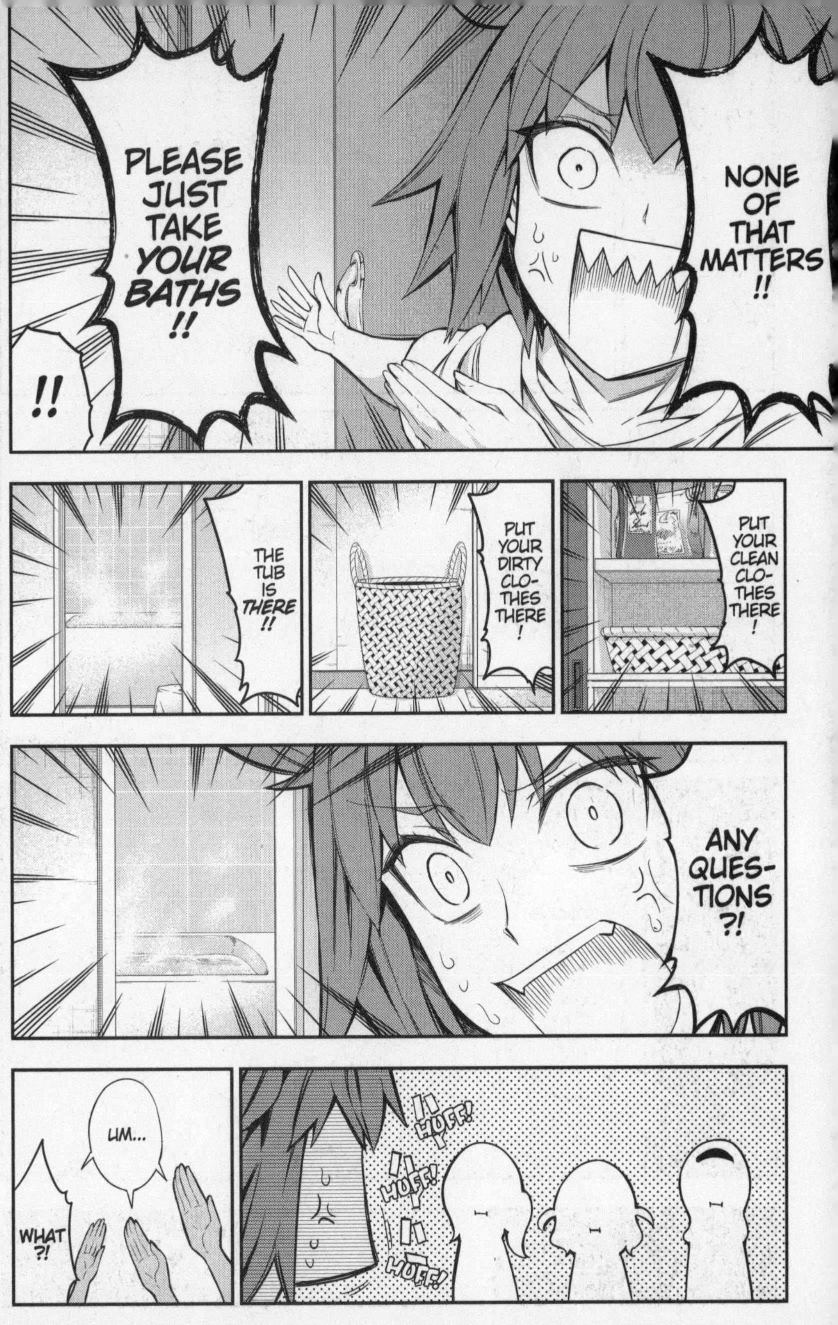
NONE OF THAT MATTERS !!
PLEASE JUST TAKE YOUR BATHS !!
!!
PUT YOUR CLEAN CLO-THES THERE !
PUT YOUR DIRTY CLO-THES THERE !
THE TUB IS THERE !!
ANY QUES-TIONS ?!
HUFF!
HUFF!
HUFF!
UM...
WHAT ?!

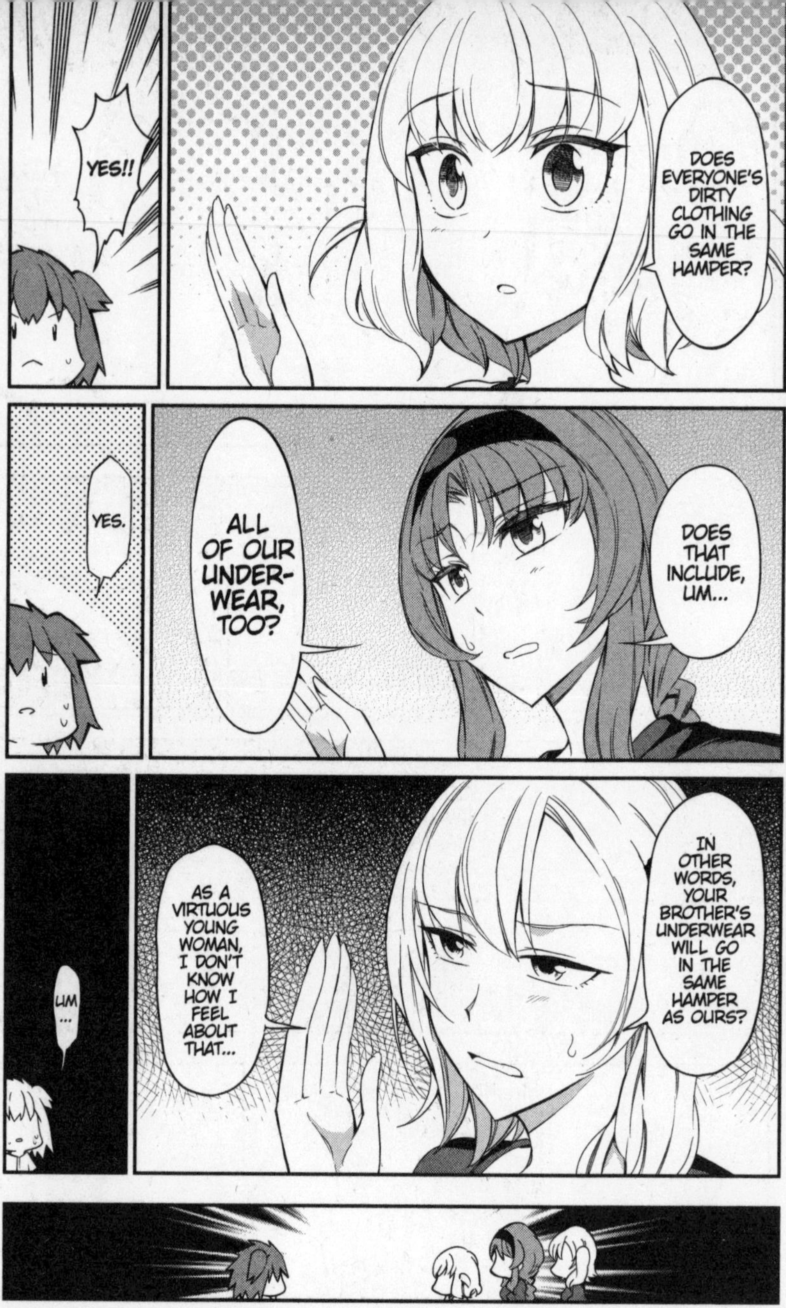
DOES EVERYONE'S DIRTY CLOTHING GO IN THE SAME HAMPER?
YES!!
DOES THAT INCLUDE, UM...
ALL OF OUR UNDER-WEAR, TOO?
YES.
IN OTHER WORDS, YOUR BROTHER'S UNDERWEAR WILL GO IN THE SAME HAMPER AS OURS?
AS A VIRTUOUS YOUNG WOMAN, I DON'T KNOW HOW I FEEL ABOUT THAT...
UM...

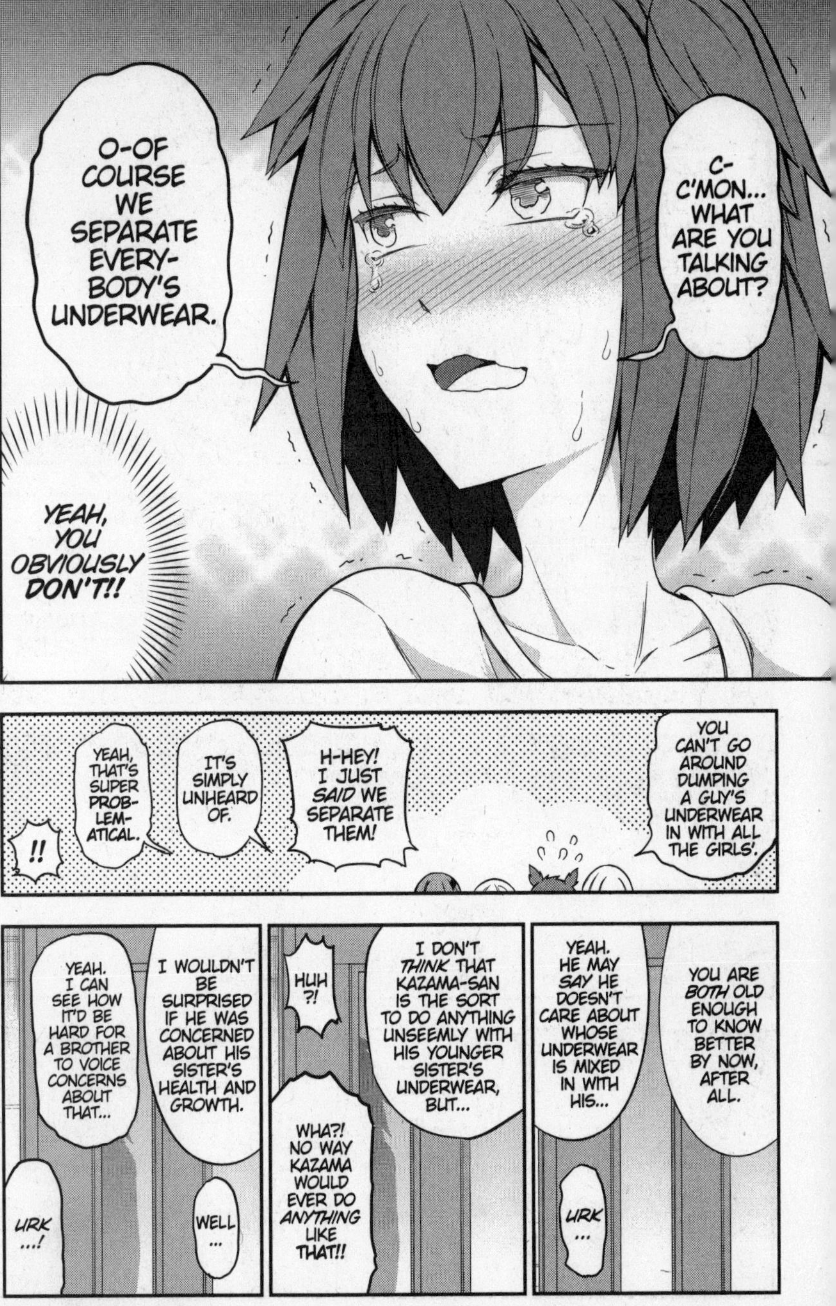
C- C'MON... WHAT ARE YOU TALKING ABOUT?
O-OF COURSE WE SEPARATE EVERY-BODY'S UNDERWEAR.
YEAH, YOU OBVIOUSLY DON'T!!
YOU CAN'T GO AROUND DUMPING A GUY'S UNDERWEAR IN WITH ALL THE GIRLS'.
H-HEY! I JUST *SAID* WE SEPARATE THEM!
IT'S SIMPLY UNHEARD OF.
YEAH, THAT'S SUPER PROB-LEM-ATICAL.
!!
YOU ARE *BOTH* OLD ENOUGH TO KNOW BETTER BY NOW, AFTER ALL.
YEAH. HE MAY *SAY* HE DOESN'T CARE ABOUT WHOSE UNDERWEAR IS MIXED IN WITH HIS...
URK...
I DON'T *THINK* THAT KAZAMA-SAN IS THE SORT TO DO ANYTHING UNSEEMLY WITH HIS YOUNGER SISTER'S UNDERWEAR, BUT...
HUH?!
WHA?! NO WAY KAZAMA WOULD EVER DO *ANYTHING* LIKE THAT!!
I WOULDN'T BE SURPRISED IF HE WAS CONCERNED ABOUT HIS SISTER'S HEALTH AND GROWTH.
YEAH. I CAN SEE HOW IT'D BE HARD FOR A BROTHER TO VOICE CONCERNS ABOUT THAT...
WELL...
URK...!

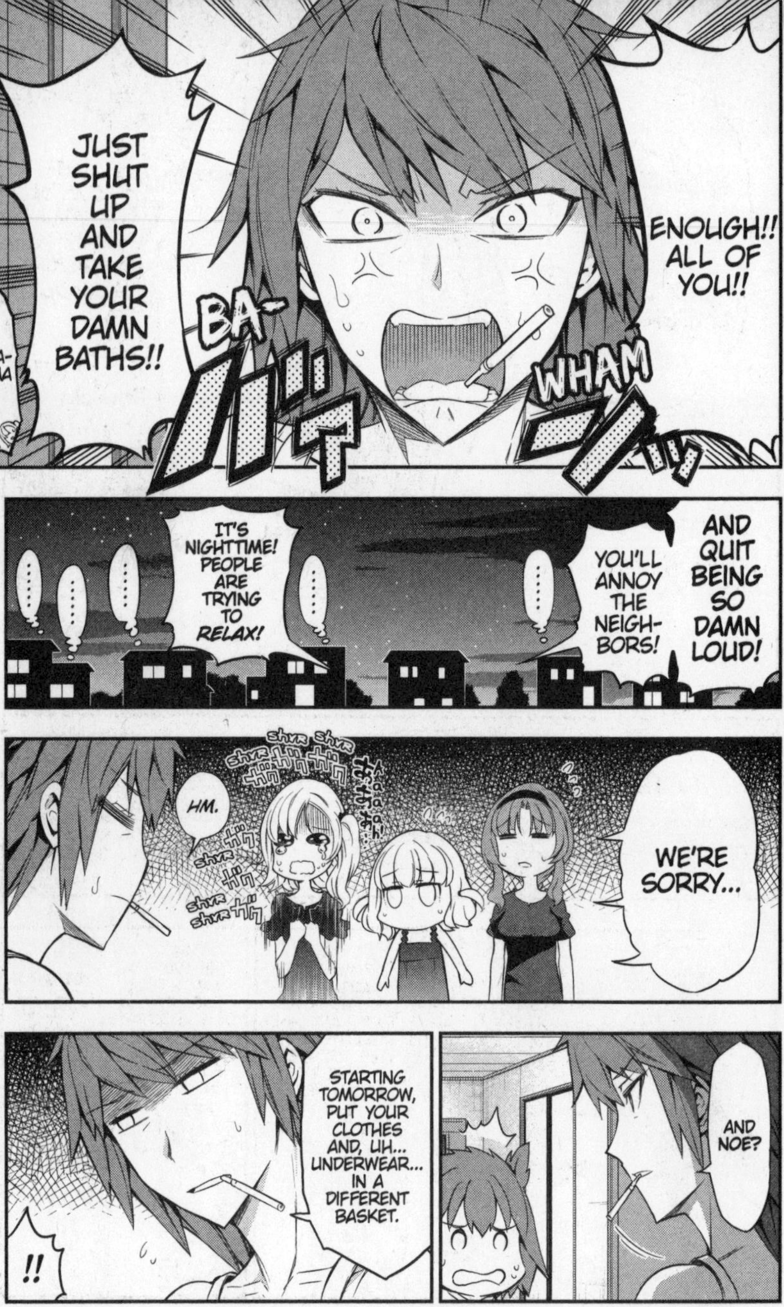
ENOUGH!! ALL OF YOU!!
WHAM
BA-
JUST SHUT UP AND TAKE YOUR DAMN BATHS!!
KAZA-MAMA!
AND QUIT BEING SO DAMN LOUD!
YOU'LL ANNOY THE NEIGH-BORS!
......
IT'S NIGHTTIME! PEOPLE ARE TRYING TO RELAX!
......
......
......
......
WE'RE SORRY...
shvr shvr
shvr
HM.
shvr
shvr shvr
AND NOE?
STARTING TOMORROW, PUT YOUR CLOTHES AND, UH... UNDERWEAR... IN A DIFFERENT BASKET.
!!

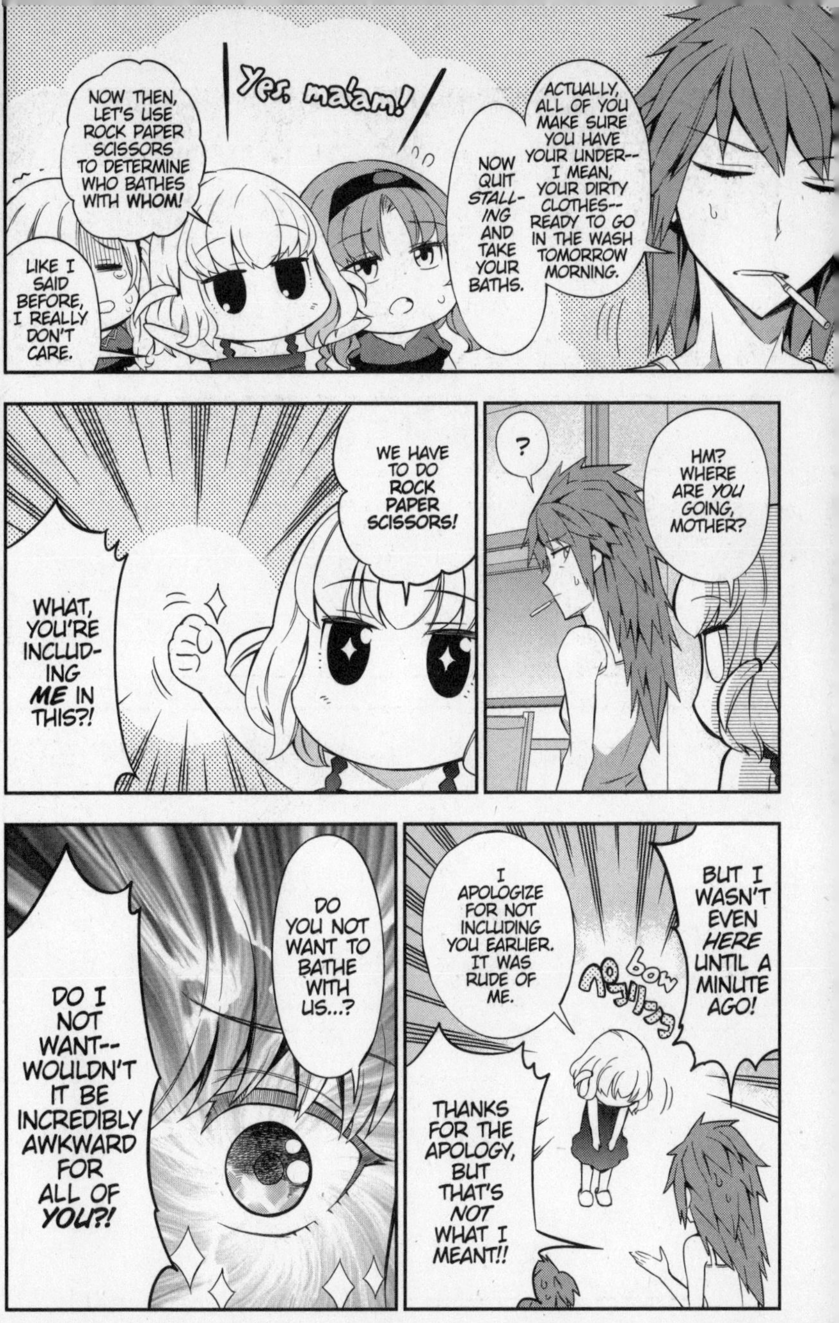
ACTUALLY, ALL OF YOU MAKE SURE YOU HAVE YOUR UNDER-- I MEAN, YOUR DIRTY CLOTHES-- READY TO GO IN THE WASH TOMORROW MORNING.
NOW QUIT STALLING AND TAKE YOUR BATHS.
Yes, ma'am!
NOW THEN, LET'S USE ROCK PAPER SCISSORS TO DETERMINE WHO BATHES WITH WHOM!
LIKE I SAID BEFORE, I REALLY DON'T CARE.
HM? WHERE ARE YOU GOING, MOTHER?
?
WE HAVE TO DO ROCK PAPER SCISSORS!
WHAT, YOU'RE INCLUDING ME IN THIS?!
BUT I WASN'T EVEN HERE UNTIL A MINUTE AGO!
I APOLOGIZE FOR NOT INCLUDING YOU EARLIER. IT WAS RUDE OF ME.
bow
THANKS FOR THE APOLOGY, BUT THAT'S NOT WHAT I MEANT!!
DO YOU NOT WANT TO BATHE WITH US...?
DO I NOT WANT-- WOULDN'T IT BE INCREDIBLY AWKWARD FOR ALL OF YOU?!

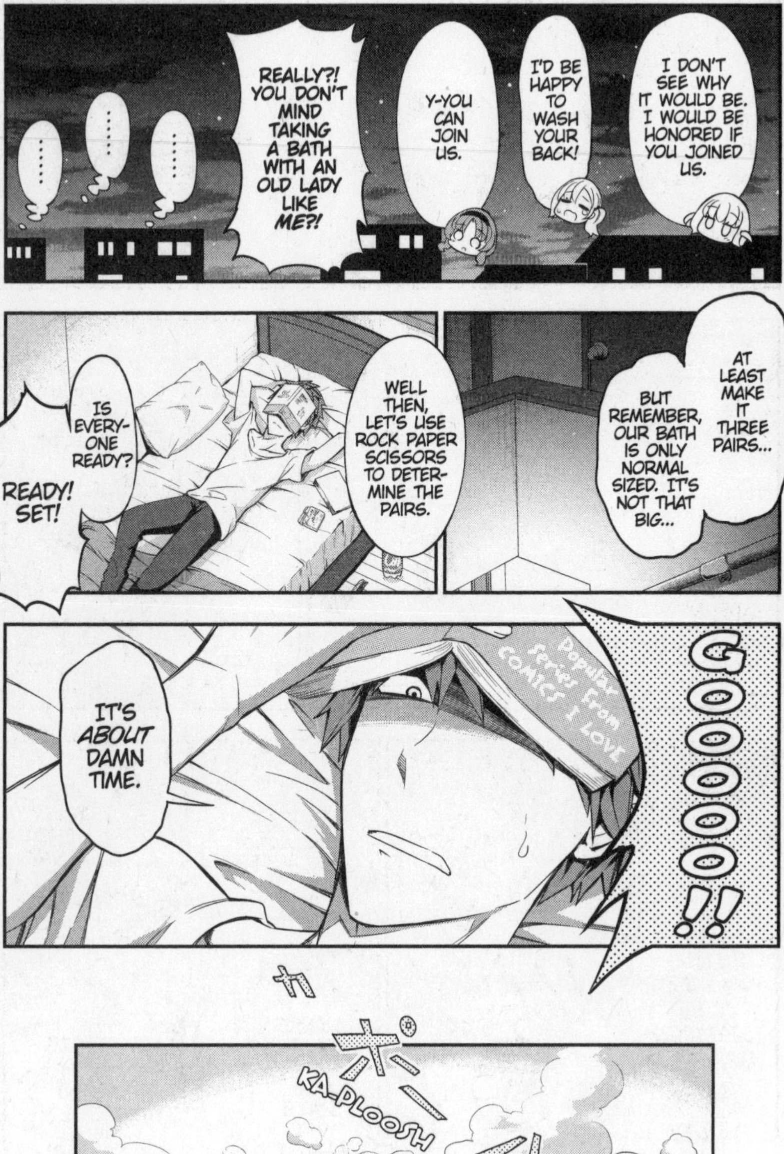
I DON'T SEE WHY IT WOULD BE. I WOULD BE HONORED IF YOU JOINED US.
I'D BE HAPPY TO WASH YOUR BACK!
Y-YOU CAN JOIN US.
REALLY?! YOU DON'T MIND TAKING A BATH WITH AN OLD LADY LIKE ME?!
......
......
......
AT LEAST MAKE IT THREE PAIRS...
BUT REMEMBER, OUR BATH IS ONLY NORMAL SIZED. IT'S NOT THAT BIG...
WELL THEN, LET'S USE ROCK PAPER SCISSORS TO DETERMINE THE PAIRS.
IS EVERYONE READY?
READY! SET!
GOOOOOO!!
Popular series from COMICS I LOVE
IT'S ABOUT DAMN TIME.
KA-PLOOSH

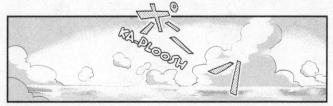

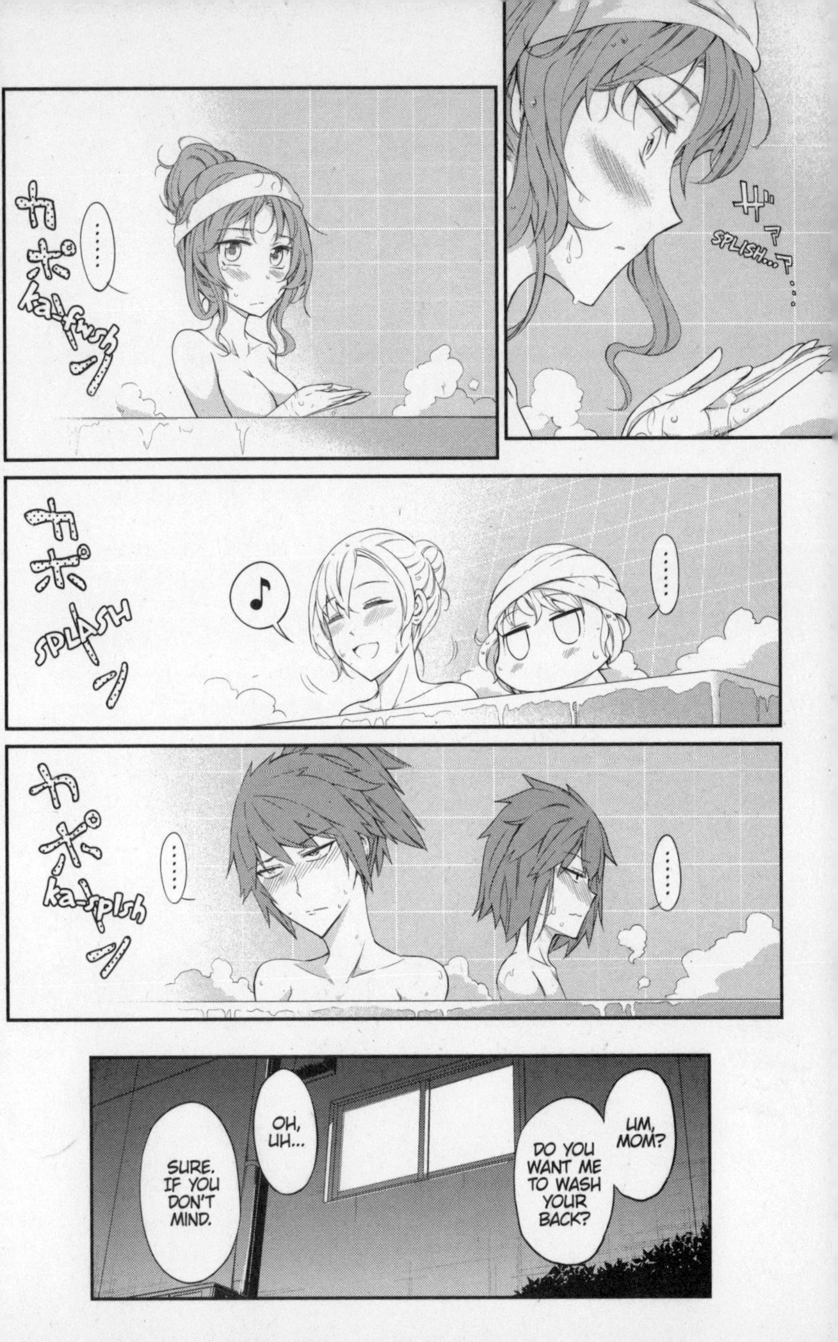
ザァ
SPLISH...
......
カポッ
ka-fwsh
♪
......
カポッ
SPLASH
......
......
カポッ
ka-splish
UM, MOM?
DO YOU WANT ME TO WASH YOUR BACK?
OH, UH...
SURE. IF YOU DON'T MIND.

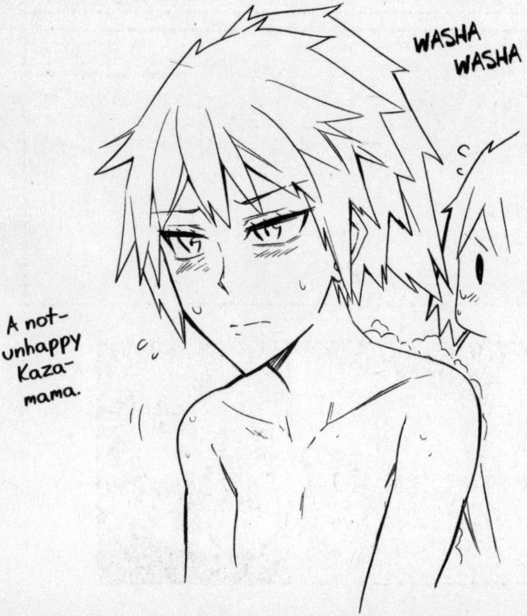
WASHA WASHA
A not-unhappy Kaza-mama.

ディーふらぐ!
D-FRAGMENTS

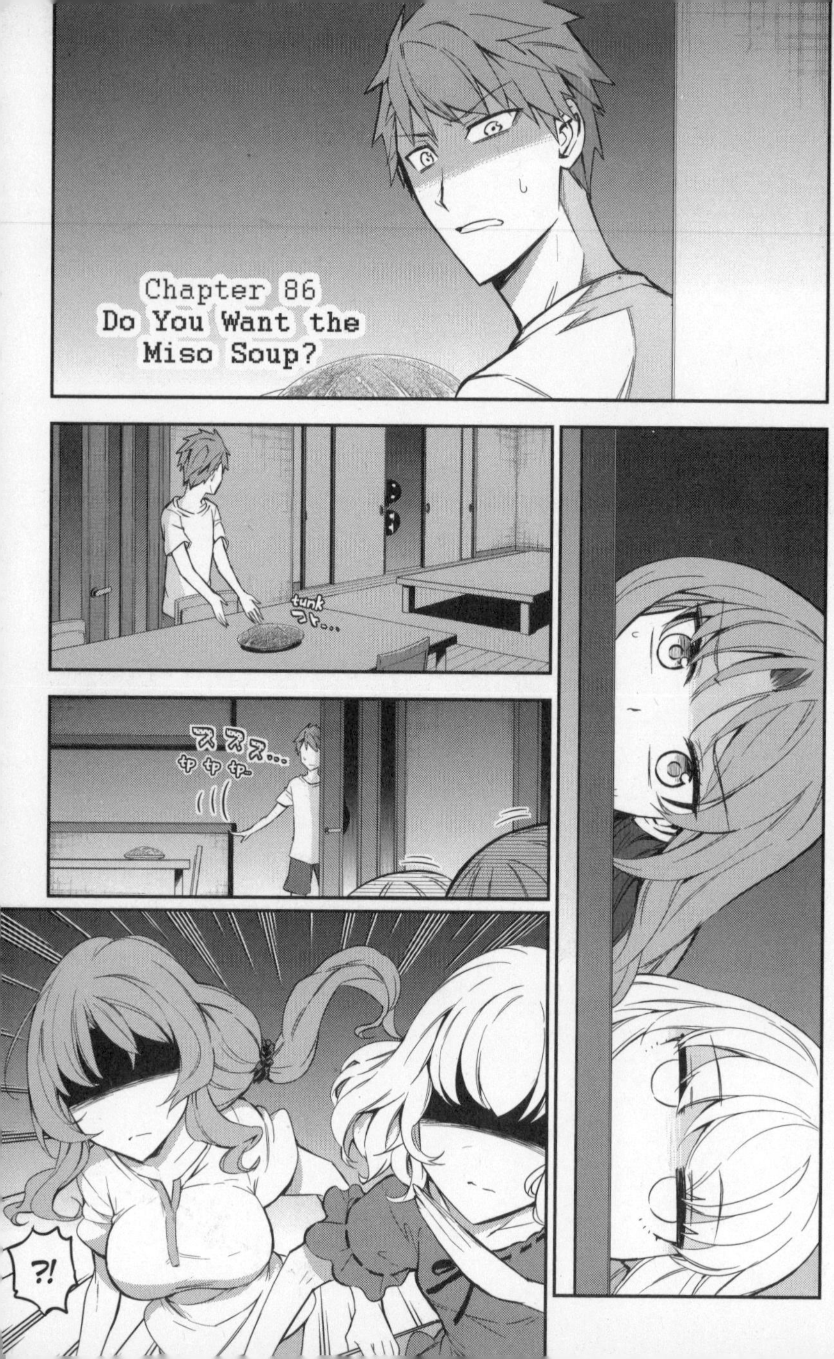
Chapter 86
Do You Want the Miso Soup?
tunk
つト…
ススス…
tp tp tp
?!

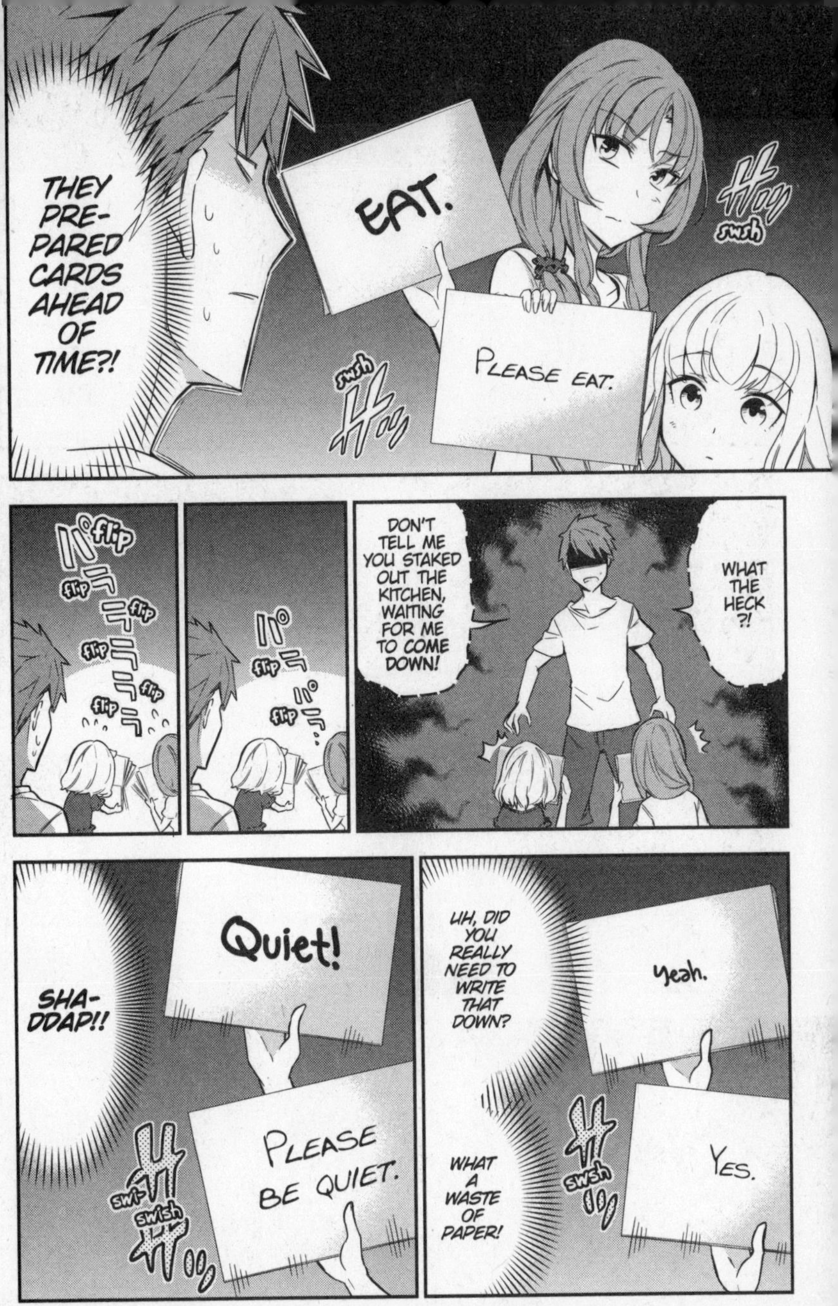
swsh
EAT.
THEY PRE-PARED CARDS AHEAD OF TIME?!
PLEASE EAT.
swsh
WHAT THE HECK?!
DON'T TELL ME YOU STAKED OUT THE KITCHEN, WAITING FOR ME TO COME DOWN!
flip
flip
flip
flip
flip
flip
flip
flip
UH, DID YOU REALLY NEED TO WRITE THAT DOWN?
yeah.
swsh
YES.
WHAT A WASTE OF PAPER!
Quiet!
SHA-DDAP!!
PLEASE BE QUIET.
swi-swish

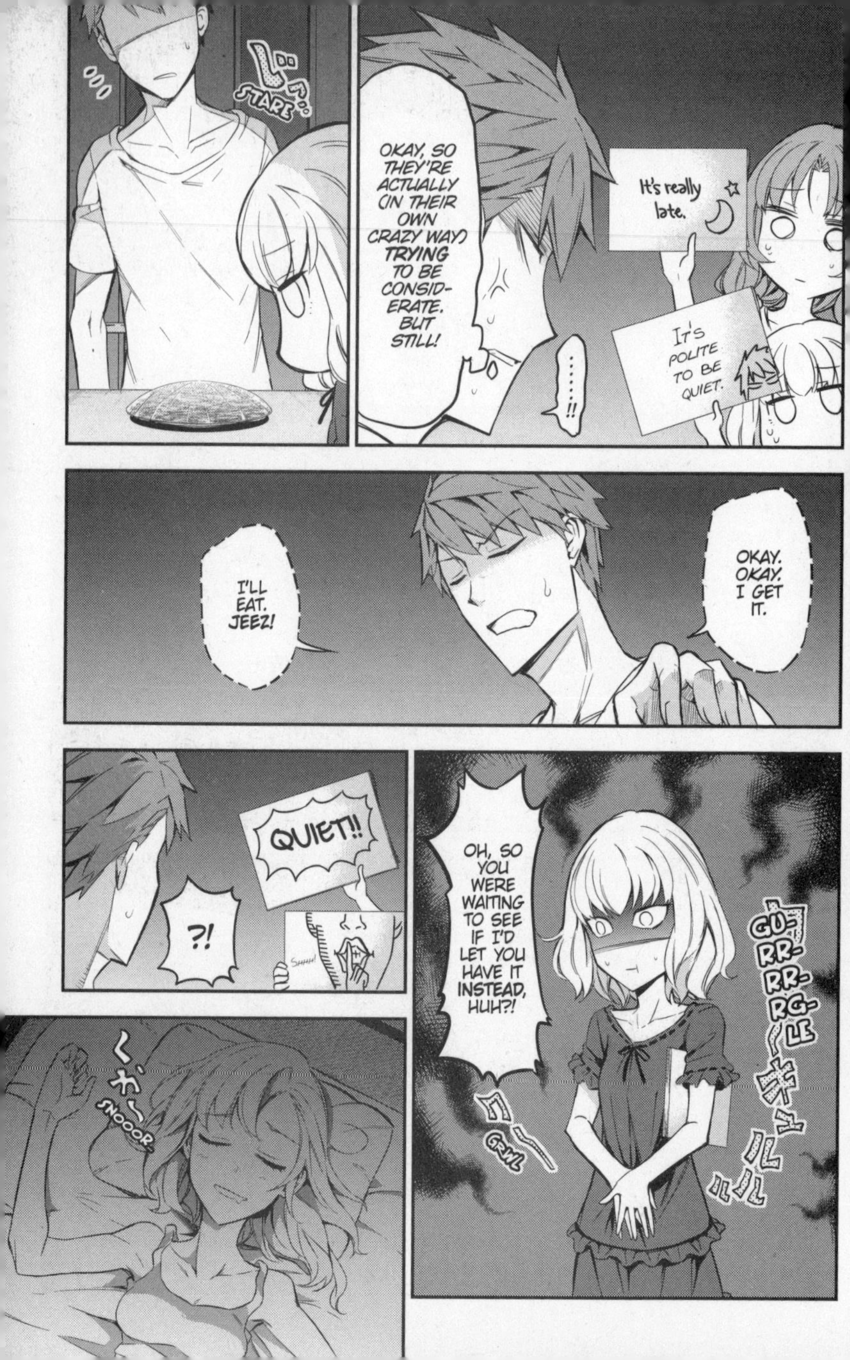
It's really late.
It's polite to be quiet.
......!!
OKAY, SO THEY'RE ACTUALLY (IN THEIR OWN CRAZY WAY) TRYING TO BE CONSIDERATE. BUT STILL!
STARE
OKAY. OKAY. I GET IT.
I'LL EAT. JEEZ!
GU-RR-RR-RG-LE
OH, SO YOU WERE WAITING TO SEE IF I'D LET YOU HAVE IT INSTEAD, HUH?!
GRWL
QUIET!!
?!
SHHH!
SNOOOR

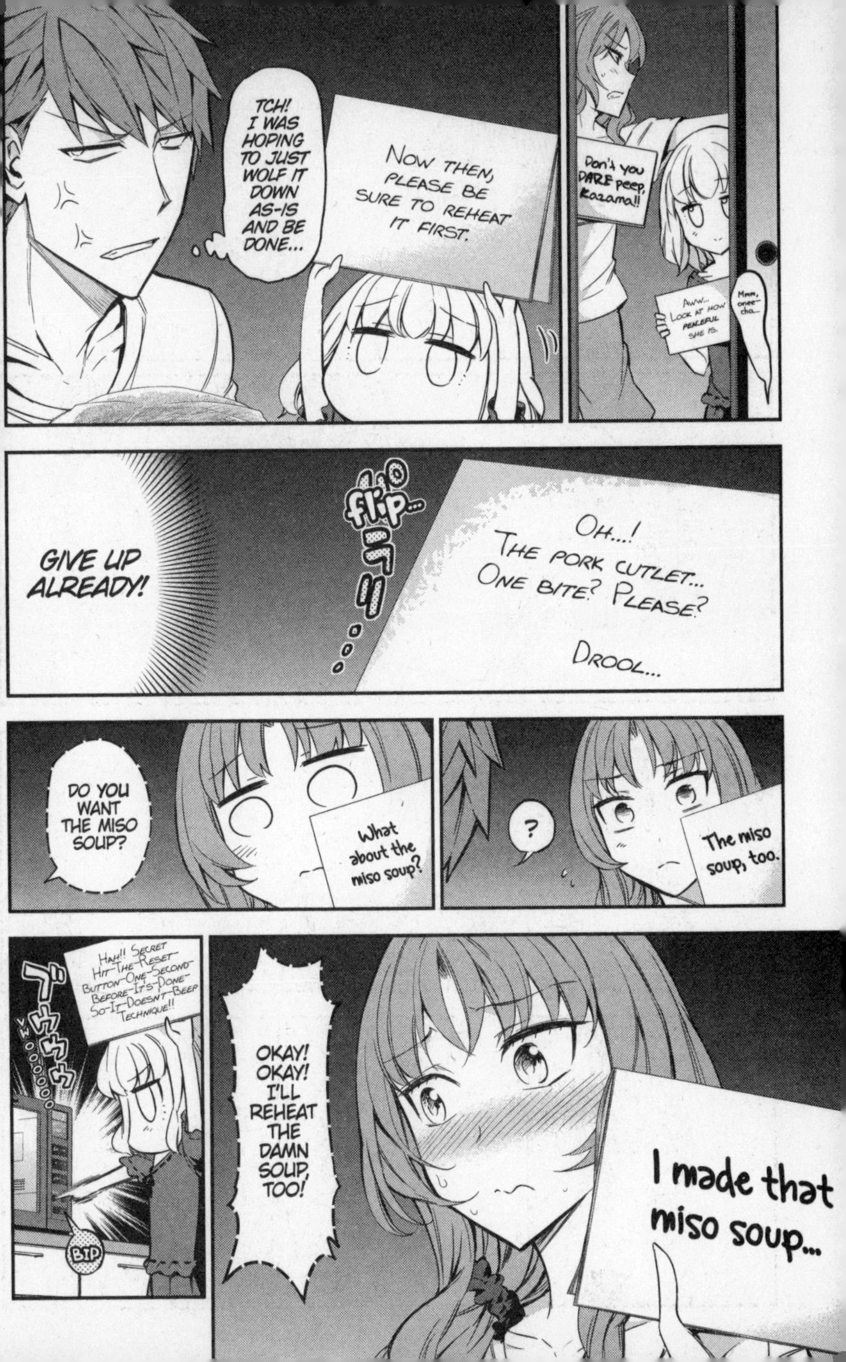
Don't you DARE peep, Kazama!!
Aww... Look at how peaceful she is.
Mmm, onee-cha...
Now then, please be sure to reheat it first.
Tch! I was hoping to just wolf it down as-is and be done...
Oh...! The pork cutlet... One bite? Please?
Drool...
flip...
Give up already!
?
The miso soup, too.
What about the miso soup?
Do you want the miso soup?
I made that miso soup...
Okay! Okay! I'll reheat the damn soup, too!
Hah!! Secret Hit-The-Reset-Button-One-Second-Before-It's-Done-So-It-Doesn't-Beep Technique!!
vwoooooo
BIP

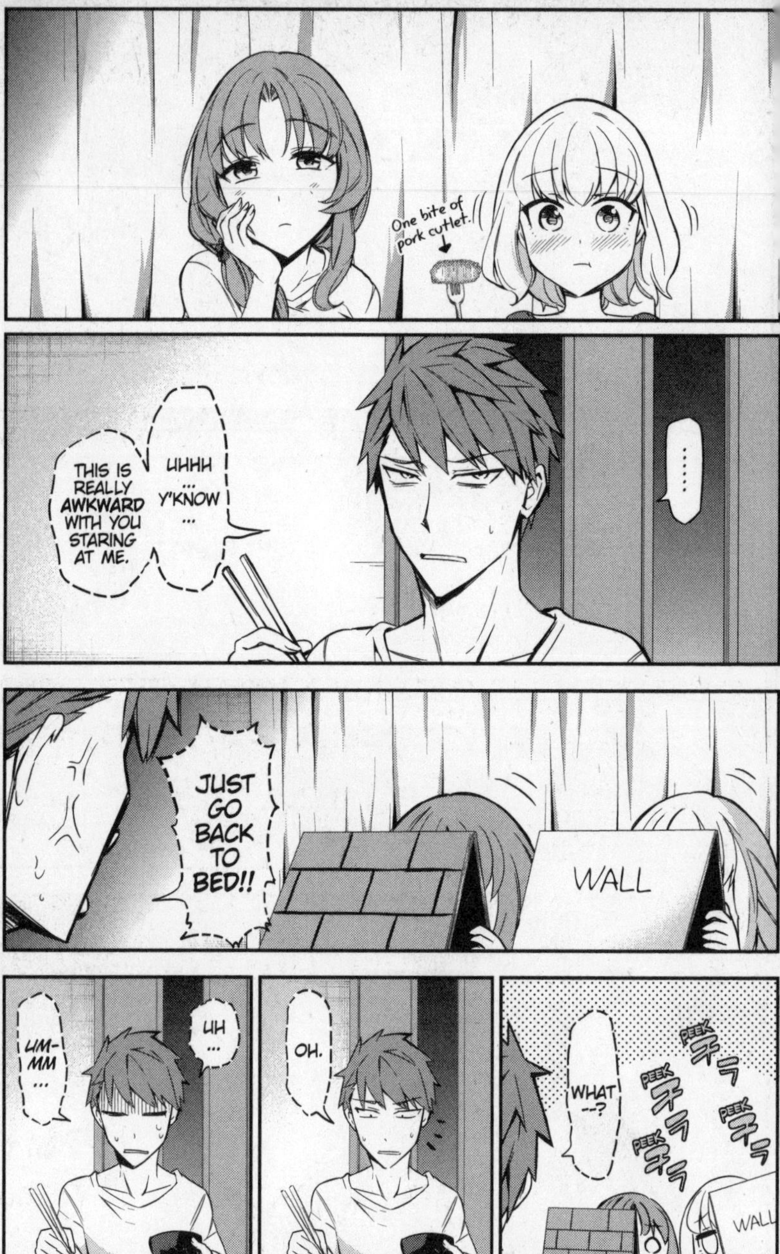
One bite of pork cutlet.
......
UHHH ... Y'KNOW ...
THIS IS REALLY AWKWARD WITH YOU STARING AT ME.
JUST GO BACK TO BED!!
WALL
WHAT--?
PEEK
PEEK
PEEK
PEEK
WALL
OH.
UH ...
UMM-MM ...

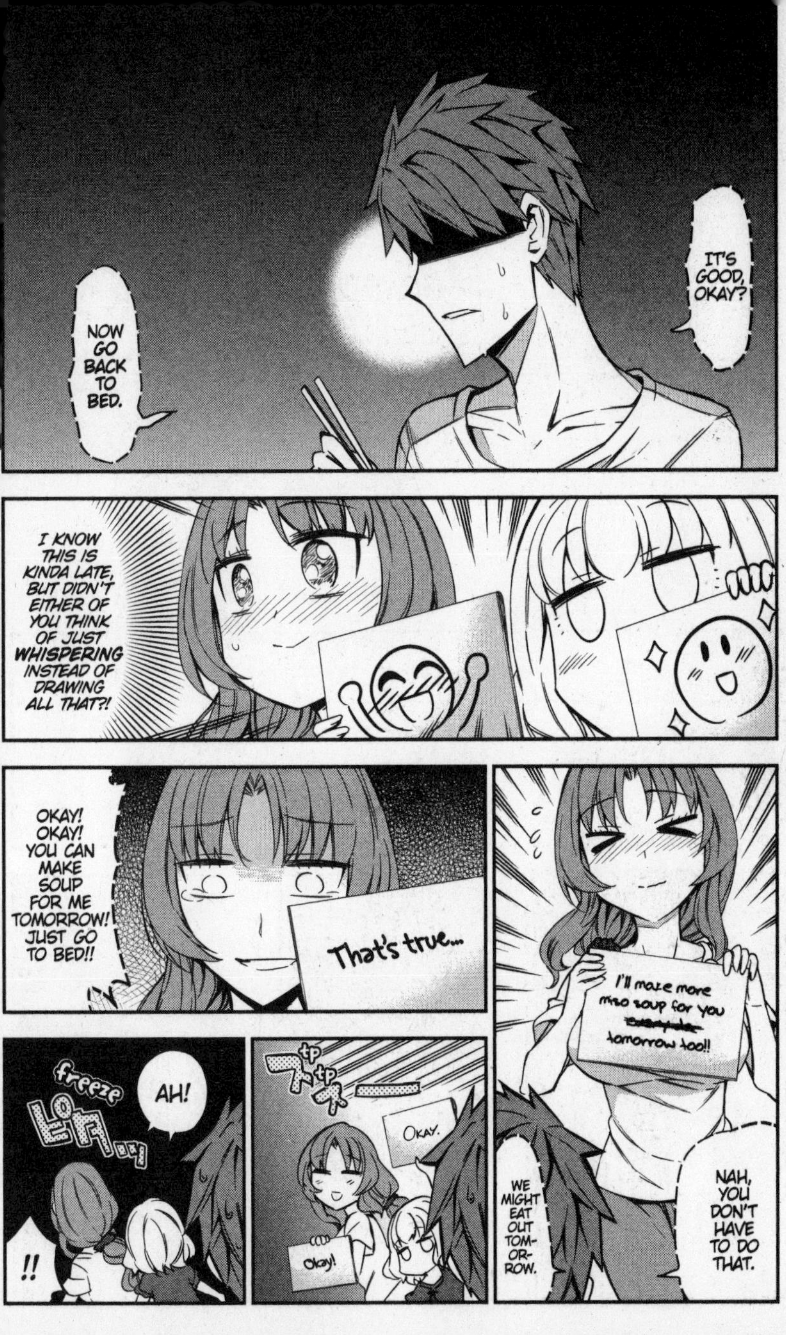
IT'S GOOD, OKAY?
NOW GO BACK TO BED.
I KNOW THIS IS KINDA LATE, BUT DIDN'T EITHER OF YOU THINK OF JUST WHISPERING INSTEAD OF DRAWING ALL THAT?!
I'll make more miso soup for you tomorrow too!!
NAH, YOU DON'T HAVE TO DO THAT.
WE MIGHT EAT OUT TOM-OR-ROW.
That's true...
OKAY! OKAY! YOU CAN MAKE SOUP FOR ME TOMORROW! JUST GO TO BED!!
tp tp
Okay.
Okay!
freeze
AH!
!!

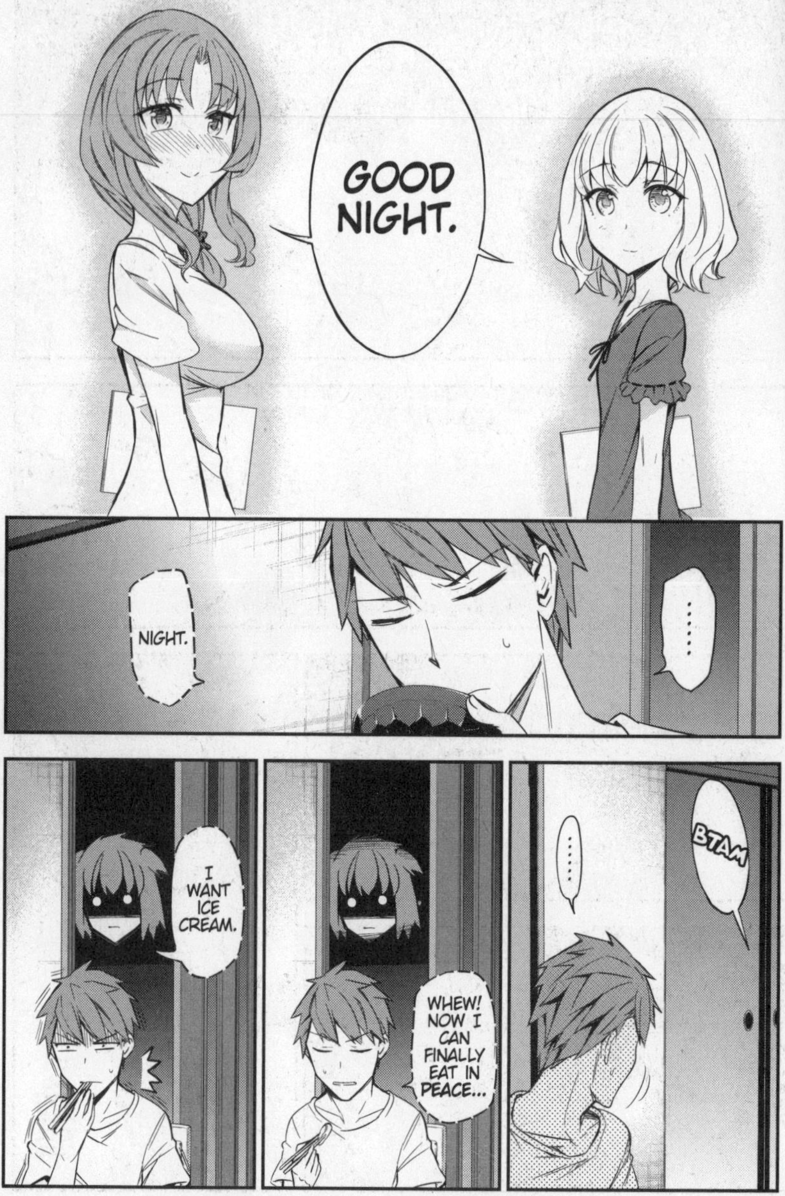
GOOD NIGHT.
......
NIGHT.
BTAM
......
WHEW! NOW I CAN FINALLY EAT IN PEACE...
I WANT ICE CREAM.

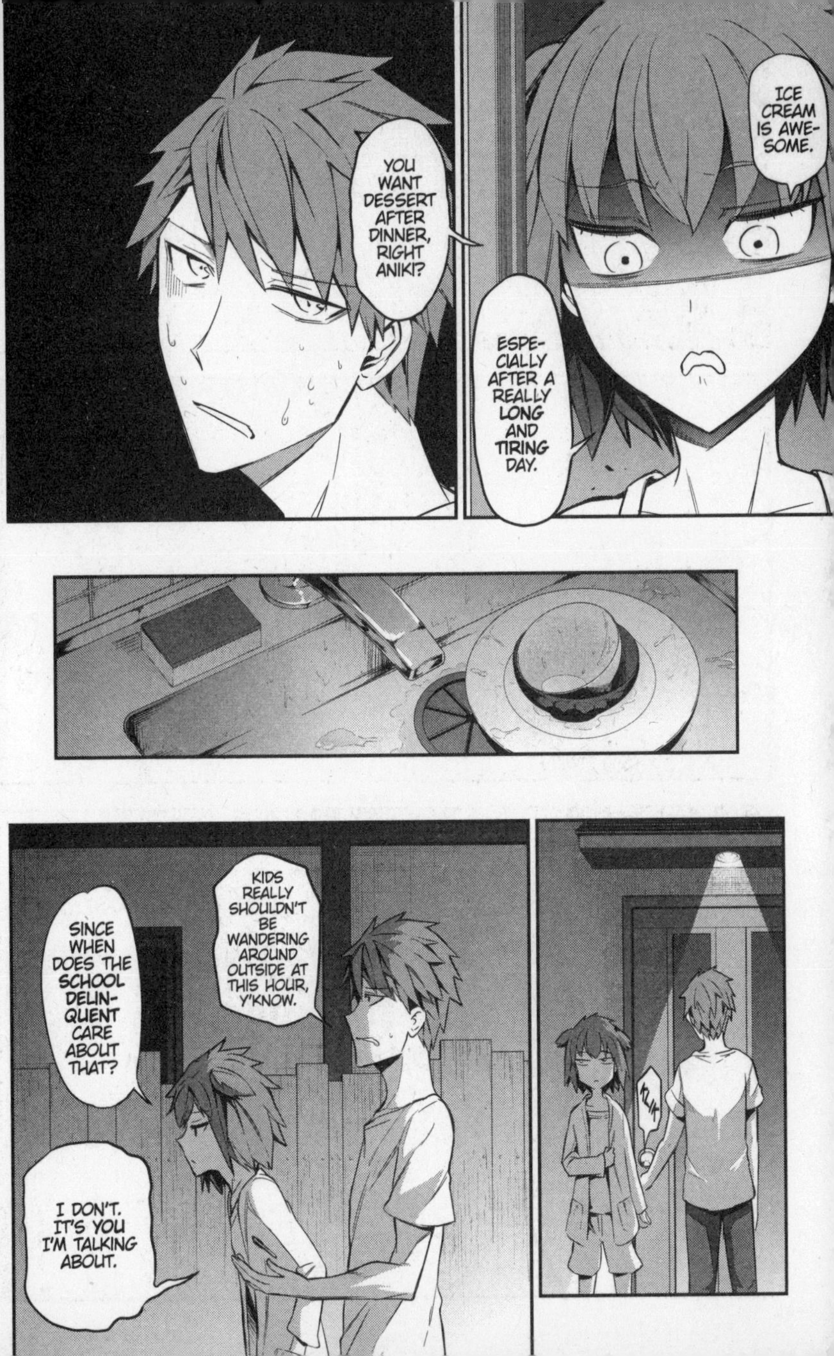
ICE CREAM IS AWESOME.
ESPECIALLY AFTER A REALLY LONG AND TIRING DAY.
YOU WANT DESSERT AFTER DINNER, RIGHT ANIKI?
KLIK
KIDS REALLY SHOULDN'T BE WANDERING AROUND OUTSIDE AT THIS HOUR, Y'KNOW.
SINCE WHEN DOES THE SCHOOL DELINQUENT CARE ABOUT THAT?
I DON'T. IT'S YOU I'M TALKING ABOUT.

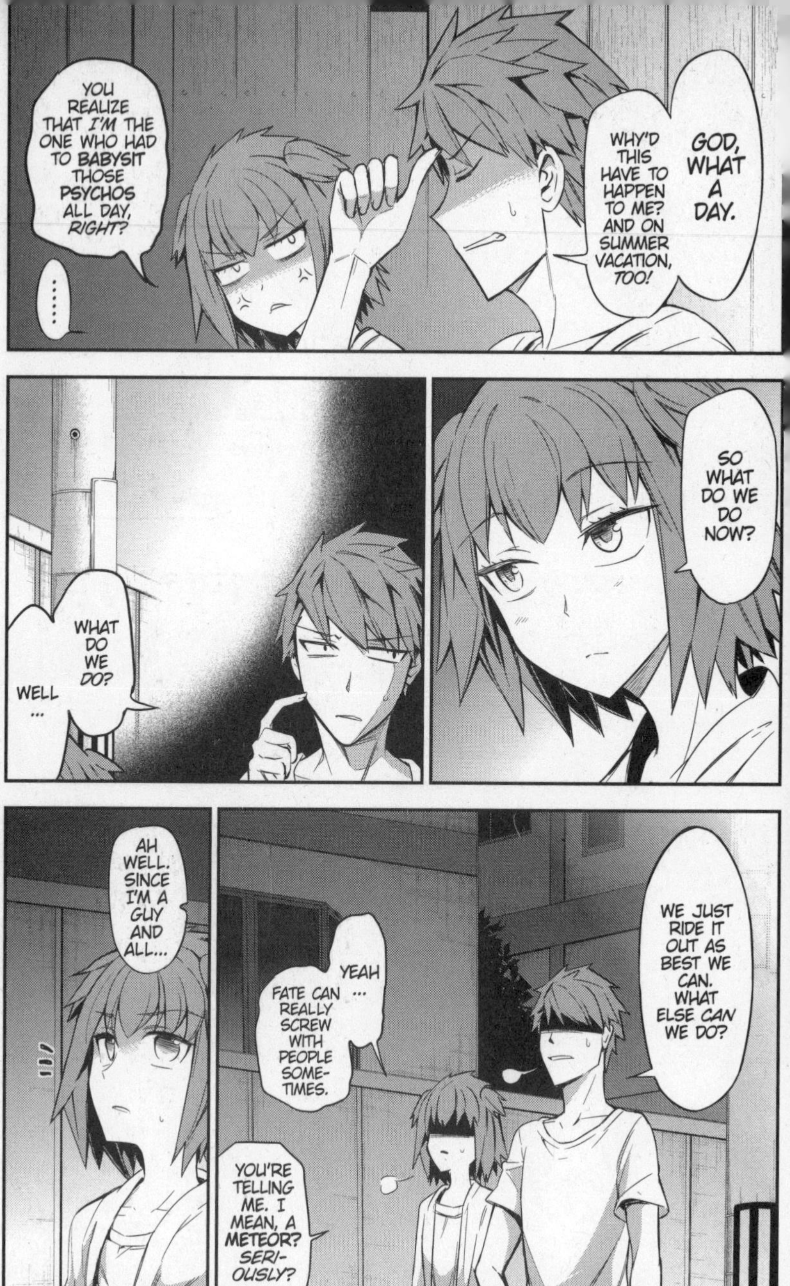
GOD, WHAT A DAY.
WHY'D THIS HAVE TO HAPPEN TO ME? AND ON SUMMER VACATION, *TOO!*
YOU REALIZE THAT *I'M* THE ONE WHO HAD TO **BABYSIT** THOSE **PSYCHOS** ALL DAY, *RIGHT?*
......
SO WHAT DO WE DO NOW?
WHAT DO WE *DO?*
WELL...
WE JUST RIDE IT OUT AS BEST WE CAN. WHAT ELSE *CAN* WE DO?
YEAH... FATE CAN REALLY SCREW WITH PEOPLE SOMETIMES.
YOU'RE TELLING ME. I MEAN, A **METEOR?** *SERIOUSLY?*
AH WELL. SINCE I'M A GUY AND ALL...

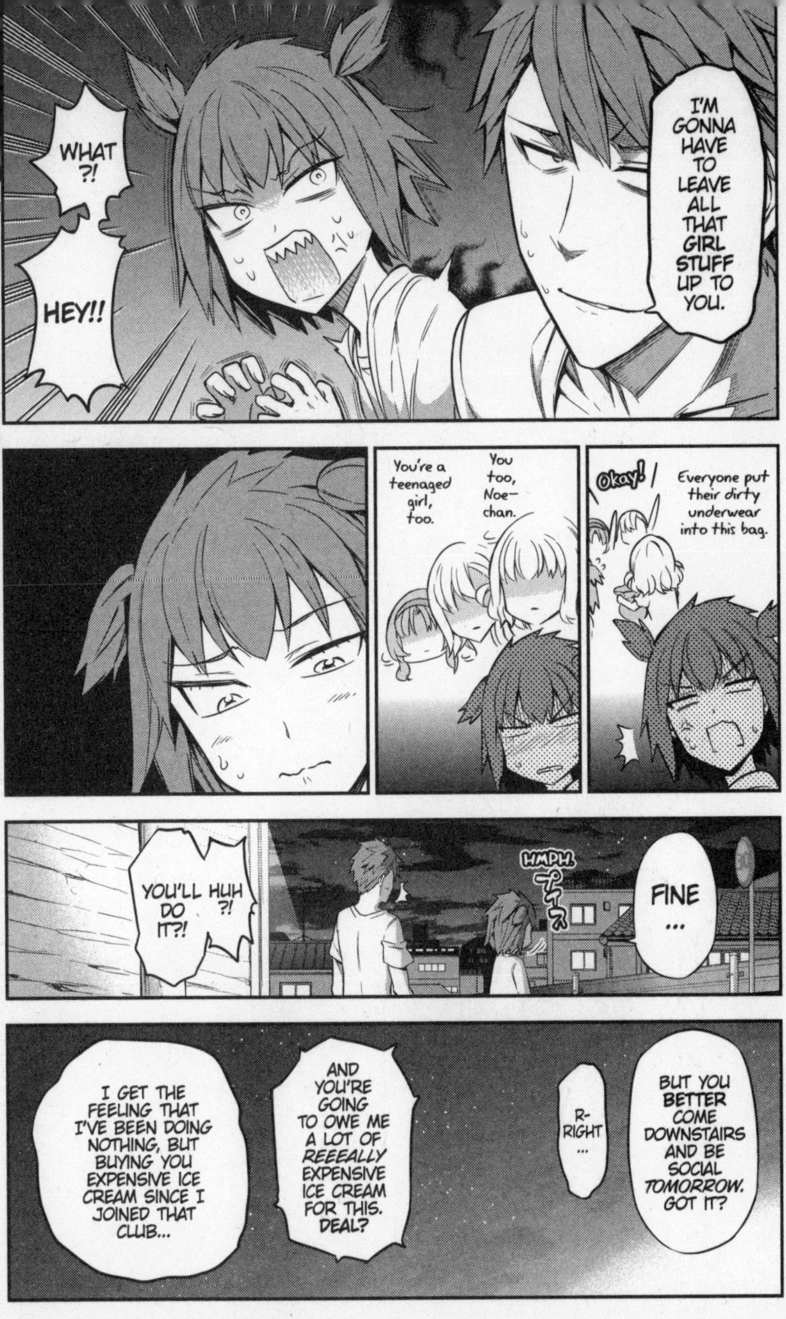

I'M GONNA HAVE TO LEAVE ALL THAT GIRL STUFF UP TO YOU.
WHAT?!
HEY!!
Everyone put their dirty underwear into this bag.
Okay!
You too, Noe-chan.
You're a teenaged girl, too.
FINE ...
HMPH.
HUH ?!
YOU'LL DO IT?!
BUT YOU BETTER COME DOWNSTAIRS AND BE SOCIAL *TOMORROW*. GOT IT?
R-RIGHT ...
AND YOU'RE GOING TO OWE ME A LOT OF *REEEALLY* EXPENSIVE ICE CREAM FOR THIS. DEAL?
I GET THE FEELING THAT I'VE BEEN DOING NOTHING, BUT BUYING YOU EXPENSIVE ICE CREAM SINCE I JOINED THAT CLUB...

D-FRAGMENTS
ディーふらぐ！

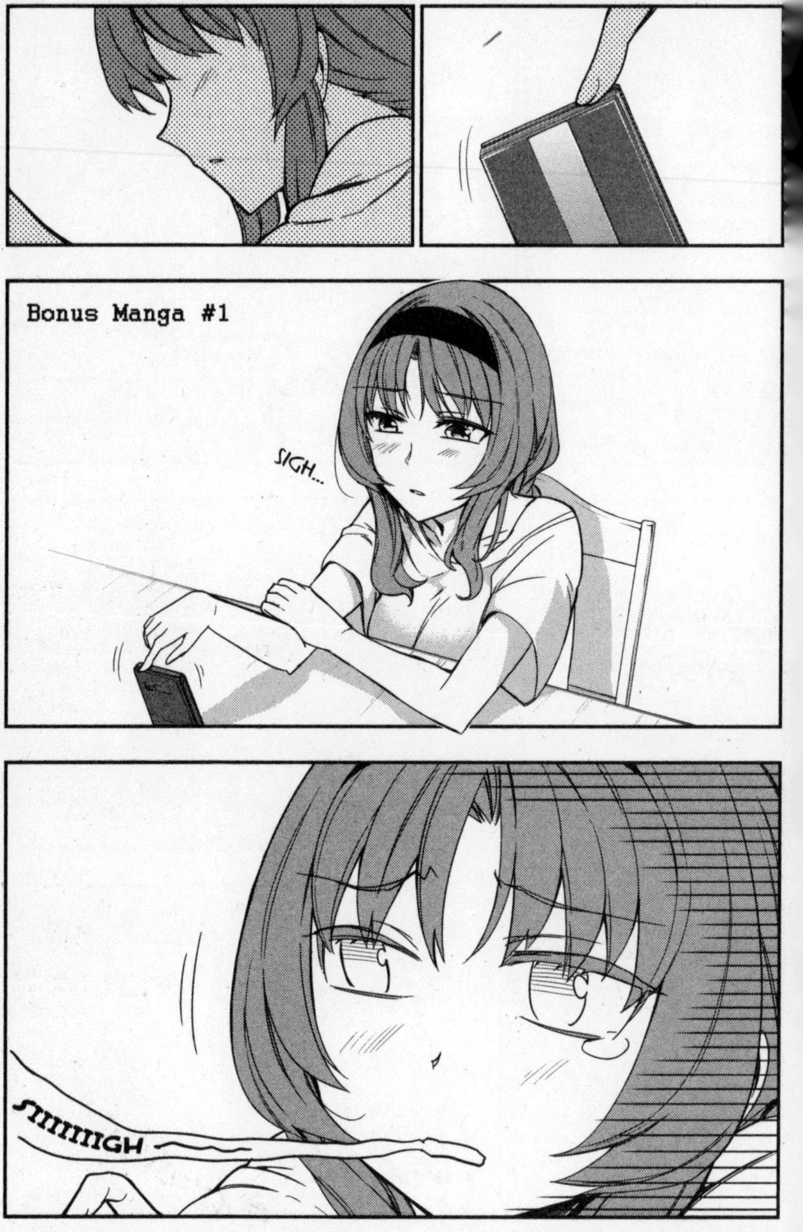
Bonus Manga #1
SIGH...
SIIIIIIGH

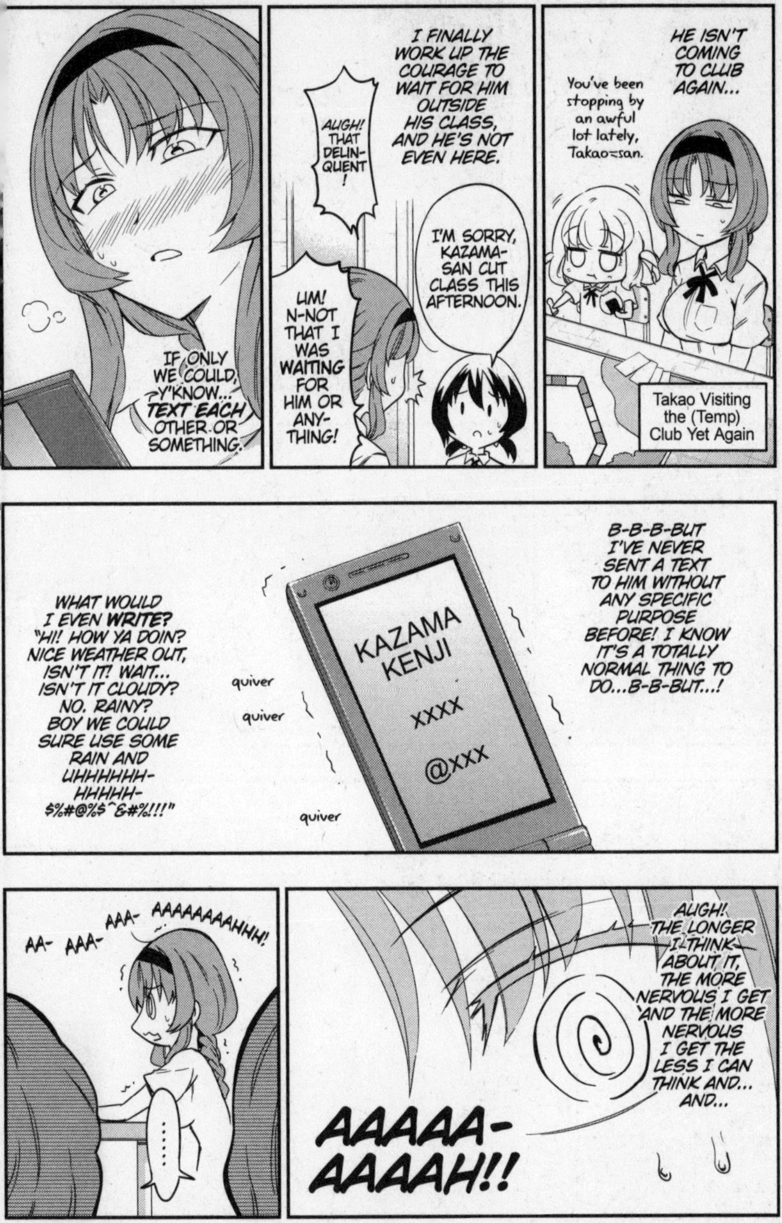
HE ISN'T COMING TO CLUB AGAIN...
You've been stopping by an awful lot lately, Takao=san.
Takao Visiting the (Temp) Club Yet Again
I FINALLY WORK UP THE COURAGE TO WAIT FOR HIM OUTSIDE HIS CLASS, AND HE'S NOT EVEN HERE.
AUGH! THAT DELIN-QUENT!
I'M SORRY, KAZAMA-SAN CUT CLASS THIS AFTERNOON.
UM! N-NOT THAT I WAS WAITING FOR HIM OR ANY-THING!
IF ONLY WE COULD, Y'KNOW... TEXT EACH OTHER OR SOMETHING.
B-B-B-BUT I'VE NEVER SENT A TEXT TO HIM WITHOUT ANY SPECIFIC PURPOSE BEFORE! I KNOW IT'S A TOTALLY NORMAL THING TO DO...B-B-BUT...!
KAZAMA KENJI
XXXX
@XXX
quiver
quiver
quiver
WHAT WOULD I EVEN WRITE? "HI! HOW YA DOIN? NICE WEATHER OUT, ISN'T IT! WAIT... ISN'T IT CLOUDY? NO. RAINY? BOY WE COULD SURE USE SOME RAIN AND UHHHHHH-HHHHH-$%#@%$^&#%!!!"
AUGH! THE LONGER I THINK ABOUT IT, THE MORE NERVOUS I GET AND THE MORE NERVOUS I GET THE LESS I CAN THINK AND... AND...
AAAAA-AAAAAH!!
AA- AAA- AAA- AAAAAAAAHHH!
......

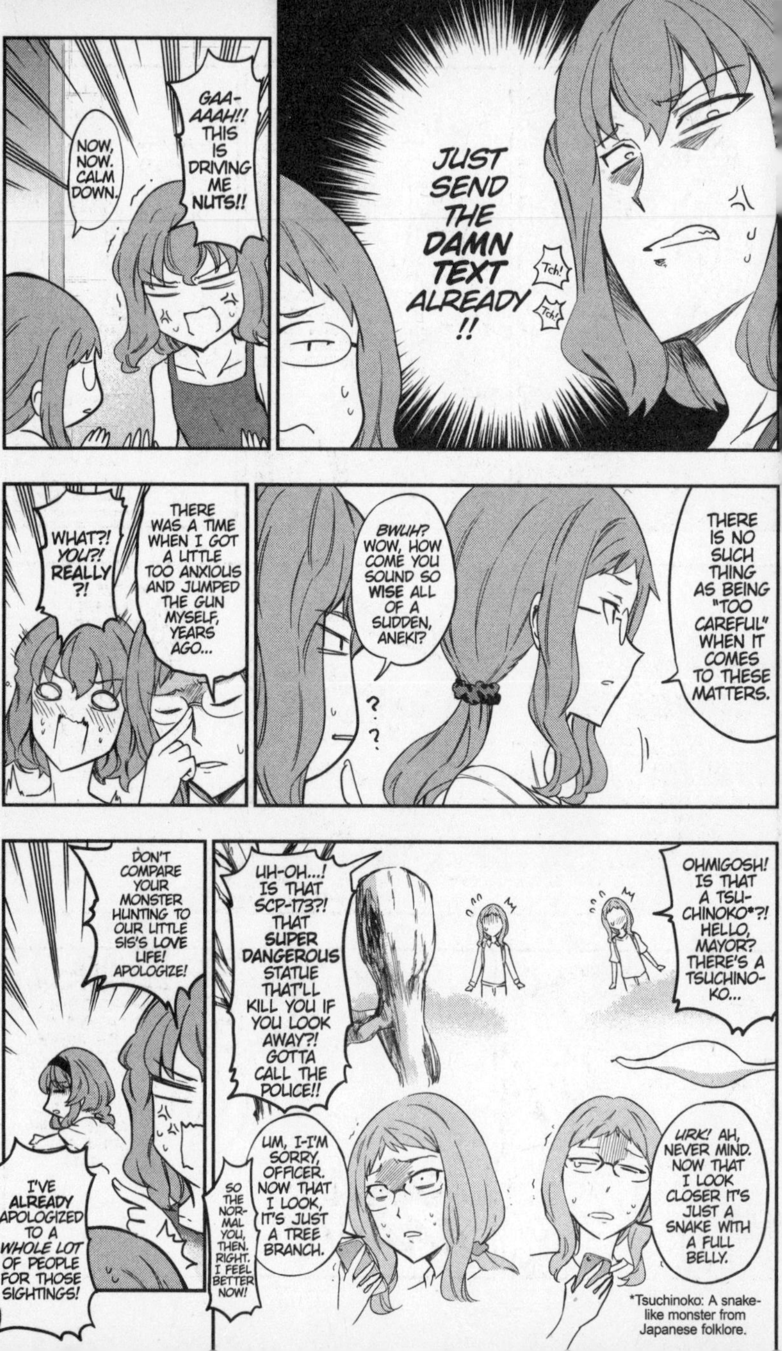

JUST SEND THE DAMN TEXT ALREADY!!
Tch!
Tch!
GAA-AAAH!! THIS IS DRIVING ME NUTS!!
NOW, NOW. CALM DOWN.
THERE IS NO SUCH THING AS BEING "TOO CAREFUL" WHEN IT COMES TO THESE MATTERS.
BWUH? WOW, HOW COME YOU SOUND SO WISE ALL OF A SUDDEN, ANEKI?
THERE WAS A TIME WHEN I GOT A LITTLE TOO ANXIOUS AND JUMPED THE GUN MYSELF, YEARS AGO...
WHAT?! YOU?! REALLY?!
OHMIGOSH! IS THAT A TSUCHINOKO*?! HELLO, MAYOR? THERE'S A TSUCHINO-KO...
UH-OH...! IS THAT SCP-173?! THAT SUPER DANGEROUS STATUE THAT'LL KILL YOU IF YOU LOOK AWAY?! GOTTA CALL THE POLICE!!
URK! AH, NEVER MIND. NOW THAT I LOOK CLOSER IT'S JUST A SNAKE WITH A FULL BELLY.
UM, I-I'M SORRY, OFFICER. NOW THAT I LOOK, IT'S JUST A TREE BRANCH.
SO THE NOR-MAL YOU, THEN. RIGHT. I FEEL BETTER NOW!
DON'T COMPARE YOUR MONSTER HUNTING TO OUR LITTLE SIS'S LOVE LIFE! APOLOGIZE!
I'VE ALREADY APOLOGIZED TO A WHOLE LOT OF PEOPLE FOR THOSE SIGHTINGS!

*Tsuchinoko: A snake-like monster from Japanese folklore.

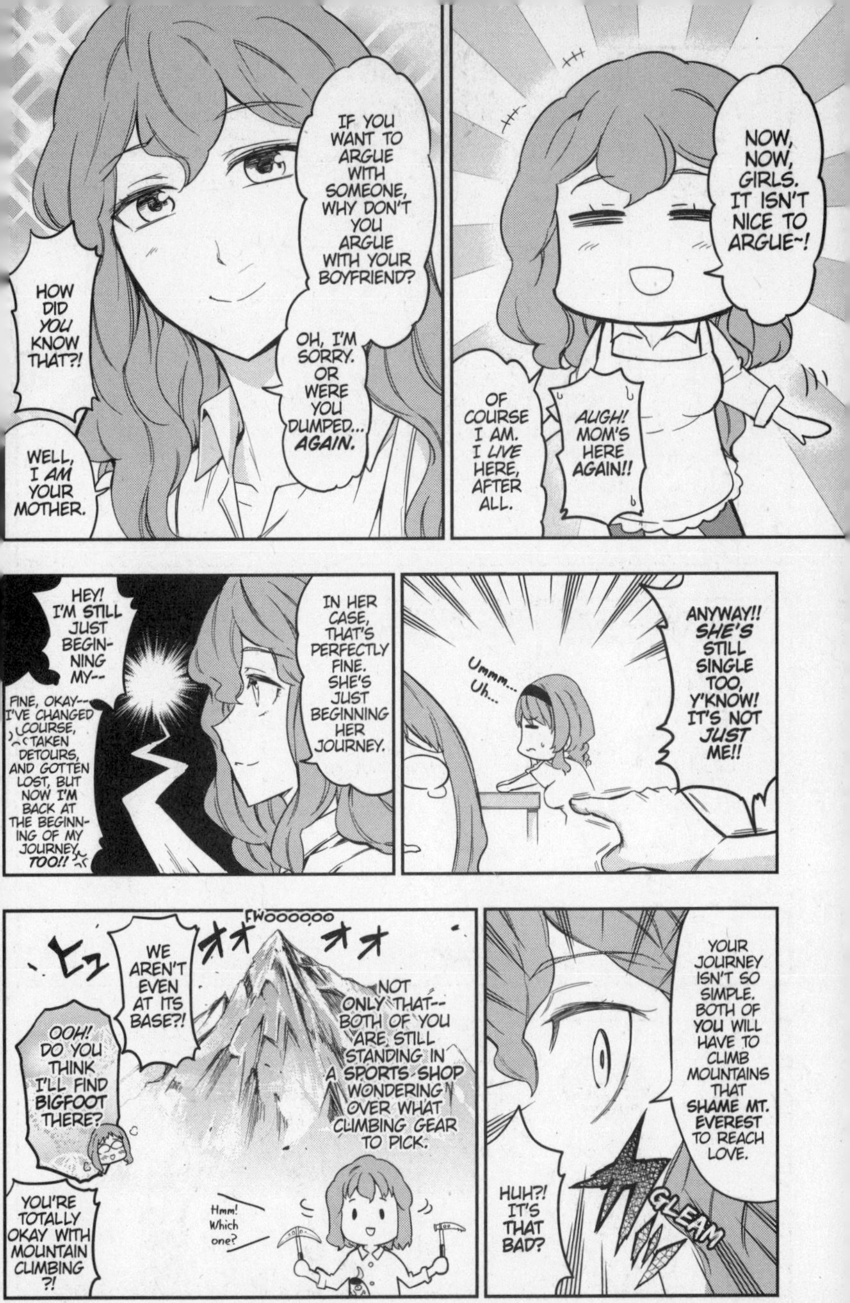
NOW, NOW, GIRLS. IT ISN'T NICE TO ARGUE~!
AUGH! MOM'S HERE AGAIN!!
OF COURSE I AM. I *LIVE* HERE, AFTER ALL.
IF YOU WANT TO ARGUE WITH SOMEONE, WHY DON'T YOU ARGUE WITH YOUR BOYFRIEND?
OH, I'M SORRY. OR WERE YOU DUMPED... ***AGAIN.***
HOW DID *YOU* KNOW THAT?!
WELL, I *AM* YOUR MOTHER.
ANYWAY!! ***SHE'S*** STILL SINGLE TOO, Y'KNOW! IT'S NOT ***JUST*** ME!!
Ummm... Uh...
IN HER CASE, THAT'S PERFECTLY FINE. SHE'S JUST BEGINNING HER JOURNEY.
HEY! I'M STILL JUST BEGIN-NING MY--
FINE, OKAY-- I'VE CHANGED COURSE, TAKEN DETOURS, AND GOTTEN LOST, BUT NOW I'M BACK AT THE BEGINN-ING OF MY JOURNEY, ***TOO!!***
YOUR JOURNEY ISN'T SO SIMPLE. BOTH OF YOU WILL HAVE TO CLIMB MOUNTAINS THAT SHAME MT. EVEREST TO REACH LOVE.
GLEAM
HUH?! IT'S THAT BAD?
FWOOOOOOO
WE AREN'T EVEN AT ITS BASE?!
NOT ONLY THAT-- BOTH OF YOU ARE STILL STANDING IN A **SPORTS SHOP** WONDERING OVER WHAT CLIMBING GEAR TO PICK.
OOH! DO YOU THINK I'LL FIND **BIGFOOT** THERE?
Hmm! Which one?
YOU'RE TOTALLY OKAY WITH MOUNTAIN CLIMBING ?!

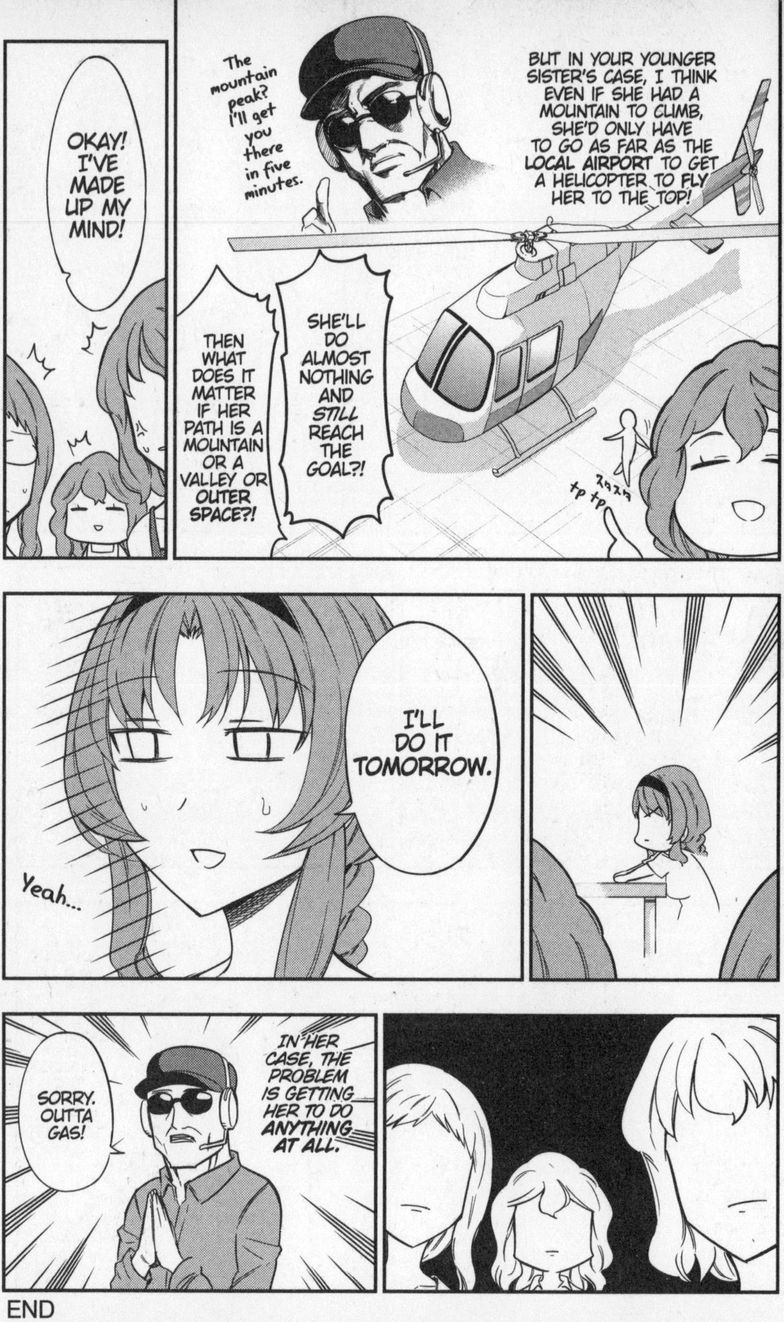
BUT IN YOUR YOUNGER SISTER'S CASE, I THINK EVEN IF SHE HAD A MOUNTAIN TO CLIMB, SHE'D ONLY HAVE TO GO AS FAR AS THE LOCAL AIRPORT TO GET A HELICOPTER TO FLY HER TO THE TOP!
The mountain peak? I'll get you there in five minutes.
SHE'LL DO ALMOST NOTHING AND STILL REACH THE GOAL?!
THEN WHAT DOES IT MATTER IF HER PATH IS A MOUNTAIN OR A VALLEY OR OUTER SPACE?!
スタスタ
tp tp
OKAY! I'VE MADE UP MY MIND!
I'LL DO IT TOMORROW.
Yeah...
IN HER CASE, THE PROBLEM IS GETTING HER TO DO ANYTHING AT ALL.
SORRY. OUTTA GAS!

END

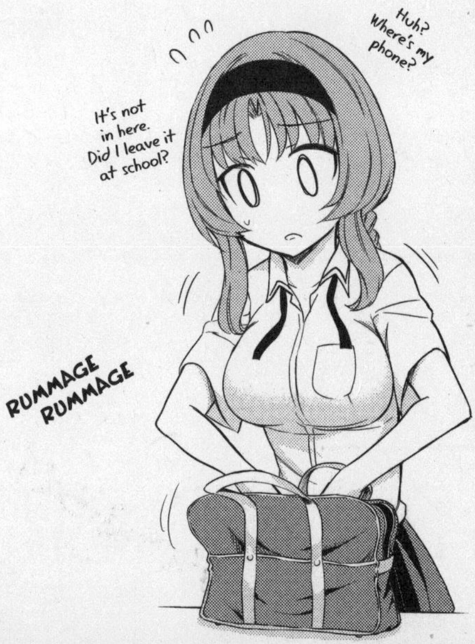
Huh? Where's my phone?
It's not in here. Did I leave it at school?
RUMMAGE RUMMAGE

D-FRAGMENTS

ディーふらぐ！

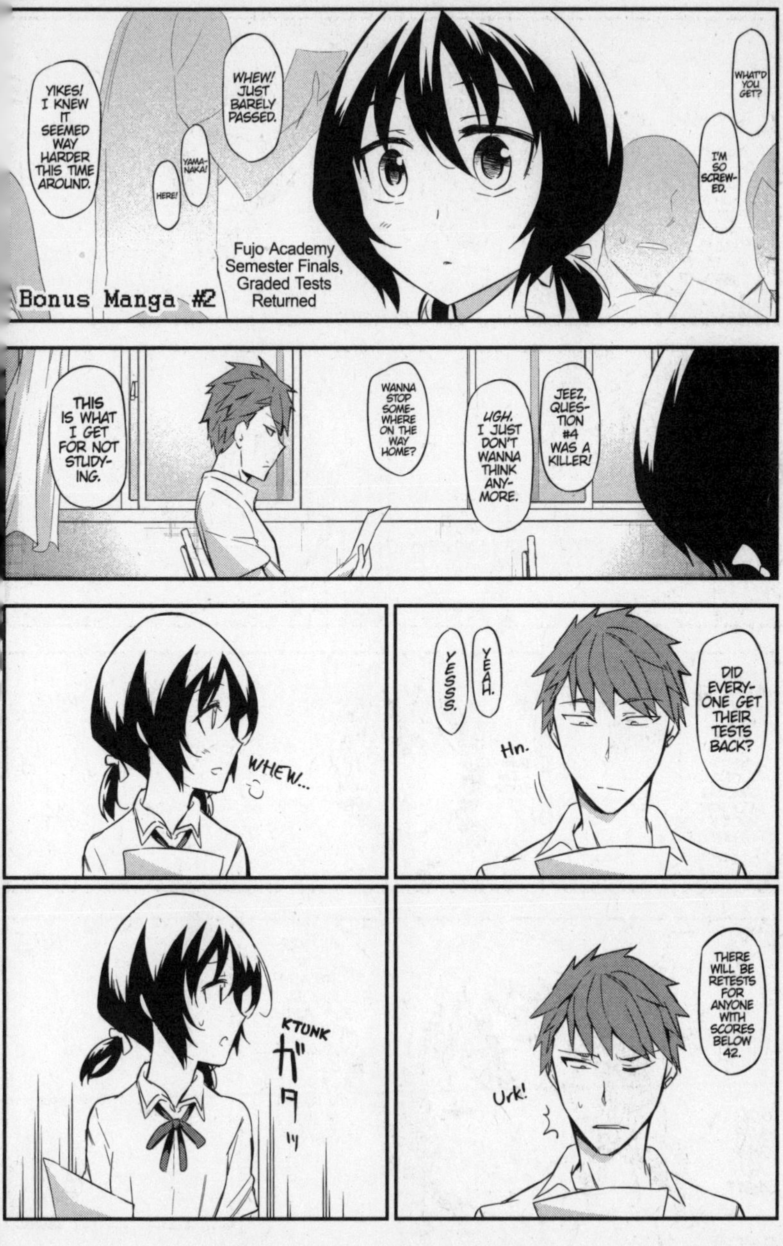
WHAT'D YOU GET?
I'M SO SCREWED.
WHEW! JUST BARELY PASSED.
YAMANAKA!
HERE!
YIKES! I KNEW IT SEEMED WAY HARDER THIS TIME AROUND.
Fujo Academy Semester Finals, Graded Tests Returned
Bonus Manga #2
JEEZ, QUESTION #4 WAS A KILLER!
UGH. I JUST DON'T WANNA THINK ANYMORE.
WANNA STOP SOMEWHERE ON THE WAY HOME?
THIS IS WHAT I GET FOR NOT STUDYING.
DID EVERYONE GET THEIR TESTS BACK?
YEAH.
YESSS.
Hn.
WHEW...
THERE WILL BE RETESTS FOR ANYONE WITH SCORES BELOW 42.
Urk!
KTUNK
ガタッ

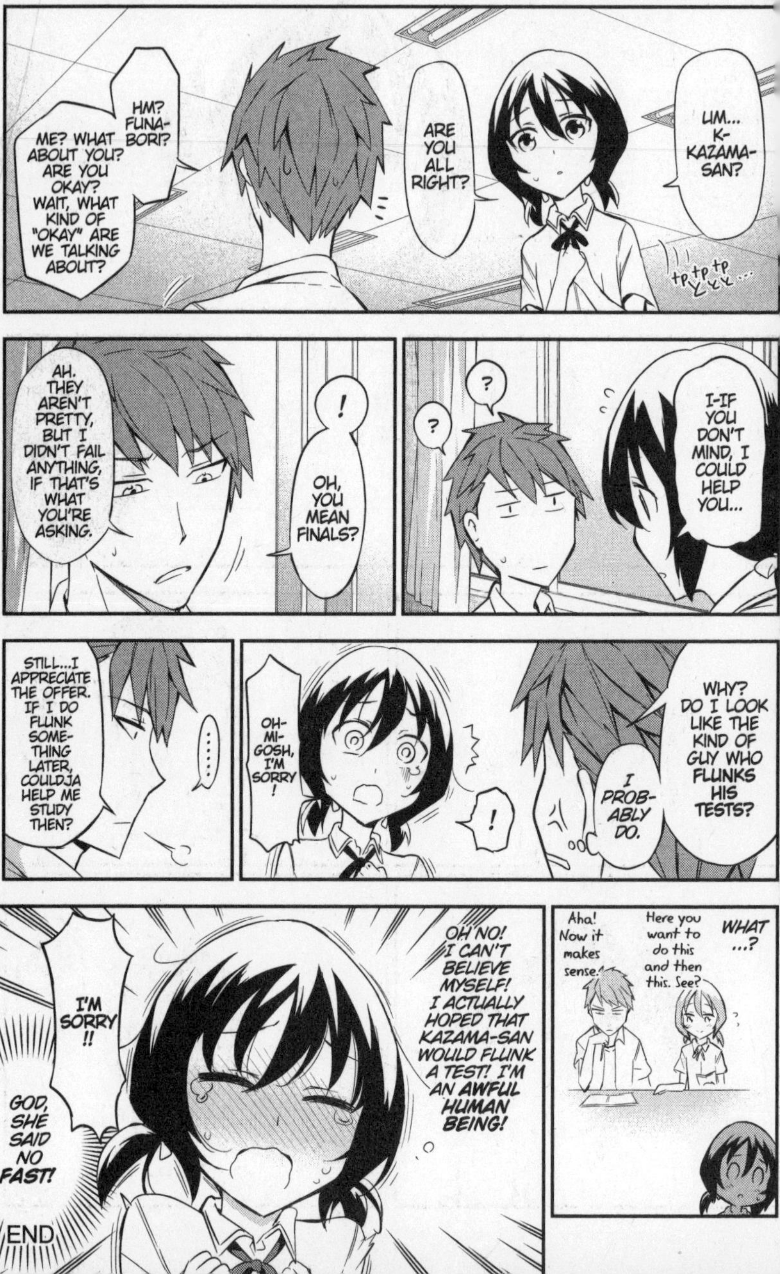
UM... K-KAZAMA-SAN?
tp tp tp...
ARE YOU ALL RIGHT?
HM? FUNABORI? ME? WHAT ABOUT YOU? ARE YOU OKAY? WAIT, WHAT KIND OF "OKAY" ARE WE TALKING ABOUT?
I-IF YOU DON'T MIND, I COULD HELP YOU...
?
?
OH, YOU MEAN FINALS?
!
AH. THEY AREN'T PRETTY, BUT I DIDN'T FAIL ANYTHING, IF THAT'S WHAT YOU'RE ASKING.
WHY? DO I LOOK LIKE THE KIND OF GUY WHO FLUNKS HIS TESTS?
I PROBABLY DO.
!
OH-MI-GOSH, I'M SORRY!
......
STILL...I APPRECIATE THE OFFER. IF I DO FLUNK SOMETHING LATER, COULDJA HELP ME STUDY THEN?
WHAT...?
Here you want to do this and then this. See?
Aha! Now it makes sense!
OH NO! I CAN'T BELIEVE MYSELF! I ACTUALLY HOPED THAT KAZAMA-SAN WOULD FLUNK A TEST! I'M AN AWFUL HUMAN BEING!
I'M SORRY!!
GOD, SHE SAID NO FAST!
END

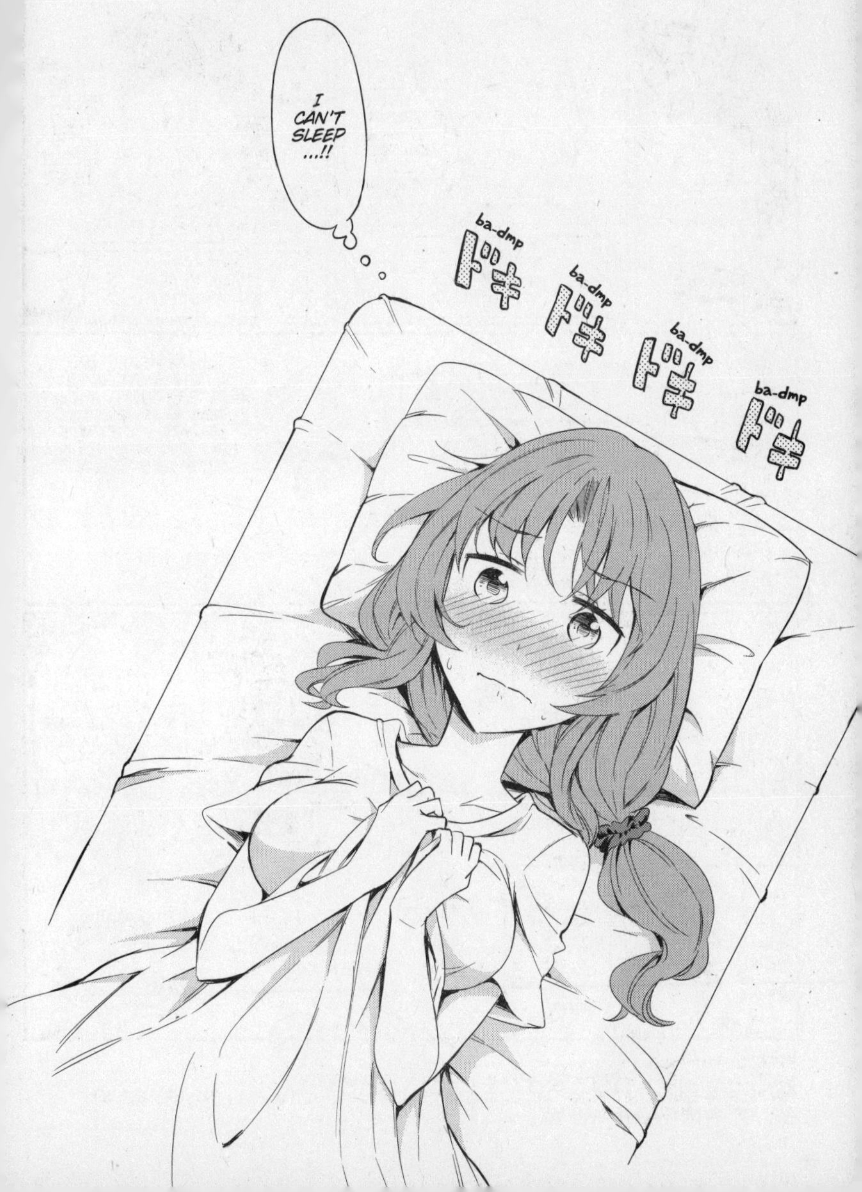
I CAN'T SLEEP ...!!
ba-dmp
ドキ
ba-dmp
ドキ
ba-dmp
ドキ
ba-dmp
ドキ

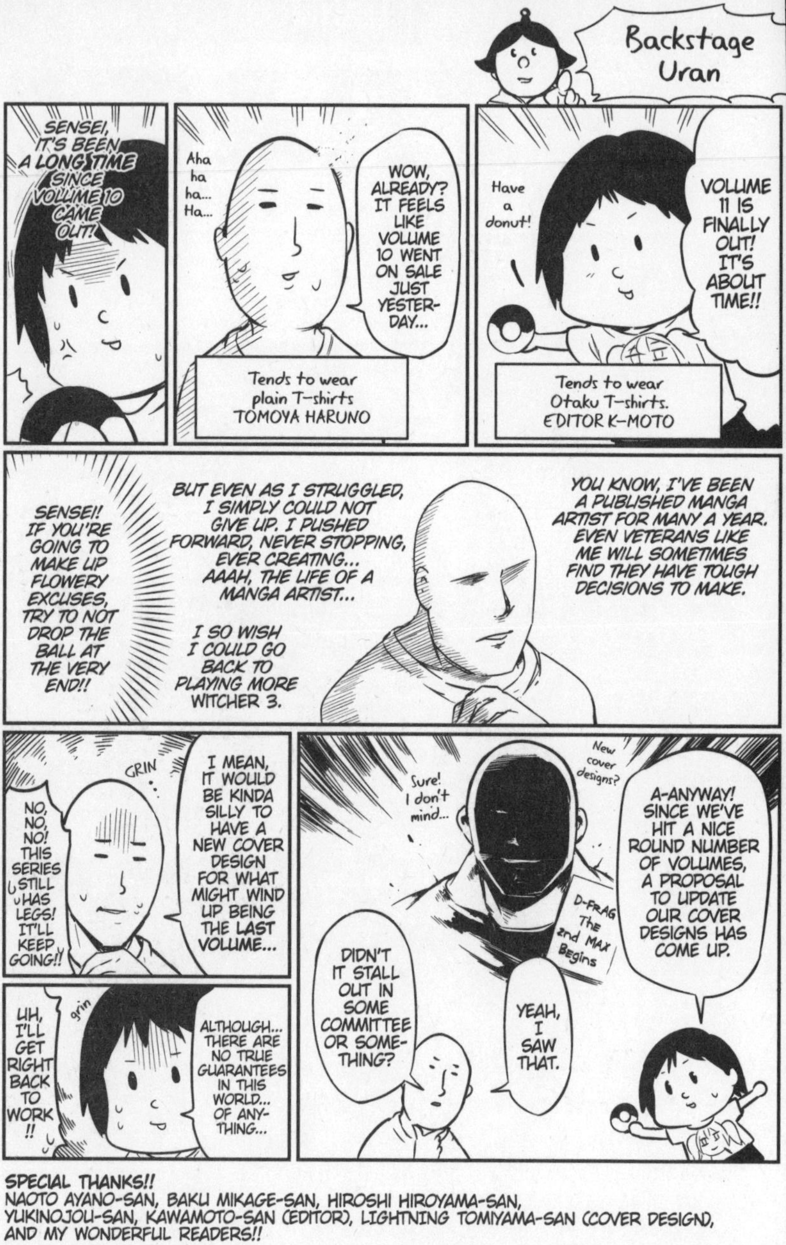
Backstage Uran
VOLUME 11 IS FINALLY OUT! IT'S ABOUT TIME!!
Have a donut!
Tends to wear Otaku T-shirts. EDITOR K-MOTO
WOW, ALREADY? IT FEELS LIKE VOLUME 10 WENT ON SALE JUST YESTER-DAY...
Aha ha ha... Ha...
Tends to wear plain T-shirts TOMOYA HARUNO
SENSEI, IT'S BEEN A LONG TIME SINCE VOLUME 10 CAME OUT!
YOU KNOW, I'VE BEEN A PUBLISHED MANGA ARTIST FOR MANY A YEAR. EVEN VETERANS LIKE ME WILL SOMETIMES FIND THEY HAVE TOUGH DECISIONS TO MAKE.
BUT EVEN AS I STRUGGLED, I SIMPLY COULD NOT GIVE UP. I PUSHED FORWARD, NEVER STOPPING, EVER CREATING... AAAH, THE LIFE OF A MANGA ARTIST...
I SO WISH I COULD GO BACK TO PLAYING MORE WITCHER 3.
SENSEI!! IF YOU'RE GOING TO MAKE UP FLOWERY EXCUSES, TRY TO NOT DROP THE BALL AT THE VERY END!!
A-ANYWAY! SINCE WE'VE HIT A NICE ROUND NUMBER OF VOLUMES, A PROPOSAL TO UPDATE OUR COVER DESIGNS HAS COME UP.
New cover designs?
Sure! I don't mind...
D-FRAG The 2nd MAX Begins
YEAH, I SAW THAT.
DIDN'T IT STALL OUT IN SOME COMMITTEE OR SOME-THING?
I MEAN, IT WOULD BE KINDA SILLY TO HAVE A NEW COVER DESIGN FOR WHAT MIGHT WIND UP BEING THE LAST VOLUME...
GRIN
NO, NO, NO! THIS SERIES STILL HAS LEGS! IT'LL KEEP GOING!!
ALTHOUGH... THERE ARE NO TRUE GUARANTEES IN THIS WORLD... OF ANY-THING...
grin
UH, I'LL GET RIGHT BACK TO WORK!!

SPECIAL THANKS!!
NAOTO AYANO-SAN, BAKU MIKAGE-SAN, HIROSHI HIROYAMA-SAN, YUKINOJOU-SAN, KAWAMOTO-SAN (EDITOR), LIGHTNING TOMIYAMA-SAN (COVER DESIGN), AND MY WONDERFUL READERS!!

SEVEN SEAS ENTERT

D-FRAG!

story and art by TOMOYA HARUNO

VOLUME 11

TRANSLATION
Adrienne Beck

ADAPTATION
Shannon Fay

LETTERING AND RETOUCH
William Ringrose

LOGO DESIGN
Courtney Williams

COVER DESIGN
Nicky Lim

ASSISTANT EDITOR
Jenn Grunigen

PRODUCTION ASSISTANT
CK Russell

PRODUCTION MANAGER
Lissa Pattillo

EDITOR-IN-CHIEF
Adam Arnold

PUBLISHER
Jason DeAngelis

D-FRAG! VOL. 11

First published in Japan in 2016 by KADOKAWA CORPORATION, Tokyo.
English translation rights reserved by Seven Seas Entertainment, LLC.
under the license from KADOKAWA CORPORATION, Tokyo.

Seven Seas books may be purchased in bulk for promotional, educational, or business use. Please contact your local bookseller or the Macmillan Corporate and Premium Sales Department at 1-800-221-7945, extension 5442, or by e-mail at MacmillanSpecialMarkets@macmillan.com.

ISBN: 978-1-626924-51-2

Printed in Canada

First Printing: April 2017

10 9 8 7 6 5 4 3 2 1

FOLLOW US ONLINE: ***www.gomanga.com***

READING DIRECTIONS

This book reads from ***right to left***, Japanese style. If this is your first time reading manga, you start reading from the top right panel on each page and take it from there. If you get lost, just follow the numbered diagram here. It may seem backwards at first, but you'll get the hang of it! Have fun!!

1
2
3
4
5
6
7
8
9

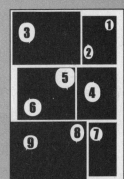